ESSAYS.

ESSAYS

IN THE

HISTORY OF RELIGIOUS THOUGHT
IN THE WEST.

BY

BROOKE FOSS WESTCOTT, D.D., D.C.L.
LORD BISHOP OF DURHAM.
HONORARY FELLOW OF TRINITY AND KING'S COLLEGES, CAMBRIDGE.

WIPF & STOCK · Eugene, Oregon

Wipf and Stock Publishers
199 W 8th Ave, Suite 3
Eugene, OR 97401

Essays in the History of Religious Thought in the West
By Westcott, B. F.
ISBN 13: 978-1-55635-741-1
ISBN 10: 1-55635-741-9
Publication date 12/3/2007
Previously published by Macmillan and Co, 1891

PREFACE.

THE Essays which are collected in this small volume are in part fragments of a design which I formed very early in life. It seemed to me that a careful examination of the religious teaching of representative prophetic masters of the West, if I may use the phrase, would help towards a better understanding of the power of the Christian Creed. Their hopes and their desires, their errors and their silences, were likely, I thought, to shew how far the Gospel satisfies our natural aspirations and illuminates dark places in our experience. The expectation, unless I am mistaken, will be found to be justified even by these isolated and imperfect sketches. If the student will extend the same method of inquiry, as I had hoped to do, to Homer, Heraclitus, Virgil, Epictetus, Plotinus—to name the men from whom I believe we may gain most—he will learn, as perhaps he can learn in no other way, what the apostolic message is as a revelation, a revelation not in thought but in life. It may seem to be a paradox—it ought to be a truism—that the Æneid is the Roman Gospel. The poem gives the ideal of the national religious hero ; and few things are more surprising in the histories of the apostolic age than that Virgil finds no place in the popular estimate of the influences at work in moulding or expressing current opinion.

To the Essays on Plato, Æschylus, Euripides, Origen and Dionysius, originally published in the *Contemporary Review* (1866, 1867, 1878, 1883), which formed part of my original design, I have added four others which illustrate the general thought which is suggested by them. The Faith welcomes all truth, while it supplements external lessons by its own peculiar witness, and places partial and limited expressions of truth in their right relations to one another and to the whole. Nothing lies outside the influence of its transfiguring power. Splendid visions burst upon us from unexpected quarters, and we find that they are included in that view of GOD the world and man which lies in the fact of the Incarnation.

It is now about five-and-twenty years since the first Essay was written. Certainly in the days which have passed since no call to effort has grown fainter and no prospect less bright. If it was possible then to make our own the memorable phrase with which Socrates closed his summons to a life of faith καλὸν τὸ ἆθλον καὶ ἡ ἐλπὶς μεγάλη, it has been brought home to us in the interval once and again by those who have proved to the last struggle of life that the Word for which Plato longed, as a sure support, has been given to us in Him Whom St John has made known.

B. F. D.

Auckland Castle,
Jan. 27, 1891.

CONTENTS.

	PAGE
THE MYTHS OF PLATO	1
THE DRAMATIST AS PROPHET: ÆSCHYLUS	51
EURIPIDES AS A RELIGIOUS TEACHER	96
DIONYSIUS THE AREOPAGITE	142
ORIGEN AND THE BEGINNINGS OF CHRISTIAN PHILOSOPHY	194
ON SOME POINTS IN BROWNING'S VIEW OF LIFE	253
THE RELATION OF CHRISTIANITY TO ART	277
CHRISTIANITY AS THE ABSOLUTE RELIGION	342
BENJAMIN WHICHCOTE	362

εὐλόγως ὁ διδάσκαλος ἡμῶν ἔλεγεν

Γίνεcθε τραπεζῖται Δόκιμοι

THE MYTHS OF PLATO.

"They that say such things declare plainly that they seek a country."
HEBREWS xi. 14.

"Truth is related to Faith as Being is related to Becoming."
PLATO.

I.

IT is an old saying that Plato combined the characteristics of Lycurgus and Pythagoras with those of Socrates. The lawgiver, the mystic, and the dialectician appear by turns in his writings; and according as the eye of the student is turned towards one of these several aspects, that for the time appears to be predominant. But even this triple form fails to include the whole range of his teaching. He was also, as Quintilian says, the rival of Homer in the grandeur of his style, and "inspired by the spirit of the Delphic oracle." He was at times, both in expression and in thought, a prophet.

So much has been done lately to bring out the dialectic and negative elements in the Platonic dialogues that it may not be without use to call attention to this positive and (so to speak) prophetic side of his work, which is now in some danger of being forgotten. Not only will the outline of his philosophic character be thus made more complete, but especially his view of the relations of philosophy and theology will appear in a striking light. For Plato more than any other ancient philosopher acknowledged alike the necessary limits of reason and the imperious instincts of faith, and when he could not absolutely reconcile both, at least gave to both a full and free expression. And so Platonism alone, and Platonism in virtue of this character, was able to stand for a time face to face with Christianity.

The myths of Plato, taken as a whole, offer the most complete and attractive summary of this prophetic positivism. For the present it is assumed that they constitute a whole. The review of their substance will, it is hoped, be a sufficient proof that the assumption is correct. At the same time it will shew that they are not, in essence, simply graceful embellishments of an argument, but venturous essays after truth, embodiments of definite instincts, sensible representations of universal human thoughts, confessions of weakness, it may be, but no less bold claims to an inherent communion with a divine and suprasensuous world. They are truly philosophic, because they answer to innate wants of man: they are truly poetic, because they are in thought creative.

Nothing indeed can be farther from Plato's view of what his myths are than the sense in which the word is now popularly understood. A myth in the common acceptation of the term is something unreal: but Plato claims that his myths are above all things true in spirit. Whatever question there might be about details of form, the central idea of the myth is affirmed absolutely, and in some cases the whole story is distinctly asserted to be historical[1]. He disclaims, in fact, the title myth in a disparaging sense for the stories to which we now apply it. They are, he says, real narratives (λόγοι) and not myths[2], and where he does use the word, he still maintains the existence of a substantial basis of fact for such myths as admit of an historical test[3], and attaches a supreme moral value to their spiritual teaching[4].

But though the word myth is commonly misapplied, it is far too valuable in its technical sense to be abandoned to vague use. It is indeed most serviceable, as expressing what the Platonic myths are. A myth in its true technical sense is the instinctive popular representation of an idea. "A myth," it has been said, "springs up in the soul as a germ in the soil: meaning and form are one: the history *is* the truth." Thus a myth, properly so called, has points of contact with a symbol, an allegory, and a legend, and is distinguished from each. Like the symbol, it

---

[1] See Timæus, 20 D; 21 A, D; 26 C. And so Critias invokes *Memory* to help him in relating the whole story, p. 108 D.

[2] Gorgias, 523 A. Compare pp. 527 A; 526 D. Meno, 81 D, E.

[3] Politicus, 268 E; 269 A, B.

[4] De Republica, x. 621 B, C.

is the embodiment and representation of a thought. But the symbol is isolated, definite, and absolute. The symbol, and the truth which it figures, are contemplated apart. The one suggests the other. The myth on the other hand is continuous, historical, and relative. The truth is seen in the myth, and not separated from it. The representation is the actual apprehension of the reality. The myth and the allegory, again, have both a secondary sense. Both half hide and half reveal the truth which they clothe. But in the allegory the thought is grasped first and by itself, and is then arranged in a particular dress. In the myth, thought and form come into being together: the thought is the vital principle which shapes the form; the form is the sensible image which displays the thought. The allegory is the conscious work of an individual fashioning the image of a truth which he has seized. The myth is the unconscious growth of a common mind, which witnesses to the fundamental laws by which its development is ruled. The meaning of an allegory is prior to the construction of the story: the meaning of a myth is first capable of being separated from the expression in an age long after that in which it had its origin. The myth and the legend have more in common. Both spring up naturally. Both are the unconscious embodiments of popular feeling. Both are, as it seems, necessary accompaniments of primitive forms of society. The legend stands in the same relation to history and life as the myth to speculation and thought. The legend deals with a fact as outward, concrete, objective. The myth deals with an idea or the observation of a fact as inward, abstract, subjective. The tendency of the legend is to go ever farther from the simple circumstances from which it took its rise. The tendency of the myth is to express more and more clearly the idea which it foreshews. Yet in many cases it seems almost impossible to draw a distinct line between the myth and the legend. The stories of St Christopher, of St Bonaventura and his speaking Crucifix, of Whittington and his Cat, and generally those which may be called *interpretative* myths, will be called myths or legends according as the thought or the fact in them is supposed to predominate.

The Platonic myths[1], while they are varied in character, and present points of similarity with the legend and the allegory, yet truly claim for the most part to be regarded as essentially genuine myths. If they are individual and not popular, they are still the individual expression of a universal instinct. Plato speaks not as Plato but as man. If at times they are conscious, yet more frequently they are taken from earlier and traditional sources. And in that which is especially characteristic of the myth, the relation between the lesson and the form, the

[1] I regret that I have been unable to see Deuschle's essay, "Ueber die Platonischen Mythen," which, from Zeller's brief references ("Die Philosophie der Griechen," ii. 363 *anm.*), appears to be full of interest.

idea is not prior to and distinct from the representation but coincident with it. The Platonic myth is, in short, a possible material representation of a speculative doctrine, which is affirmed by instinct, but not capable of being established by a scientific process. The myth is itself the doctrine so far as it is at present capable of apprehension by men.

There are, however, some Platonic stories commonly included among the myths, of which this description will not hold true. Though Plato stands alone in the adoption of the myth as the natural expression of a common human instinct, others before him had made use of allegory as a graceful and agreeable vehicle of popular instruction. Every one will recall the exquisite story of the choice of Hercules, in which Prodicus painted for all ages the rival charms of Virtue and Pleasure, as they meet man when he enters on the journey of life; and the myth in the "Protagoras" indicates that this form of illustration was also employed by the Sophists in the discussion of political subjects. It was natural, then, that in this as in many other points of form, Plato should avail himself of the example of his predecessors. We may even say, without exaggeration, that the labours of the Sophists made a Socrates and therefore a Plato possible; and it is probably more than a mere fancy which traces the artificial elegance of the Sophistic style in the earlier Platonic dialogues. One example of allegory modelled on this earlier type—the Birth of Love—will serve as an instructive contrast, in

THE MYTHS OF PLATO.

spirit and conception and application, to the genuine myths which follow. Fruitful and expressive as we feel the story to be, yet it is evident that the whole conception precedes the imagery in which it is clothed, and transcends it, and gains nothing from it but a momentary distinctness.

The narrative is given by the "sage Diotima" in answer to Socrates, who had spoken of Love as a glorious god. She said[1],—

"He is no god, Socrates, but a spirit (Δαίμων), a great spirit, one of those beings who occupy a middle place between gods and men; for God himself can hold no intercourse with man, and all the fellowship which exists between heaven and earth is realized through this intermediate order, which bridges over the chasm between them. These spirits, then, are many and manifold, and Love is one of them. It is a long tale to give the history of his parentage, but I will tell it you. At the birth of Aphrodite the gods held a feast, and among them was Resource, the son of Counsel. So after the banquet began, Poverty, knowing of the good cheer, came there to beg, and lingered about the doors. As the day crept on, Resource, having drunk freely of the nectar—for wine, the drink of men, was not yet discovered—went into the garden of Zeus and sank overpowered to sleep. Poverty, when she saw it, thinking on her own resourcelessness, sought his company, and according to her desire, bore him, in due time, a son, who was called Love. And so it is that Love is the attendant and

[1] Symposium, 203 A, *et seq*. It must be remarked, once for all, that the renderings of the myths are not close translations. Condensation and paraphrase have been freely used when either seemed desirable for the sake of space or clearness.

squire of Aphrodite, because it was on her birthday that Poverty first met Resource, and he is also naturally an enthusiast for the beautiful. Love, then, as being the child of Poverty and Resource, has a strange fate. He is always poor; and so far from being delicate and fair, as most people suppose, is rough and squalid, unsandaled and homeless, sleeping upon the bare earth beneath the open sky, and, according to his mother's nature, is always mated with want. But on the other hand, as he takes after his father, he aims at the beautiful and the good, and is brave, vigorous, and energetic, clever in the pursuit of his object, skilful in invention, passionately fond of knowledge, and fertile in resource, unceasingly devoted to the search after wisdom, and withal an inveterate trickster, charlatan, and sophist. Moreover, his being is neither truly immortal nor mortal; but in a single day he enjoys the full vigour of life, and dies, and is raised to life again through the essence of his father's nature. The resources which he gathers melt away, and so he is neither resourceless nor wealthy. He stands midway between wisdom and ignorance. He is not like the gods, who do not seek wisdom because they *are* wise. He is not like the ignorant, who do not seek wisdom because they *are* ignorant. Love desires wisdom, which is the noblest beauty, and strives to gain it, because he knows what it is and that he needs it. This is the prerogative of his birth."

Somewhat similar in nature is the story told by Aristophanes of the origin of passion and the original complete form of man, if it be not rather a dim reflection of an Eastern belief[1]; and the myth in the "Protagoras" has many allegoric traits, though in its

[1] Symposium, 189 D, *et seq.*

present form it contains so much that is a prophetic interpretation of the laws of life that it may be rightly considered as a true myth.

But there is yet another story, which Plato himself calls a myth—a fable—a mere poetic fiction,—which claims notice as answering to the interpretative myths of popular tradition. It is a deliberate endeavour to invent a semi-historical explanation of difficulties which may practically remove them; and the apology which is made for the pious fraud shews with what earnestness of faith Plato must have held to the truth of his genuine myths, for which he sets up the claim of substantial reality. Socrates has sketched the principles on which the education of the different classes in his ideal commonwealth must be conducted. It remains to find a bond of unity between men whom he has thus widely separated in work and dignity. With doubt and hesitation[1], and a great show of unwillingness, he proposes his scheme[2]. "We must have recourse," he says, "to a splendid falsehood to win the State to our views. It has the authority of poets in its favour, though now there will be need of great power to convince men of its truth." And then, in answer to the encouragement of his friends, he continues,—

"I tell you my plan; and yet I know not how I shall arm myself for the task, or what words I shall use in ex-

[1] Compare De Republica, ii. 377 B; 382 C, D.
[2] *Ibid.* iii. 414 D, *et seq.*

plaining it. I shall, then, endeavour to persuade our rulers and warriors, and afterwards our whole State, that in real fact the training and education which we gave them was a mere dream, that all they suffered and all that was done to them was mere fancy, while they were in fact at that very time being moulded and trained beneath the earth, where also all their equipment and their arms were fabricated, and that, when they were perfectly fashioned, then the earth, their mother, sent them to the light above, and that they must now take thought for the country in which they are, and defend it against every foe, as believing that it is their mother and nurse, and also regard all their fellow-citizens as brethren, being, like themselves, children of the earth. 'For all ye who are in the State,' we will say to them, following out our fiction, 'are brethren; but God, when He moulded you, at the time of your birth, mixed gold in the substance of all of you who were fit to rule, and therefore they are the most honoured. He infused silver in the military caste, iron and bronze in the husbandmen and craftsmen generally. The offspring of these several classes will, as a general rule, preserve the character of their parents. But if the signs of gold or silver appear in the children of the bronze or iron castes, they must then be raised to their due place. And if bronze or iron appear where we look for gold, that too must be reduced to its proper rank.'"

He concludes,—

"We shall not persuade the first generation that this is so, but it may be that in time their descendants will believe our tale. And the belief would contribute greatly to their devotion to the good of the State and to the good of one another."

Elsewhere, as we shall see, Plato has a deeper theory of the origin of the external differences between men. Here those points which are the true mythical elements of the story,—the common origin of mankind, the divinely appointed diversities of human capacity, the general laws of the propagation of character—are very slightly dwelt upon from their spiritual side: or rather they are contemplated as facts first, already assumed in the constitution of the State, and simply combined in one striking picture. Another difference between this story and the legitimate myth will appear in the course of the exposition. The latter, as it will be seen, belongs properly to views of the Universe or of the Individual. The instinctive power of which it is the expression strives necessarily towards unity—the unity of the single being, or the unity of the sum of being. The Manifold is a stage of preparation or transition, and not a limit of repose.

Thus there are two great problems with which the Platonic myths deal, the origin and destiny of the Cosmos, and the origin and destiny of man. Both problems obviously transcend all experience and all logical processes of reason. But no less both are ever present to the student of life, though he may neglect them in the investigation of details, or deliberately set them aside as hopelessly insoluble. Plato can acquiesce in neither course, and therefore he follows his poetic instinct in interpreting and combining the phenomena which force themselves upon his notice and the notice of all men. He sees more clearly, but with the same power of vision as others: he speaks more articulately, but with the same voice. He looks upon the world as others look upon it; but the truth which is for them a blurred and dim picture is borne in upon his soul in grand and solemn scenes: and each scene is transcribed in a myth.

II.

It is difficult not to begin an examination of the myths with the well-known portraiture which Plato has drawn of the fortunes of a human soul. But his views will be more truly apprehended in their whole bearing if we begin with the most general aspect of the Cosmos, and pass from that to the Individual. The Individual, according to him, exists only as a part of the Cosmos; it is by reference to that alone that he is seen in his full and just proportions.

Here we are met by three questions which can never grow old, and never be so answered as to leave nothing for future ages to ponder over in anxious and mysterious doubt. What was the origin of the Cosmos, and the relation of man to it? What are the general laws by which the course of the Cosmos is regulated? What are the special laws which affect that part of it with which man is most closely connected? Plato answers each question by a myth, and, as it seems, his words have yet a meaning which we have not outlived. His meaning has been often

THE MYTHS OF PLATO. 13

obscured by the ingenuity of later Sophists, who sought to extract by the understanding what must be felt by the heart; but it is none the less still intelligible to the same common instinct of humanity of which it is the utterance.

The origin of the Cosmos came about in this way[1],—

"All existences are divisible into two classes. Of these, the one consists of that which *is* always, and has no source, and is comprehensible only by reason; the other, of that which is always *becoming* but never really *is*, and is cognizable by sensation, and must necessarily be dependent on some cause. To this latter class the Cosmos belongs, for it is perceptible by the senses of vision and touch, and it therefore must have had a Maker and Father[2], whom it is a hard matter to discover, and when one has discovered Him it is impossible to declare Him to all. He[3], however, was good, and a good Being is incapable of envy in any case; and therefore He wished everything to become as far as possible similar to Himself. And this wish was the cause of the origin of the Cosmos. For when God found the sum of visible existences in discordant and disorderly movement, He brought the chaos from disorder to order. And as His work was made after an eternal and suprasensuous pattern[4] it was perfect of its kind, essentially one and only-begotten ($\mu o \nu o \gamma \epsilon \nu \eta s$)[5], including in itself every absolute form of life, and at the same time endowed with a rational and vital soul. And when the Father who gave it birth saw it possessed of motion and life He rejoiced and ·

[1] Timæus, 27 D.
[2] Ibid. 28 C.
[3] Ibid. 29 E.
[4] Ibid. 29 A.
[5] Ibid. 31 B; 30 B.

was glad[1], and to make the visible Cosmos more like to the invisible and intelligible pattern, He called into being Time, as a moving image of Eternity, and the bright Gods of heaven, and to them He gave the charge of peopling the world with the other orders of animal life[2]. 'O Gods of Gods,' he said, 'Lords of the works (the stars) of which I am Framer and Father, which as they have come into being through Me are indissoluble if so I will. Everything which is compound is dissoluble, yet an evil being only would wish to dissolve that which is fairly fitted together and fulfils its functions well. You therefore, since you have come into being, are not absolutely immortal or indissoluble, but yet you will not be dissolved or suffer death, for my will is a greater and surer bond of your natures than those bonds by which you were first compacted. Hear then my will. Three classes of mortal creatures are still unformed. Till these are formed the Cosmos will be incomplete. If I make them, they will be like Gods. Do you therefore, as far as in you lies, imitate my action. The immortal element, as far as such creatures may receive it, I will supply. For the rest, do you form them by adding a mortal element to an immortal, and bring them to their full maturity, and when they die again receive them to yourselves.' When He had thus spoken, He poured into the bowl in which He mixed the soul of the universe, what was left of the elements which He used before; but they were not now pure as at first. From this compound He formed souls equal in number to the stars, to which He attached each one severally, and shewed them the laws of their future destiny. At their first embodiment each, He said[3], would be born a man, the most pious of creatures,

---

[1] Timæus, 37 c.   [2] *Ibid.* 41 A.
[3] *Ibid.* 41 D.

and in life would have to master the temptations of sense and passion. If he succeeded in doing this for the appointed term he would pass to a home in his kindred star, and live a congenial and happy life. If he failed of this, at his second birth he would be born a woman. If in this life also he lived badly, then he would in his next embodiment assume some animal shape answering to his character, and gain no respite from suffering till at length his reason should be brought into harmony with the eternal reason, and overcome the manifold accretions by which its action was hindered. Thereupon the Supreme Father reposed in His eternal rest, and His children fashioned the body of man, imitating, as best they could, the laws which their Father had followed in shaping the Cosmos. And to supply the necessary waste of man's frame, they composed another order of creatures—plants and trees[1]. And thus the Cosmos was fully furnished, for beasts, and birds, and reptiles, and aquatic animals, were produced by the transformations of men[2]."

Even in this brief summary some details are introduced which are rather logical than mythical, and in the "Timæus" itself the mythical basis is overlaid with elaborate speculations which are wholly foreign to the spirit of a myth. But the grand outlines of the conception, the origin of the Cosmos from the infinite goodness of a heavenly Father, its inherent unity and common life, the complexity of man's nature, his divine soul implanted in him by God Himself, his possible affinity with lower beings, form a noble answer to importunate questionings of the

---

[1] Timæus, 77 A. [2] *Ibid.* 91 D.

heart. The answer goes beyond and yet falls short of the diviner lessons in which we rest, but it is no less a precious witness to what man seeks to know and what he craves to believe.

So the Cosmos came into being and was peopled. And from the date of its origin it has been subject to laws of cyclic change[1]:—

"Faint traces of the crises through which it has passed are preserved in popular traditions, as when we read of the age of Kronos, and that the course of the sun was reversed in the days of Atreus, and that men were once born from the earth. But these ancient legends are scanty and isolated memorials of a great and marvellous truth, which is this. The course of the universe is not always the same. At one time God Himself assists in directing it in its revolution, and again, when the measure of the time is full, He leaves it to itself; whereupon, by its spontaneous power, it revolves in the opposite direction, since it was endowed with life and reason by its first Framer. The necessity for this change happens thus:—To remain absolutely undisturbed and unchanged is the prerogative only of the divinest existences; and glorious as are the attributes of the Cosmos, still it has a body. It must therefore be liable to change; but this change is the least which could be, as it revolves about one axis with the least possible deviation. But again, it cannot always move itself, for that belongs to One only; nor can a god (nor yet two gods) move it in two contrary ways—as tradition shews it does move. We are forced, then, to suppose that at one time it is guided by a Divine power, during which period it acquires fresh stores of life, and then again that it is left to

[1] Politicus, 268 E, *et seq.*

its own action under such conditions that it revolves backwards for many myriads of revolutions, because its weight is balanced most nicely upon the delicate point on which it revolves. The crises of transition are the greatest through which the Cosmos can pass, and few living beings survive them[1]. Those who do, suffer a marvellous change. The progress from youth to age is checked, and life flows backward; grey hairs grow black, the bearded chin grows smooth, the boy passes into the infant, the infant fades away and vanishes, and then the order begins afresh, for the dead rise up again from the earth in full maturity to trace a backward life,—all at least whom GOD has not transferred to another fate. At such a period Kronos is said to reign over men, who find, without care, or pain, or social effort, all they need; and under him are other spirits, who provide for all the wants of lower animals. Thus the opportunities of men at these times are boundless[2]. They have leisure and capacity for intercourse with every creature. But they may miss their highest blessings, and fall short even of our fortune, amidst the rich luxuriance of their material happiness. However this may be, the appointed end comes. The Pilot of the universe lets go, so to speak, the tiller of his vessel, and retires to his watchtower; and with him follow the gods who had shared his dominion. Fate and inborn Desire succeed to his place, and, with an awful crash and ruin, the Cosmos revolves in the opposite direction. By degrees order is restored, as it recalls the lessons of its Framer and Father; but these lessons are again forgotten, and when all is on the verge of destruction, GOD sees the distress of the universe, and, placing Himself at the rudder, restores it to order and endues it with a fresh immortality. But if we fix our at-

[1] Politicus, 270 c, *et seq.* [2] *Ibid.* 272 c, *et seq.*

tention on the course of the world when left, as at present, to direct, with absolute power, its own course, we shall see results in all respects the exact converse of those in the reign of Cosmos. When the change from its former motion first took place, the downward progress of life was at once checked in those who survived the crisis. The infant, then ready to vanish, grew towards maturity. The greybeard, who had just risen from the ground, sank again into the grave. Men were born of men, and not from a common mother, Earth. All creatures, alike deprived of special Divine rule, gave full play to their natural instincts. Then was a time of dire distress and peril, till, with the needful training, men received from the gods the gifts of fire and arts and seeds, by the help of which they fashioned their lives, following in their independent action the condition of the whole Cosmos."

This remarkable myth, which finds no parallel to its central conception in the Platonic writings, appears to derive its form simply from the popular traditions of "earth-born" races, and changes in the courses of the heavenly bodies[1]. So far it is simply an interpretative myth. But its proper mythical meaning lies deeper. In this respect it is an attempt to work out the moral consequences of a paradisiacal life as contrasted with our present life. A universal instinct has led men to imagine a golden age of peace and wealth and happiness, before the stern age of struggle and freedom in which they now live. Plato draws out the picture at length. We might be

[1] The well-known passage in Herod. ii. 142, is a remarkable example of these strange traditions.

tempted to think that he has a vision of Eden before him when he describes the intercourse of man and animals, the maturity of each new-formed being, the rural ease of a life which is a gradual disrobing of the spirit from its earthly dress. But even so he shews that the perfect order of a Divine government, and boundless plenty, may leave man's highest nature undisciplined. It may be that when GOD has left the world to the action of a free will, not as forgetting or neglecting, but only ceasing to control it, man, by remembering the precepts of the Great Father which he bears within him, and battling with opposing powers, may yet live a noble and a godlike life, even if year by year he gathers round him the material chains of earth. His highest strength lies in the right exercise of the freedom of his will, and not in the circumstances of his condition.

In another dialogue, Plato has traced out somewhat more fully the progress of our present human society, which is very rapidly sketched in the "Politicus." The myth is attributed to Protagoras, and there is very much in the elaborate elegance of its form which seems to have been derived from him[1]:—

"There was a time when the gods only existed; but when the appointed time came that mortal creatures should come into being, the gods moulded them within the earth, compounding them of earth and fire, and when they were about to bring them to the light, they bade Forethought (Prometheus) and Afterthought (Epimetheus)

[1] Protagoras, 320 c, *et seq.*

array them severally with suitable powers. Afterthought begged Forethought to allow him to make the distribution alone: 'When I have made it,' he said, 'do you come to see.' And so his wish was granted; and he proceeded with his task, providing for the safety, the comfort, and the support of the different tribes. Some he protected by size, others by speed, others by weapons of offence. One kind he clothed in fur, another he covered with thick hides. And he appointed to each their proper food. But when his store of endowments was exhausted, he found to his dismay that man was left unarrayed, naked and unarmed, and the fated day was already close at hand on which man must enter on the upper world. Forethought, when he saw the fatal error, found but one way to remedy it. He stole the craftsman's skill of Hephæstus and Athene, and fire with it—without which art is valueless,—and gave this to man. Thus man was furnished with all he needed for his separate life; but he had not yet the wisdom by which society is formed. This wisdom was kept in the citadel of Zeus, and into that awful sanctuary Forethought could not enter. As time went on, the power and weakness of man were seen[1]. He established ordinances of worship; he defined language; he invented clothing, and procured food for himself. But he lived in isolation, and he was unfit for social union. Thus, if men were scattered, they were in danger of perishing from wild beasts. If they tried to combine, they were scattered again by mutual violence. Thereupon Zeus, fearing for the safety of our race, sent Hermes with self-respect (αἰδώς) and justice, that their presence among men might establish order and knit together the bonds of friendship in society. 'Must I distribute them,' said Hermes, 'as the various

[1] Protagoras, p. 322 A.

arts have been distributed aforetime, only to certain individuals, or must I dispense them to all?' 'To all,' said Zeus; 'and let all partake of them. For states could not be formed if they, like the arts, were confined to a few. Nay more, if any one is incapable of self-respect and justice, let him be put to death, such is my will, as a plague to the state.'"

So it is, according to the myth, that states are framed. The essential bond by which they are held together is that which is common to all, while their efficiency depends upon the diversity of gifts with which their members are endowed. But the contemplation of any special state blinds us to the enormous scale on which the life of man is exhibited in the world. And so it was that the priest of Sais said to Solon[1],—

"You Greeks are always children. I never saw an aged Greek. You are young in soul—lost in the contemplation of your little fragments of history, over which your own records reach: you cherish no ancient belief, borne down by primeval tradition: you preserve no lesson gray with the growth of time. Your fable of Phaëthon—for at first sight it seems a fable—is but a dim recollection of one of the periodic catastrophes by fire to which the earth is subject. Your history of Deucalion is but the story of one cataclysm out of many by which nations have been and will be submerged. Thus it happens that the memory of the untold ages of the past is lost, through these crises of secular ruin by fire and water, which few survive, unless,

[1] Timæus, 22 B.

as with us in Egypt, the character of the country averts from some favoured spot the general desolation."

With this prelude Plato opens his discussion on the Universe, on which we have already touched. It is as if he wished to extend his view as widely in time as in space. The outline is bold and clear, and there is something strangely grand in this conception of æons of human life, bounded by the result of the accumulated action of natural causes, whose tendency we can trace even in the little period of our own existence. Moreover, just at present the theory is of universal interest, because recent speculations lend some support to the belief in secular physical catastrophes on which it rests. But Plato uses the myth to illustrate a moral truth. Revolutions of the earth recur, and history also tends to repeat itself. The day before the dialogue of the "Timæus" was supposed to be held, Socrates had developed his view of a perfect state. Having done this, he feels, as he says, like one who has seen animals only in painting or at rest; he wishes now to see them in vigorous action. For this pleasure he looks to the young statesmen, Timæus and Critias and Hermocrates, who have invited him to be their guest. Nor in vain: Critias tells the story of what had befallen Solon in Egypt, and Socrates hears, in what professes to be an authentic record, the achievements of a primitive Athenian state, constituted like his own. "Your Greek traditions," so the priest continues, in his address to Solon[1], "are little better than children's tales; and—

"You do not know that the noblest and bravest race upon the face of the earth once lived in your land. Yes, Solon, before the last great flood, that which is now Athens was the best and the best governed of all states. Its exploits were the most glorious, and its institutions the noblest, of all whose fame has reached us. What I speak of happened nine thousand years ago, and I will now simply indicate briefly the laws of the commonwealth and the greatest of its triumphs. We will afterwards examine at our leisure, with the help of the original documents, the exact details of its history. For its laws, then, you will find many parallels here in Egypt, as in the division of castes (priests and craftsmen and warriors), and in the style of arming, and in the provisions for learning. All these ordinances your patroness Athene (who is the same as our Neith) gave you, and she chose the spot in which your forefathers dwelt, being herself devoted to war and wisdom, because she saw that it was likely to bear men most closely resembling her own character. Many, therefore, and great are the marvellous deeds of your city which are recorded, but one deed surpasses all for grandeur and courage. For our records tell of the mighty power from the Atlantic which it checked in its proud advance against all Europe and Asia. For at that time the Ocean was accessible. In front of the Pillars of Hercules, as you call them, lay an island larger than Libya and Asia, from which you might reach the other islands, and from these the mainland opposite, which extended along the real Ocean. In this island, Atlantis (so it was named), a great

[1] Timæus, 23 B.

and wondrous league of kings arose, who conquered the whole country, and many other islands and parts of the mainland, and besides this they held dominion over Libya as far as the borders of Egypt, and over Europe as far as Tyrrhenia. So then, having combined all their forces together, they essayed to enslave by one bold assault your country and ours, and all the district of the Mediterranean. Whereupon your state, Solon, proved gloriously conspicuous for valour and might; for first at the head of the Greeks, and then alone and deserted, as all else abandoned her, pre-eminent in courage and martial arts, she was brought to the extremity of peril, but at last triumphed over the invaders, and saved for ever all who had not yet been enslaved from the fear of slavery, and generously restored their freedom to all others within the Pillars of Hercules. But at a later time, after unnatural earthquakes and floods, a wild day and night followed, and all your warrior race was swallowed up by the earth, and the island Atlantis sank beneath the sea. And so it is that the sea there is impassable, because all progress is hindered by the shallow banks of mud which were caused by the sinking of the island[1]."

[1] The existence of Atlantis has been a favourite subject of discussion with modern geologists. Dr Unger, of Vienna, has published a remarkable lecture upon the subject (translated in the *Journal of Botany*, 1865, pp. 12, *et seq.*), in which he shews, from the consideration of the Floras, that "in the Tertiary period Europe must have been connected with North America;" and again, that at a later period this "Atlantis assumed the form of an island separate from both continents."

Plato expressly distinguishes the island from the mainland beyond it. His shallow, muddy sea is an evident allusion to the great sargassum-bed, of which Aristotle has an interesting notice (De Mirab. Aud., § 136).

The further development of this myth of epic magnificence is reserved for the "Critias," of which only a fragment, as it seems, was ever written, but that a fragment of unrivalled richness. The description of the wealth of Atlantis is almost Oriental in the profusion of detail, and almost prophetic in its anticipations of the triumph of modern commerce and art. Every production of the earth was gathered to the marts of the favoured people of Poseidon[1]. Their docks were built of marble; their buildings were varied in fanciful polychrome; their palaces were of stupendous size and beauty; their walls were plated with metal; their harbours were crowded with vessels from every quarter of the world, and filled day and night with the voice of merchants and the manifold din of ceaseless traffic. For a time they bore meekly, as it had been a burden, the large measure of their wealth. But at last the Divine element within them was overpowered by human passion. Unjust aggrandizement and power seemed the greatest blessings, and they were blind to their own shame; whereupon Zeus devised their chastisement, and called the gods together to hear his purpose. . . And so the poem ends; for in the "Critias" the myth has grown into a poem. The conception of secular cataclysms is lost in the episode of Athenian greatness, or the symbolic struggle of martial wisdom against material power. The teaching of instinct is replaced by the creations of fancy. Yet even so the last picture in the noble

[1] Critias, 113 B, *et seq.*

series is one on which the Platonist, and not he only, could look with devout thankfulness. For it taught him that He who made the universe into a living whole, and rejoiced when He looked upon it,—He who with wise alternations of control and freedom directs the cyclic periods of its common course,—He who by the action of general laws renews the face of the earth on which we live,—looks also to separate nations, and ordains judgment for their excesses, "that they may learn uprightness by correction[1]."

III.

The Personal Myths of Plato, in which he deals with the history of the individual soul, are better known than the Cosmical Myths which we have hitherto noticed, and have left a deeper impression upon popular thought. They have also more obvious and closer affinities with the genuine Socratic teaching. It is indeed very significant that no cosmical myth is attributed to Socrates. These broad and venturous speculations are assigned to Timæus, the physical philosopher of Locri; to an anonymous Eleatic stranger; and to Critias, the brilliant and unscrupulous statesman. Socrates applauds[2], it is true, "the marvellous success of Timæus upon the stage," in his view of the Cosmos, but it is impossible not to feel that such investigations lie beyond the limits of human morals, within which he purposely

[1] Critias, 121 B.   [2] Critias, 108 B.

confined himself. It is otherwise with the personal myths. These are all delivered by Socrates himself, and all bear upon the questions to which his life was devoted, the eternal principles of justice and duty and truth. This contrast in the treatment of similar forms of exposition is important, and not without interest, as shewing under what restrictions Plato felt himself at liberty to bring forward Socrates as the interpreter of his own opinions. Socrates speaks when the doctrine is that out of which his lessons flowed, or in which they could find their essential confirmation, or where the process of inquiry is itself the end: he listens when new topics are opened, harmonious it may be with his practical teaching, but larger in scope and farther removed from life.

Plato's mythical history of the soul is given in several distinct scenes. The slight sketch in the "Meno" is elaborated into a complete picture in the "Republic." Between the two come the descriptions of the Soul in Heaven in the "Phædrus," of the Judgment in the "Gorgias," and of the Unseen World in the "Phædo," which severally bring out special aspects of the one great subject.

In the "Meno," Socrates is preparing the way for his assertion that knowledge is recollection.

"I have heard," he says, "from men and women wise in divine matters a true tale as I think, and a noble one. My informants are those priests and priestesses whose aim it is to be able to render an account of the subjects with

28   THE MYTHS OF PLATO.

which they deal. They are supported also by Pindar and many other poets,—by all, I may say, who are truly inspired. Their teaching is that the soul of man is immortal; that it comes to an end of one form of existence, which men call dying, and then is born again, but never perishes. Since, then, the soul is immortal, and has been often born, and has seen the things here on earth and the things in Hades,—all things, in short,—there is nothing which it has not learned, so that it is no marvel that it should be possible for it to recall what it certainly knew before about virtue and other topics. For since all nature is akin, and the soul has learned all things, there is no reason why a man who has recalled one fact only, which men call learning, should not by his own power find out everything else, should he be courageous and not lose heart in the search. For seeking and learning is all an act of recollection[1]."

In the "Phædrus" we read how that true and absolute knowledge is gained, which it is thus the highest object of an earthly life to recall. Socrates has first given a metaphysical proof of the immortality of the soul, after which he describes its nature, under the famous image of a chariot, guided by a charioteer, and drawn by two winged steeds, of which, in the case of man, the one is good, the other not so[2]. He then employs the image in one of his grandest myths. At a certain time there is a great procession in heaven[3];—

"Zeus advances first, driving his winged car, ordering all things and superintending them. A host of deities and

[1] Meno, 81 A.   [2] Phædo, 246 A. Compare p. 253 c.
[3] Phædrus, 246 E, *et seq*.

spirits follow him, marshalled in eleven bodies, for Hestia remains alone in the dwelling of the gods. Many then and blessed are the spectacles and movements within the sphere of heaven which the gods go through, each fulfilling his own function; and whoever will and can follows them, for envy is a stranger to the divine company. But when they afterwards proceed to a banquet, they advance by what is now a steep course along the inner circumference of the heavenly vault. The chariots of the gods, being well balanced and well driven, advance easily, and others with difficulty; for the vicious horse, unless the charioteer has thoroughly broken it, weighs down the car by his proclivity towards the earth. Whereupon the soul is exposed to the extremity of toil and effort. For the souls of the immortals, when they reach the summit, go outside and stand upon the surface of heaven, and as they stand there the revolution of the sphere bears them round, and they contemplate the objects that are beyond it. That super-celestial realm no earthly poet ever yet sang or will sing in worthy strains. It is occupied by the colourless, shapeless, intangible, absolute essence which reason alone can contemplate, and which is the one subject of true knowledge. The divine mind, therefore, when it sees after an interval that which really *is*, is supremely happy, and gains strength and enjoyment by the contemplation of the True, until the circuit of the revolution is completed, in the course of which it obtains a clear vision of absolute (ideal) justice, temperance and knowledge; and when it has thus been feasted by the sight of the essential truth of all things, the soul again enters within the vault of heaven and returns home. And there the charioteer gives his steeds ambrosia to eat and nectar to drink. This is the life of the gods. But the fate of the other souls is far otherwise. The soul which follows GOD closest, and is made most like to Him, lifts the head of its charioteer into the super-celestial realm, and so he is carried round; but still he is constantly disturbed by the steeds which he drives, and gains only with difficulty a clear vision of the absolute truth of things. Another soul rises for a time, and then sinks, and through the violence of its steeds obtains only a partial view. The rest follow, all eagerly desirous of reaching the upper region; but being unable to do so, are borne round within the elements of the material Cosmos, struggling and trampling one another down in their efforts to reach the foremost place. And in the tumult and strife many souls are lamed, and many have their wings broken, and all, in spite of their earnest efforts, catch no sight of that which really *is*, and when they return are forced to feed upon the food of fancy. For the reason why they strive so zealously to see the plain of truth is this, that the food which suits the noblest element of the soul is found in the meadow there, and that it is by the help of this the wings grow by which the soul is lifted from the earth. So the procession ends, and the irrevocable judgment follows. Every soul which has gained a clear vision of truth remains in the society of the gods till the next time of review. The rest, which have been unable to follow their divine guides, or have met with any accident, or have suffered forgetfulness to overpower them, or have lost their wings, are implanted in some human form, varying in character according to the impressions which each soul still retains of its former vision of truth[1]. Ten

[1] Phædrus, 248 D, E. The exact order is very remarkable, and as it does not appear to be noticed by the commentators, it may be worth while to indicate the law which it presents:—

Pure Spirit— SOUL.		SOUL dominant	Absolutely	i. φιλόσοφος.
			Relatively { Morally	ii. ἀρχικός.
			{ Physically	iii. οἰκονομικός.
	MAN (Soul Body)		Individually	iv. γυμναστικός.
		SOUL neutralized		v. μαντικός.
		BODY dominant	Individually	vi. ποιητικός.
Pure Matter— BODY.			Relatively { Physically	vii. δημιουργικός.
			{ Morally	viii. δημοτικός.
			Absolutely	ix. τυραννικός.

thousand years pass before they can regain their former state. The soul of the philosopher alone can recover its wings in three thousand years, if at each time of choice it faithfully chooses the same lot: for at the close of each life follows a period of retribution for a thousand years, after which each soul is free to choose its destiny. A human soul may pass into a brute; the soul of a brute, which was once a man, may return to a man. For no soul which has *never* seen the truth can reach the human form; for man must be able to understand general terms which answer to *ideas*, and he does so by recalling those objects which his soul once saw when it followed in the train of GOD, and was lifted above what we now say *is*, and gained a sight of that which *is* truly."

In no other place has Plato given so clear a statement of his doctrine of ideas, which gives fixity to the doctrine of recollection. And the reason is evident. The doctrine itself represents an intuition or an instinct, and not a result. It is a beginning and not a conclusion. And therefore a mythical exposition alone can place it in its true relation to the general system of the universe. By using this, Plato sketches in a few ineffaceable lines what he holds to be the divine lineaments of the soul, seen in its power to hold fellowship with GOD and apprehend absolute truth. It may fall from the heights of heaven which it has been privileged to climb, but even so the transitory images of earthly things are for it potential symbols, and memorials of glories which it has seen; and in its degradation it yet can feel that the way of return to supra-celestial joy is not finally closed.

The myth of the "Phædrus" opens a glimpse of a judgment after death. The judgment itself is portrayed in the "Gorgias." As suits the character of the dialogue, the treatment of the subject here is "most purely moral," and the accessories and scenery of the myth are taken directly from the Homeric poems[1]. Socrates has maintained that to act unjustly is the greatest of evils. In illustration of the proposition he says[2],—

"'I will tell you a very beautiful story, which you, I fancy, will regard as a fable, but I hold to be very truth. Well, then, as Homer tells us, Zeus and Poseidon and Pluto divided between them the empire which they received from their father. In the time of Kronos there was a law, which is still, even now as always, in force among the gods, that after death men should go to the Islands of the Blest, or to Tartarus, according as they had lived holy or godless lives. Till Zeus had reigned some little time, the judgment took place on the day on which they were to die. Judges and judged were living men. So, many errors were committed, and when complaint was made to Zeus, he said, "I will put an end to this. The present mode of trial is faulty. The subjects of the trial are still clothed when they undergo it, for they are yet living. And many men with wicked souls are arrayed in beauty, and rank, and wealth; and at the time of their trial many come forward to give evidence that they have lived justly. So the judges are influenced by these witnesses, and moreover are clothed themselves, for the veil of sense lies before

[1] This is pointed out by Mr Cope—*Gorgias, Introd.*, p. lxxiv.

[2] Gorgias, 523 A, *et seq*.

their souls. First, then, I must prevent men from knowing the time of their death; and next, judges and judged must be unclothed by death before the trial takes place, and the judge must give his sentence as he regards simply with his soul alone simply the soul of each, at the moment after dissolution, when the subject is bereft of all his kinsmen, and has left on earth all the fair adornment in which he was arrayed. This I had observed," he added, addressing the complainants, "before you, and determined to appoint as judges my own sons, Minos and Rhadamanthus from Asia, and Æacus from Europe. After their death, these shall give sentence in the meadow where the crossroads meet, of which one leads to the Islands of the Blest, and another to Tartarus. Rhadamanthus shall judge the dead from Asia, Æacus those from Europe. Minos shall hold the supreme place of honour, and finally decide if the two others are in any doubt, that the judgment which determines the road men must tread may be as just as possible."
'This,' Socrates continues, 'is the story which I have heard, and believe to be true. And the conclusion which I draw is this:—Death, in my opinion, is simply the separation of two things, soul and body, from one another. And after their separation, each preserves the character which it had when the man was alive. The body, as we can see retains its natural characteristics, the results of care and discipline, the traces of accident and suffering. So it is also, I believe, with the soul. When the soul is stripped of its bodily vestment, it also presents all the traits of nature, and the consequences of individual habits, distinctly visible. And so, when the dead come to the judges, the judge regards the soul of each, not knowing whose it is: very frequently he lays hands on the great King, or some other prince or potentate, and sees that his soul is all rotten, covered all over with slavish scars, and

full of wounds inflicted by perjuries and injustice, which his own conduct has impressed upon the soul of each; he sees that every member of it is distorted by falsehood and ostentation and the utter absence of the discipline of truth; he sees that it has lost every trace of harmony and beauty, through licence and luxury and arrogance and intemperance; and when he sees it, he despatches the soul in dishonour straightway to the prison-house, where it is doomed to bear the sufferings which it deserves. For some this suffering is remedial, for others it is simply exemplary[1]. As it is on earth, so it is below. Those whose sins can be healed, can be healed only by sorrow and pain, which here and hereafter are used to restore them. Those whose guilt is incurable, from the extreme magnitude of their crimes, draw no longer any profit from their sufferings, for they are past healing, but others draw profit from them, when they see them suffering for ever for their sins the greatest and most terrible pains, hung up simply as examples in the dungeon of Hades, as spectacles and warnings to all the guilty who come there. And such characters are, I fancy, generally found among the great, for these, if they have the will, have also the power, to act most wickedly. Whenever, then, Rhadamanthus[2] finds such an one he only knows that he is a guilty wretch, and nothing else about him, neither who he is nor whence he comes, and so he sends him away to Tartarus, affixing a mark upon him to shew whether he seems to be curable or incurable. And sometimes, when he has looked upon another soul, which has lived with holiness and truth,—that of a plain citizen it may be, or more frequently of a philosopher, who has devoted himself to his own pursuits, and not meddled in the affairs of others,—he is filled with admiration, and

[1] Gorgias, 525 B, *et seq*.   [2] *Ib*. 526 B, *et seq*.

sends it away to the Islands of the Blest. And thus also does Æacus. And Minos looks on from his throne, alone, holding a golden sceptre, as Odysseus says in Homer[1],—

> 'There Minos, child of Zeus, sceptred with gold,
>   I saw dividing justice to the dead;
> Who round his throne, in the wide-gated hold
>   Of Hades, stand or sit, and him, their head,
> Cry to for judgment.'"

So pitilessly stern and impartial is the judgment of the dead; and even according to Plato's instinct there are some who cannot receive forgiveness "either in this world or in the world to come," for whom the wings of the soul are lost for ever. And it is remarkable that the material aspect of the unseen world is a subject on which he seems to delight to dwell. This, in his imagination, has no likeness to the supersensuous region of ideas on which the unembodied souls gaze, but akin to man, who is for a time its tenant. So when Socrates had exhausted his arguments on immortality, he is represented in the "Phædo" as concluding his last discourse with a mythic delineation of the future resting-place of the blessed dead, and the seats of torture for the wicked. There is, he admits, adequate ground for questioning the truth of his reasoning, from a consideration of the greatness of the subject and the weakness of man; but yet practically he is convinced, himself, of his immortality, and therefore of the infinite importance of right action[2],—

[1] Od. xi. 576 (Worsley).   [2] Phædo, 107-A, B.

"For the soul[1] takes with it to Hades nothing but the results of its education and growth, which immediately begin to manifest their effects. The story is, that after death the genius to whom each man was committed during his lifetime, proceeds to take him to a place where the dead must be gathered together to obtain their sentence, before they go to Hades in the charge of the guide to whom the task of conducting them is committed. And when they have received there their due recompence, and remained the appointed space, another guide brings them back to earth. The road to Hades is not, then, so simple as Æschylus tells us : '*One single path conducts us to the shades.*' If it were so, there would have been no need of guides; but the road is really branching and circuitous. And so the well-disciplined and wise soul follows the guide and recognises its present position: that soul, on the other hand, which is passionately attached to the body, fluttering about it and the world of sense with lingering desire, after a violent resistance and grievous suffering, is forcibly removed by the appointed genius. And when such a soul, stained by impurity and crime, reaches the common gathering-place, every one flies from it and avoids it: companionless and guideless, it wanders about in dire distress till the time comes when it must be carried to its appropriate habitation. But that soul which has lived in purity and justice, after enjoying the companionship and guidance of the gods, dwells in its proper place. Yes, and there are many marvellous places in the earth; and the earth is not, either in nature or extent, such as geographers suppose. For I am convinced[2] that we who live along the borders of the Mediterranean are like frogs living around a swamp; and that there are many other basins like that in which

---

[1] Phædo, 107 D.   [2] *Ib.* 108 *et seq.*

we live, similarly occupied, which are receptacles for a sediment of water, and mist and air; and that the true earth rises far above, all radiant and pure in the pure radiance of heaven. But we who live in these deep basins fancy we live upon the earth, whereas our case is just as if creatures living at the bottom of the sea were to fancy that they lived *upon* the sea, and when they saw the sun through the water, were to hold the sea to be heaven. For we call our hollows earth and the atmosphere heaven, and cannot any more than the tenants of the deep rise to the surface of the element which covers us, and see the true brightness of the celestial bodies, whose dimmed glory only reaches us, and the true beauty of the objects of earth, of which we see only starved and corroded and decaying types. The earth, in fact[1], when looked at from above, is said to be like a particoloured ball, such as children play with, marked out into regions of various hues, purple and gold and white, and so on, brighter and purer and more manifold than those which artists use. Even the hollows in which we live, like lakes, add brilliancy to the assemblage of tints, and complete their harmony. So again the trees and flowers in that higher region are proportionately more beautiful than ours. The mountains are solid gems, of which our jewels are little fragments. The precious metals are seen everywhere; to look upon the real earth alone is happiness. There are also living beings there, and men, some of whom dwell on the shores of the atmosphere, others on islands which it encircles; for our atmosphere is their sea, and their atmosphere is æther. Moreover, the inhabitants have temples of the gods, in which the gods really dwell, and hold intercourse with their worshippers. And as there is this true earth above us, so are there awful and

[1] Phædo, 110 B, *et seq*.

mysterious caverns below[1], through which flow immeasurable streams, and rivers of fire and torrents of mud, which centre all in Tartarus. Of these, four rivers[2] are chiefly to be noticed: Ocean, the greatest of all, which flows outermost round the earth; and opposite to this Acheron, which, passing through desert places, comes to the Acherusian lake, where the mass of the souls of the dead assemble. The third river, directly after its rise, falls into a place burning with fire, and forms a lake of boiling mud, and after a circuitous course reaches the Acherusian lake, but does not mingle its current with the water. This is Pyriphlegethon, and lava-streams are casual jets from its molten flood. The fourth river falls into a dreary and savage spot, where it forms the Stygian lake, and afterwards passes through the Acherusian lake, without mingling with it, opposite to Pyriphlegethon; and this, the poets say, is called Cocytus. This being so, when the dead reach the place whither their genius carries them, they obtain their sentence, and those whose lives have been neither very good nor very bad are conveyed along Acheron to the Acherusian lake, where they are purified of their wickedness by punishment, and receive the rewards of their good deeds. Those who are judged to be incurably guilty, owing to the greatness of their sins, are thrown into Tartarus, from which they never come out. Those, again, whose sins are very great, but yet not past all cure, are thrown, for so it must be, into Tartarus; but after a year they are carried by Cocytus or Pyriphlegethon to the Acherusian lake, where, with loud cries, they call upon those whom they wronged, beseeching them for pardon, that so they may leave their place of torment and come to them; and if their prayer is heard, it is well; if not, they return

[1] Phædo 111 c, *et seq.* [2] *Ib.* 112 E, *et seq.*

to their place of suffering, for they gain no respite till it is granted by those whom they injured. Those, lastly, who have lived with conspicuous holiness are they who are freed from their prison-house in the lower realms, and rise aloft to radiant habitations, and dwell upon the earth which I have described. And such as have purified themselves sufficiently by philosophy live wholly without bodies for the future, and rise to habitations more glorious than these, which it were hard to paint; and now time presses. But I think what I have said shews that we must strive by all means to gain virtue and wisdom in our lives. The prize is glorious and the hope is great."

The words are surely memorable words, and in the place which they occupy, of more than tragic interest. The last great discourse of Socrates in Plato's narrative is like his last charge, which was given so soon afterwards. There is the same spirit in the injunction to offer the customary sacrifice[1]—"the cock to Æsculapius"—as in the delineation of the material paradise. In the final moments of his earthly sojourn the philosopher seeks, as it were, some sacramental pledge of his highest faith. He clings dutifully to the rights of traditional worship which he had sought to ennoble. He dwells lovingly among the images of common beauty, which he transfigures with a diviner grace. In that supreme crisis the man reposes not on the subtleties of argument, but on the broad foundations of natural instinct. He dies with the vision of a home still before his eyes,

[1] Phædo, 118 A.

such as he had known, but purer, brighter, abiding in heaven.

One myth still remains, the story of Er the Pamphylian, with which the "Republic" closes. In this the destiny of the soul is traced out with more completeness than in any other, and if it is inferior to the myth of the "Timæus" in magnificence, and to that of the "Phædo" in pathos, it is yet on the whole perhaps the richest in thought and the most artistic in treatment of all the Platonic myths. Er, so the story runs[1], was slain in battle, and when his corpse was recovered and laid on the twelfth day upon the funeral pile, he came to life again, and thereupon he related what he saw in the interval. He said,—

"When his soul left his body, it went with many others to a mysterious place where there were two openings in the earth, and two in the heaven opposite to them; and between judges were sitting. These, after giving sentence, ordered the just to go upwards to the right, fastening on their breasts tokens of their decision: the unjust downwards to the left, carrying on their backs tokens of their actions. When he went up to them, they said that he would have to tell men what passed in the world below, and straitly charged him to hear and observe everything. So he saw some souls go away by the two openings above and below, and others returning by the two corresponding openings, of which those which descended from heaven were pure and clean, those which ascended from the earth were soiled and dusty. It seemed that they had come from a long journey, and they were glad to meet in the

[1] De Republica, x. pp. 614 B, *et seq.*

meadow and speak of their various lots during their passage, of a thousand years, the one class telling of their unspeakable enjoyments, the other, with tears and lamentations, of their sufferings ; for the recompence of virtue and crime, he said, was tenfold as great as the acts themselves. Moreover, he saw one spirit asked by another where Ardiæus the Great was, who had made himself a despot in a city of Pamphylia a thousand years before, after murdering his father and elder brother, and committing, as was said, many atrocious crimes. 'He has not come,' was the reply, 'nor will he come up here, for among other terrible sights we saw this. When we were near the mouth of the pit[1], and on the point of ascending, we suddenly saw him, and others with him, most of them despots; and when they thought that they should ascend, the mouth would not receive them, but began to bellow whenever one of those who were incurably vicious, or had not yet paid the adequate penalty of his guilt, endeavoured to ascend. Whereupon[1] he continued, 'men savage of aspect and all fiery, seized some of them and led them away, but Ardiæus and others they bound hands and feet and head, to cast them into Tartarus. And though we had suffered many and manifold terrors,' he added, 'this terror was the greatest of all, lest we should hear the voice when we tried to ascend, and we each rejoiced greatly that we were allowed to ascend, as the mouth uttered no sound.'"

After they had spent seven days in the meadow, Er said, they were obliged to resume their journey on the eighth day, and after four days they came to a spot from which—

"They saw a column of light like the rainbow, but

[1] De Republica, x. 615·D, *et seq.*

brighter and purer, which they reached in half a day's march, and then they saw that the light was the bond which encircled heaven, and that through its extremities passed the spindle of Necessity, round the base of which revolved, as on the rims of gigantic cups fitting closely into one another, the eight planets; and as the spindle turned, so too they turned with their proper motions, and on each rim a Siren sat, giving forth a single note, so that from the eight arose one grand harmony[1]. And three others sat round at equal intervals, each on a throne, the daughters of Necessity, the Fates, white-robed, with chaplets on their heads, Lachesis, Clotho, and Atropos, and sang to the harmony of the Sirens, Lachesis of the past, Clotho of the present, Atropos of the future. The souls, he said, when they came there, were obliged to go directly to Lachesis. Whereupon a prophet first marshalled them in order, and then, taking lots and samples of lives from the knees of Lachesis, mounted on a lofty tribune, and said, 'O souls of short-lived men, now begins a new course of mortal existence. Your fate will not be assigned to you: you will choose your fate yourselves. Virtue is the peculiar prize of none. Each, as he honours or dishonours her, will enjoy her favour. Blame rests with the chooser: GOD is blameless.' When he had so said he threw down the lots, and each picked up that which fell beside him, except himself (for he was forbidden), and saw the order of his choice. And afterwards the prophet placed the samples of lives on the ground before them, far more in number than those present. These were of all kinds, he said, including those both of men and animals, and marked by every variety of gifts and failings in external station and personal endowment. The character of the soul was alone left undeter-

[1] De Republica, x. 617 B, *et seq*.

mined, for this necessarily depended upon the nature of
the life chosen in each case. The prophet thereupon[1]
warned the souls of the supreme importance of their choice,
and said, 'He who comes last in order, if he chooses with
intelligence and lives with energy and self-control, has the
assurance of a happy life. He who chooses first must not
be careless: he who chooses last must not despond.' On
this he to whom the first lot fell came up and grasped the
greatest sovereignty, and in his greedy folly he had not
observed that it included the necessity of his feeding on
his own children; and when he discovered this on a calm
investigation, he began to bewail and lament his fate, accusing every one but himself of the evils of his destiny.
This, he said, was one of those who had come down from
heaven, and had lived in his former life in a well-ordered
commonwealth, and been virtuous by habit without the
salutary discipline of philosophy. And those who came
from heaven, he said, were thus deceived in their choice
quite as often as others, because they were undisciplined
by suffering; while those who came from the earth, since
they had suffered themselves, and had seen others suffer,
were generally slow and cautious in choosing. And from
this, among other reasons, the souls, as a general rule, experience a transition from good to evil, and the reverse;
though the sound pursuit of philosophy would go far to
secure happiness on earth, and a smooth and heavenly
passage through the shades below. It was indeed, he said,
a strange sight to watch the choice of lives—piteous at
once and ludicrous; for the souls were chiefly influenced
by their former experience. For example, he saw the soul
of Orpheus choosing the life of a swan; that of Ajax avoiding a human destiny from the remembrance of his wrongs;

[1] De Republica, x. 619 B.

that of Agamemnon taking the life of an eagle. Among the last he saw the soul of the buffoon Thersites choose the life of an ape: and last of all, the soul of Ulysses went to make its choice. This soul, cured of ambition by the recollection of its former sufferings, went about for a long time in search of a life of a quiet, simple citizen; and when it found it, after great trouble, lying in an obscure corner, and neglected by all the rest, took the life gladly, and said that it would have done the same if it had the first choice. At the same time the souls of animals passed into other animals and into men. And when the choice was completed, all went to Lachesis, and she charged the genius which each had chosen, to accompany him through life, and accomplish the fate which he had selected. Afterwards they visited Clotho and Atropos, and passed forth through the throne of Necessity, and all marched to the plain of Oblivion, through terrible and suffocating heat. As it was now drawing towards evening, they encamped by the stream Forgetfulness, whose water no vessel can hold, of which all were forced to drink a measure, and those who were not preserved by prudence drank more than the measure; and straightway the drinkers forgot everything. They then fell asleep, and when midnight came there was a clap of thunder and an earthquake, and suddenly all the souls were carried, like shooting stars, in different directions to their birth. He himself, he said, was not allowed to drink the water; and yet he could not tell how he came into his body, but suddenly looking up in the morning he saw himself lying on the funeral pyre. So the story was saved," Socrates continues[1], "and not lost, and it will save us if we give heed to it, and we shall then cross happily over the river of

[1] De Republica, x. 621 B, *et seq*.

Oblivion, and not defile our soul. Yes, if we all give heed to my counsel, and believe that the soul is immortal, and capable of every woe and every good, we shall keep close to the upward path, and practise justice with active wisdom in every way we can, that we may be at peace with ourselves and with the gods while we abide on earth, and when we reap the rewards of justice, like victors in their triumphal course, and may ever fare well, not only in our present life, but also in that pilgrimage of the thousand years which we have described."

IV.

Such briefly are the Myths of Plato. Even when thus presented they form undoubtedly one of the most fruitful chapters in the history of the religious thought of Greece; for though scattered they have a real unity, and though romantic they are truly Greek[1]. The proof of their unity lies in the connection of the stories among themselves, and it seems impossible not to see in them a proper whole. But their unity is derived not from any conscious plan, but from the character of the subjects with which they deal, and

[1] To point out the connection of Plato's myths with the Ancient Mysteries, with Pythagoras, and with Egypt, would require an independent essay. For it is not meant that the conception of the Platonic myths is everywhere original, which is manifestly untrue, but that Plato made what he borrowed his own. He was himself perhaps the most catholic of Greeks, and the myths are Greek in the same way that he is.

the unconscious symmetry with which the works of the highest genius are always invested. Each myth, as will have been seen, stands alone as if it were a single and complete creation; and yet each gains new fulness when placed in its true relation to the others. They overlap and intersect each other, and yet room is left for each separate development. Nothing, indeed, is more remarkable than the careless prodigality, as it might seem, with which Plato brings out his treasures, never again caring to look back upon them; and yet, with a master's art, he continues to the last to throw new lights and fresh adornments on what he might appear to have forgotten.

It is not, therefore, strange that the Myths were accepted by common consent as the text for the deepest speculations of the later Platonic schools, and so have contributed, through them, more largely than any other part of Plato's writings to the sum of common thoughts. The popular notions of Platonism, again, are almost exclusively derived from the myths. And it is easy to see why it is so. The value of a method may be estimated differently at different times. The delight of mere discussion without result at last ceases to charm. But there are subjects of positive belief on which the soul is never wearied in dwelling; and it is with these the myths deal.

In bold and vigorous outlines, they offer a philosophy of nature, a philosophy of history, and a philosophy of life, deformed, it may be, by crude speculations in physics, and cramped by imperfect knowledge and a necessarily narrow sphere of observation, but yet always inspired by the spirit of a Divine life, centring in the devout recognition of an all-wise and all-present Providence, and in the inexorable assertion of human responsibility. In form, in subject, in the splendour of their imagery, and in the range of their application, they form, if we may so speak, an Hellenic Apocalypse. And if we compare our popular theories of the world and man with the aspirations which they embody, we may well doubt whether we have used the lessons of eighteen Christian centuries as Plato would have used them.

The earnestness of Plato is indeed a strange contrast to our indifference in dealing with the same topics; for as has been said before, the Myths were not for him poetic fancies, but representations of momentous truths. The details might or might not be exact, but their general scope was that for which he was ready to contend to the uttermost. Thus Socrates says, at the close of the myth in the "Phædo[1],"—

"To confidently affirm that the narrative which I have given is literally true becomes no reasonable man. But I do think it becomes him to believe that what I have said about our souls and their habitations is either literally true or like the truth, if, at least, the soul is shewn to be immortal; and that it is worthy of him to face peril boldly in such a belief, for the peril is glorious; and such thoughts he ought to use as a charm to allay his own misgivings:

[1] Phædo, 114 D.

in which spirit I have myself dwelt thus long upon the story."

The last words point to two characteristics of the Myths which can now be appreciated better than when they were first indicated in the opening section. The Myths transcend the domain of pure reason, and their moral power springs out of their concrete form. In the first respect, to take an illustration which will make the notion clear, they answer to Revelation, as an endeavour to enrich the store of human knowledge; in the second, to the Gospel, as an endeavour to present, under the form of facts, the manifestations of Divine Wisdom[1].

Whatever may be the prevailing fashion of an age, the Myths of Plato remain an unfailing testimony to the religious wants of man. They shew not only that

[1] This idea is stated very forcibly by Mr Maurice, *Moral and Metaphysical Philosophy*.—Plato:—"Plato...was...certain that somehow or other all great principles must have an investiture of *facts*, and cannot be fully or satisfactorily presented to men except in facts. And if no such series of facts, embodying and revealing truths, were within his reach, rather than leave it to be fancied that his truths are bare, naked conceptions of his mind, he will invent a clothing for them; it is the least evil of the two....Then what pretence have those to the name of Platonists who wish to believe that there is no series of facts containing a revelation of supersensual and transcendent truths, who think it an à *priori* probability, that the deep want of such facts which Plato experienced has not been satisfied, who are determined, even by the most violent treatment of historical evidence, to prove that whenever a supposed fact manifests a principle, it must be a fable?"

reason by its logical processes is unable to satisfy them, but also in what directions its weakness is most apparent and least supportable. They form, as it were, a natural scheme of the questions with which a revelation might be expected to deal,—Creation, Providence, Immortality,—which, as they lie farthest from the reason, lie nearest to the heart. And in doing this, they are so far an unconscious prophecy, of which the teaching of Christianity is the fulfilment.

But more than this: the Myths mark also the shape which a revelation for men might be expected to take. The doctrine is conveyed in an historic form: the ideas are offered as facts; the myth itself is the message. With what often appears unnecessary care, Plato appeals to popular tradition or external testimony for the veracity of his mythical narratives. He knows that their power of influencing life depends directly upon their essential connection with life. If the myth belongs really to our world, not as a thought but as an event, it is homogeneous with man as man in his complex nature. In this way, again, Plato is an unconscious prophet of the Gospel. The Life of Christ is, in form no less than in substance, the Divine reality of which the Myths were an instructive foreshadowing.

It is well, then, that we should remember that what we look back upon as accomplished events, were once looked forward to as aspirations of the heart. The problem of life is not changed by the lapse of centuries, but the conditions are changed. What the problem is, and what the conditions were in old times, and what they are now, Plato himself may teach us[1]. Socrates said to his friends on the evening of his execution,—

"Do you think that, when I speak of my present fate as no misfortune, I am a less skilful diviner than the swans, who sing longest and sweetest in the prospect of death, because they are on the point of going to the god whose servants they are? Nay rather, I am bound by the same service as they are, and devoted to the same god, and my lord inspires me with prophetic insight no less than them, and therefore I ought to depart from life as cheerfully as they do."

And Simmias answers:—

"Still, Socrates, I feel some difficulty. I think, and perhaps you think with me, that it is impossible or extremely difficult to obtain distinct knowledge on such subjects in our present life. On the other hand, it is utterly unmanly to desist from investigating, by every means in our power, whatever is urged about them, before we are exhausted by a complete inquiry. For we must gain one of two results. We must either learn or discover the truth about them; or if this be impossible, we must take the best and most irrefragable of human words, and, supported on this as on a raft, sail through the waters of life in perpetual jeopardy, unless we might make the journey on a securer stay,—some *Divine Word*, if it might be,—more surely and with less peril."

The Word for which the wavering faith of Simmias thus longed, has, we believe, been given to us; and once again Plato points us to St John.

[1] Phædo, 85 a, *et seq.*

THE DRAMATIST AS PROPHET:
ÆSCHYLUS.

οὗτοι, νόμον μὴ ἔχοντες, ἑαυτοῖς εἰσὶν νόμος· οἵτινες ἐνδείκνυνται τὸ ἔργον τοῦ νόμου γραπτὸν ἐν ταῖς καρδίαις αὐτῶν.

EP. AD ROM. ii. 14.

ἔσθ᾽ ὅπου τὸ δεινόν εὖ
καὶ φρενῶν ἐπίσκοπον
δεῖ μένειν καθήμενον·
ξυμφέρει σωφρονεῖν ὑπὸ στένει.

EUMEN. 491.

I.

IN reading the works of a Greek tragedian it is very difficult to realize practically the circumstances of their composition. Their similarity in form to later dramas is constantly tending to hide their difference in idea; and though otherwise a true understanding of the text is impossible, there is need of a steady effort to feel that the play was essentially an element of a religious rite: that those who took part in its representation were for the time devoted to the service of a god, and hallowed by his protection: that the altar, in front of the stage on which it was acted, was really destined for sacred use, and built on consecrated ground. The Greek theatre was indeed a national temple; and, more than this, the tragic poets were the national preachers. In the early days of Athenian glory the teaching of philosophy was unheard or concealed. When it obtained a popular voice in Socrates, his practical sagacity could not save the strange doctrines from the condemnation of impiety. Even when their influence was greatest, the schools reached but a small section of the citizens: on the general tone of thought and belief, their direct influence was inconsiderable. The Athenian, the typical Greek, received his characteristic training on a grander field. His secular discipline came from an active participation in the government of the State; his religious instruction—if we except the initiation at Eleusis—from the sacred festivals, and especially from the tragic representations at the Dionysia. In a word, he learned the practice of life from the debates of the public assembly; he learned the theory of life from the poems of the theatre.

For it must ever be remembered that the Greek tragedies were poems and not illusions : they were interpretations and not pictures of life. The facts, so to speak, were given; the business of the writer was to explain their meaning and their lessons. The outline of the plot was a familiar text; the filling up was the sermon of the preacher. And so it is that the remains of the Greek tragedians furnish a remarkable picture of the history of popular religion during the period over which they reach. Or rather, when we bear in mind the marvellous rapidity of the moral and intellectual development of Athens in the fifth century before our era, they shew the complete cycle of forms of national religious thought, ending on the one side in schools of philosophy which became more and more estranged from the old belief, and on the other side in the comedy of manners which was destitute of all spiritual significance.

In this aspect, the position occupied by Æschylus is of commanding interest[1]. He is the prophet of Greek tragedy, as Sophocles is the artist, and Euripides the realist. The succession of character is one which reappears in every literature, but in this first example it is most marked and most spontaneous. Events are first viewed on their divine side, then on the side of order or beauty, and lastly on the side of nature. The same story which furnishes Æschylus with an occasion for reconciling the claims of revenge and forgiveness, the powers of earth and the powers of heaven, furnishes Sophocles with a powerful dramatic

[1] The references to the plays are made throughout to Mr Paley's Æschylus, "re-edited with an English Commentary" (London, 1855), which has the signal merit (unless I am mistaken) of being the first English edition of a Greek tragedian in which the author is treated as a real poet. The fragments are quoted from Dindorf's *Poetæ Scenici*.

Klausen's essay, *Theologumena Æschyli Tragici*, Berolini, 1829, is very full and instructive. He alone of the writers whom I have consulted justly estimates the character of Prometheus.

study of female character, and Euripides with a graceful picture of life. It is no reproach to the later poets that they were different from the first. The difference between the three was inevitable; and the respective value which is assigned to each of the three views of life which they give will vary from age to age. There is no supreme standard to which they can be brought. Every critic will have a judgment of his own. But to decide the question on absolute principles would be as reasonable as to arrange on the same method the colours of the rainbow in order of beauty: for perfect light we need them all.

In his prophetic function, Æschylus stands in relation to the fragmentary and inharmonious teachings of antique rites and early religious traditions, as we may believe Homer to have stood as a poet in relation to the traditional ballads of a former generation. He takes up into his own teaching all that had in it the element of divine life: he reconciles and combines what had been separately and exclusively wrought out before: he inspires—by the depth and sincerity of his own faith, no less than by the grandeur of his genius—a spirit of unity into the whole which he thus creates. The poems of Homer betray, as we believe, the work of different hands: the religious teaching of Æschylus exhibits equally a diversity of sources. His theology everywhere bears marks of the conflict out of which it has arisen, and in two of his seven extant plays, he deals specifically with the reconciliation of divine powers, which in some

degree reason—in accordance with ancient legends—
represents as antagonistic. In this, indeed, his truest
prophetic work lay. It was his task to harmonize, as
best he might, the claims of fate and will, of law and
life, of GOD and man, in this present world; to con-
nect suffering with sin, and strip guilt of the boast of
impunity; to indicate the majesty of Providence, and
the absolute wisdom of the Divine voice revealed in
appointed ways.

To fulfil this task Æschylus was fitted by great
external advantages. He was a native of Eleusis,
and so connected by his birth with the most solemn
mysteries of the Greek faith. He lived through the
great struggle with Persia, when gods and heroes were
still supposed to have fought on the side of Greece.
He belonged to a family of warriors. One brother,
the colleague of Miltiades, fell with signal glory at
Marathon; another carried off the prize for bravery
at Salamis; and he himself took part, not without
honourable wounds, in the battles of Marathon,
Salamis, and Plataeae. His parents, moreover, were
noble, and so he was naturally connected with the
party of order and tradition, to whom reverence is a
ground of conviction, and interpretation the rule of
progress. Thus it was impossible that, being born a
poet, he should not receive with a solemn awe all that
was consecrated by old belief; that he should not see
the action of gods everywhere, when he had witnessed
such marvels from their interposition; that he should
not dwell upon the problems of retribution and the

56   THE DRAMATIST AS PROPHET:

continuity of action, when he had lived through the close of that great contest of the East and West, which, according to ancient traditions, began with the abduction of Io and Helen[1]. It does not fall within our scope to discuss his genius. His writings shew that that at least corresponded with his position. As a religious poet, Dante alone stands by him; both were children of their age, both were schooled in sorrow, but both were above all that was merely personal and local, and remain, to those who will read them, prophets for all time.

II.

But though it is admitted that Æschylus was peculiarly qualified, by his historical and literary position, to give an accurate and living portraiture of Greek theology, it may be urged that his extant tragedies are but a very imperfect fragment of his actual works. Of ninety plays which he is said to have written, only seven have been preserved, and the remnants of his lost tragedies are comparatively few and unimportant. It is indeed impossible to estimate our loss. The first and last plays of the Promethean trilogy, the "Niobe" and the "Psychostasia" (the Soul-weighing), would probably have cleared up much that is now conjectural or obscure

[1] This is brought out remarkably by the introduction with which Herodotus opens his history: Herod. i. 1—5.

as to his religious views; but on the other hand, the selection of plays which remains is singularly rich. It was apparently made of deliberate purpose out of a larger number of extant tragedies; and both by its variety and unity it is calculated to assure us that the outline of the Æschylean creed which it contains is not deficient in any conspicuous article.

The manifoldness of the subjects of the Æschylean tragedies prepares the way for the fulness of their teaching. The "Prometheus" is purely mythical: all the actors are divine, for Io is destined for divine honours: the interest of the play is personal and moral. The "Suppliants" brings us to the verge of the heroic age: the gods take part in the action only through the ordinances of their worship: the interest of the play is national and religious. In the typical heroic plays, the "Seven against Thebes" and the "Orestea," we have the two great tragical legends of Northern and Southern Greece drawn out in their characteristic differences. In the former the State is the centre, in the latter the family: the one closes with death, the other with deliverance. Finally, in the "Persians," a scene of contemporary history is brought into clear relationship with mythical times. Whatever may have been the exact subjects of the other plays with which it was grouped, it seems certain that the object of the poet was to link the events of his own day to the ages of gods and heroes, and shew the fulfilment of a divine will in the actual course of national fortunes,

For however wide the field which Æschylus covers, he sees all equally in the light of a divine presence. Primitive myths, ancient traditions, historic events, are alike regarded by him from a spiritual point of sight. His view of life and society is in every case theocratic; and it is only by keeping this truth steadily in view that we can gain the central idea of his separate plays. No one of his tragedies is complete in itself. A single episode, a single generation, was insufficient for the display of the dependence of life upon life, and the moral infinitude of action, which it was his design to exhibit. Thus he habitually composed groups of three connected plays, which gave full scope for the development of thought and work. And so it happens that four of his seven plays are really fragments of greater wholes. The "Prometheus Bound," the "Suppliants," and the "Persians," were the middle plays of trilogies; the "Seven against Thebes" the concluding play[1]. In the "Orestea" alone, and yet surely there in its most complete grandeur, the full pattern of his mode of treatment is visible. And from the "Orestea" we can faintly imagine the outlines of the other trilogies, of which parts only remain.

It would be out of place to attempt to give now any detailed analysis of the tragedies. A slight indication

[1] This is established, against the conjectures of earlier scholars, by the express testimony of the Didascaliæ given in the Medicean manuscript. The other plays were Laius and Œdipus.

of the general conception of each will be enough to show how Æschylus dealt with his materials, and in what spirit he approached the interpretation of national mythology. The "Prometheus" is necessarily the foundation of his system, for it treats of the original problem of life and revelation, the relation of the free will of a finite being to the supreme will, of limited reason to divine wisdom, of their first dissension, of their open antagonism, of their final reconciliation. Unhappily the central piece of the trilogy alone survives. We know little more of "Prometheus the Firebearer" than the name: of "Prometheus Released," than the most meagre outline of the plot. So it is that the "Prometheus Bound" is in danger of being misunderstood. Throughout we are spectators of what seems to be an undecided conflict. There is no calm. From first to last the storms of earth hide the clear light of heaven. While Zeus is represented chiefly by the words of his adversaries, Prometheus is represented by his own. We forget that his sufferings were the consequence of an act of faithless distrust in Zeus, and of disobedience to his counsels. We forget again that his daring boasts were afterwards exchanged for lamentations, and that his threats against Zeus were mere idle vauntings. For the time he appears as a martyr; but he was first a rebel, and afterwards a pardoned subject. This true view of his character is illustrated by the appearance of Io, the second figure in the play. In Prometheus we have reason challenging Zeus: in Io, Zeus making himself known to men. The contact in both cases brings for the present overwhelming suffering, but in all other respects the fate of the two sufferers is contrasted. Prometheus, strong in will and power, has seized a divine boon; he is reckless of consequences; he forgets his own sufferings; the consciousness of his immortality assures him of final deliverance: such is reason. Io has been the involuntary recipient of divine fellowship; she is lost in the greatness of her own suffering; she has no self-dependence, no foresight: such is feeling. And yet it was from Io that the hero sprang by whose vicarious[1] sufferings Prometheus was in due time delivered. The weak woman was in the end stronger than the Titan[2].

The "Suppliants" is in every respect far simpler in its structure. It is indeed little more than a record of the reception of the daughters of Danaus, descendants of Io, under the shelter of the gods of Greece. Sought by their cousins in an unholy marriage, they flee to Argos, and there make good their claim to an inviolable sanctuary. There is no contrast or complexity of principles in the plot. The whole interest of the play centres in the absolute validity of external religious ordinances against self-

[1] Prom. 1047.
[2] One of the Greek commentators on the play notices that the subject is treated episodically by Sophocles in one play, and is not found in Euripides at all. The fact is itself a commentary on the difference between the tragedians which has been already pointed out.

interest and force. The suppliant claims protection with a divine right, and the right prevails. As the complement to this view of what may be called the power of external religion, the portraiture of Zeus himself is singularly pure and majestic. In no other play is he represented in more sublime and serene grandeur; and he who appeared for a time in the "Prometheus" as the betrayer of Io is here seen to have wrought out blessings for men through her.

The "Persians" has a singular interest. It is the earliest extant Greek history, and it is a poem. It is a record of one of the noblest achievements of human courage, and the conception is wholly theological. From the names of the other plays of the trilogy to which it belonged[1], it seems certain that the triumph of Greece over Persia was connected with ancient prophecies of the time of the Argonauts, and probably extended to the triumph of Greece over Carthage at Himera[2]. The scope of the providential view of history would thus be more complete, but the play itself preserves the full spirit of the treatment. The failure of the Persians was due to the transgression of the bounds which the gods had fixed to their empire. The sovereignty of the sea was not for them[3]. The destruction of their armies was a direct judgment for their impiety. They had desecrated the temples of Greece. And as if in mockery of human splendour,

---

[1] Phineus and Glaucus Pontius (or Potnieus).
[2] Klausen, p. 81. Comp. Æsch., Fragm. 25.
[3] Pers. 102.

the shade of Darius is called up to tell the tale, and declare the lessons of humility. He is addressed as a god, and his last words are,—And now

> "I go beneath the gloom of earth below;
> But you be glad even in the midst of woes,
> And give your souls to joy while it is day;
> For wealth, my friends, availeth not the dead."

The "Seven against Thebes" introduces us to a new form of thought, the conflict of self-will with national duties. Their relation to the State is the test by which actions are weighed. Laius was warned to save the State by dying childless; and for a time the sacrifice of Eteocles preserves it. It is only by seizing this idea that we can enter into the catastrophe of the play rightly. Personally the claim of Polynices was just: Eteocles broke a solemn compact in retaining the sovereignty. But nationally his attempt to secure his claim by violence, with the help of strangers, was unnatural and impious. Eteocles again, under the circumstances in which he was placed, was right in defending his country to the uttermost; but in seeking to meet his brother face to face he yielded to personal passion. The city was saved and the brothers fell; but by the manner of their death occasion was given for a fresh cycle of woe.

Of the "Orestea" it is difficult to speak shortly. No poet has ever drawn such another picture of human selfishness and guilt, of divine judgment and mercy. Each play has its special burden, and so far is complete in itself, and yet each is bound to the others by a continuity of moral purpose. In the "Agamemnon," human will is seen working out its own designs, freely indeed, but with the shadow of the curse behind. Paris indulges his impious passion; Menelaus his unmanly uxoriousness; Agamemnon his inordinate ambition; Ægisthus his cherished hatred; Clytemnestra her guilty love: and all succeed. Each gains his selfish object, and by gaining it, opens the way to his punishment. Even Cassandra—the one remaining character—exhibits the working of the same law. She had listened to the voice of Apollo voluntarily, and deceived him. Her reward was to know her fate and to be powerless to avert it. In this her lot was the converse of that of Io. The weakness of Io—the involuntary recipient of divine love—issued in divine blessings: the strength of Cassandra—the voluntary contemner of divine love—issued in death.

"The Choëphoræ" differs from the "Agamemnon" in its whole conception. In the "Agamemnon" man acts throughout of his own will. In the "Choephoræ" the action is at every point moulded by divine interposition. Revelation pronounces on human duty, and man obeys in doubt and sorrow. Thus the structure of the plot is simpler, but not less subtle. Every point which marked the guilt of Clytemnestra is reversed in the case of Orestes. She acted simply from her own resolve; he by an express command: she had a guilty passion to gratify; he a natural affection to conquer: she exults when the deed is done; he is filled with remorse: she in her blindness is ready to treat the old curse as satisfied; he looks forward to unknown sufferings: she enjoys a present triumph; he is visited by present punishment: and so the end is prepared; she dies, and he is purified by sorrow and delivered by the gods.

This deliverance is the theme of the "Eumenides;" and in this play again the action is divine. Man throws himself wholly on the word revealed to him, and his fellow-men are unable to pronounce a judgment: their voices are equally divided. But the god who destroyed Cassandra saves Orestes. The divine counsel is justified by the divine wisdom. And so it is that the special case of Orestes is merged, at the end of the play, in the broader lesson which it exhibited. Pallas not only restrains the action of the avenging Erinyes, but converts them into beneficent powers (Eumenides); and her victory is won, not by force but by persuasion. The truth is an old one, and yet perhaps it is not fully learnt yet. Æschylus could see that true worship and honour, the offerings of a loyal and wise obedience, can convert into sources of endless good the awful and inexorable laws of the external world, whence come on him who does them violence, untold plagues, and suffering.

Such, in brief outline, appear to be the central conceptions of the extant tragedies of Æschylus. His treatment of his subjects answers to their dignity, but of that nothing can be said now; nothing of his bold and pregnant language, which almost, like St Paul's, breaks down beneath the pressure of thought committed to it; nothing of the personal intensity of his faith, which, like that of an old prophet, applies to the present and the future. the divine teaching of the past; nothing of the personal devotion with which he evidently bows himself before the beings whose power he vindicates.; nothing of the tragic irony, more awful than that of Sophocles, with which he draws the fate of the wicked; nothing of the unconscious art by which he shews that pathos, no less than sublimity, is within his reach. For the present we listen to him simply as an exponent of religious belief; and the sketch which has been given of his position and his poems is sufficient to justify the expectation that we may find in him the general features of a theology consistent and tolerably complete.

III.

The first characteristic, perhaps, of the Æschylean theology which strikes a student is its true nationality[1]. The gods of Greece were not less real divinities

[1] Cicero's vague statement that Æschylus was "non poeta solum, sed etiam Pythagoreus: sic enim accepimus" (Tusc. ii. 10), if it refers at all to his religious opinions, rests on no adequate authority, and is certainly not supported by internal evidence. No passage *characteristically* Pythagorean can be

to Æschylus than they were to Homer, though they are differently apprehended. Æschylus approaches them, not as a poet simply, who finds in old legends ornaments for his work,—nor as a philosopher, who uses a popular phraseology to veil new teaching,— but as a devout believer, tracing out in life the realization of his faith. The sacred names which he uses, are spoken with heartfelt reverence. The sublime powers which he invokes are adored with genuine awe. According to an early and constant tradition he was accused of publishing the Eleusinian mysteries; and, strange as it may seem, the charge is in itself likely to be true. For him divine mysteries were "open secrets." He lived face to face with them, and they became axioms of life. For while he is a believer he is a poet and a prophet too. He looks beneath the manifold to the one: he translates, unconsciously it may be, the symbol into the lesson. He receives the common creed of his Athenian countrymen, embodied in conflicting stories and rival ceremonies, and he gives it back again simplified and harmonized. In his tragedies the will and destiny of man are reconciled with the claims of sovereign justice. The conflicts of the gods are traced to the necessary development of partial and imperfect attributes. The hierarchy of Olympus is marshalled in a noble order; and far above all weakness and change

pointed out in his writings; and, on the contrary, his whole teaching on a future state is eminently un-Pythagorean.

Zeus is throned supreme, whose will is Right, and whose name is the Saviour[1].

But these results are not gained by an arbitrary eclecticism. On the contrary, the fulness of Greek polytheism is nowhere more clearly seen than in Æschylus[2]. His work, as he seems to have understood it, was to reconcile and combine the conflicting factors of fate and will of which life is made up—the offspring of earth and the offspring of heaven,—and not to ignore their antagonism, or suppress either element in the great battle. This he does even in the earliest view which he opens of the dynasties of heaven. Like a true Greek, he sees in the celestial world the progress which he observes on earth. There was a time when Zeus was not yet king. But under his treatment the successive sovereignties of Uranus and Cronus and Zeus are a noble parable of the history of natural religious thought. The cycle of change was inevitable, and its lessons fruitful to the latest time.

Far back in the earliest ages, Uranus (Heaven) was supreme. This was the first instinctive embodiment of power. Men bowed themselves before the vast, silent, changeless expanse which covered them. But such a worship was soon supplanted by one more definite. The progeny of Uranus and Gaia (Earth), the manifestations of the forces of nature in their

---

[1] The character of Zeus the Saviour is well brought out by Müller, *Dissertations on the Eumenides*, § 94 (Eng. Tr.).

[2] Klausen, p. 5.

fullest activity, succeeded to the homage of mortals. The ancient ocean, the towering Atlas—which bore heaven upon its shoulders,—the fiery volcano, the wild storm, and all the brood of the Titans, with Cronus at their head, were acknowledged as divine[1]. And then was a time of strife and anarchy. The gods themselves were divided. But meantime Earth, their mother, revealed a nobler lesson, for she gave birth to Themis (Right), by whose voice it was declared that the victory should be decided by wisdom and not by might. The Titans were deaf to her warnings. "No power, they thought, could shake their rule of force," and so they fell in turn. The cycle was at length complete. Zeus, the son of Cronus, welcomed the counsels of prudence, and seized the sceptre which was offered him. The powers of nature were bound[2]; strength and force were made subject to will[3]; and a sway of sovereign reason was established, rising out of, and yet above, the grandest displays of physical energy[4].

In the portraiture of this reign of Zeus Æschylus uses language of Eastern sublimity. Zeus is "Prince of princes, most blessed of the blessed[5]," "Sovereign of eternity[6]," "Almighty Father[7]," "the cause and worker of all things[8]," "He who seeth all[9]," "invin-

[1] Prom. 356 *et seq.*; 432 *et seq.* Suppl. 554.
[2] Prom. 227.   [3] Prom. 1 *et seq.*
[4] *Ibid.* 205, *et seq.;* comp. 978.   [5] Suppl. 518.
[6] *Ibid.* 568.   [7] S. c. Th. 111; comp. Eum. 878.
[8] Ag. 1461.   [9] Eum. 999.

cible[1];" "His mind is an unplumbed abyss[2]," "His providence burns everywhere as a great light, even amidst the darkness of human life: his counsels meet with no reverse: but tangled and dark are the ways of his thoughts, inscrutable to mortal eye. He needs no arms of force to work his purpose. Seated afar upon his holy throne he carries it to its issue. For him the word and work are one[3]." And so it is that in life all is rightly referred to him, victory and defeat, the decision of the wavering council, the distribution of national power[4]. He "alone is free;" and "the harmonious order of the worlds which he has fixed no human plans can violate[5]."

Nothing can be plainer than that the supremacy of a Divine Will is affirmed here in every phrase; and yet it is commonly supposed that Æschylus placed a fate above Zeus to which he himself was subject. The difficulty is started by Prometheus, but the true answer is indicated at the same time. "Zeus has no refuge from the law of Fate," Prometheus says, when he looks forward to his illusory vengeance, and the Chorus answers, "Well, what is fated but his endless reign?" The Fates themselves draw their power from him[6]. Fate is, indeed, but another name for the will of Zeus. "That which is *fated* will most surely be:

[1] S. c. Th. 509.   [2] Suppl. 1043.
[3] Suppl. 81 *et seq.*; 588. The first passage is one of sublime grandeur in the original.
[4] Ag. 564; Pers. 534; Suppl. 617; Pers. 758.
[5] Prom. 50, 561.   [6] Ch. 288.

no power can thwart the mighty will of Zeus[1]." The very commonest words for fate,—μοῖρα, the lot assigned; αἶσα, *fatum*, the voice uttered,—bear witness to its dependence on a personal will: and yet, when once the allotment is made and the word spoken, both, in a certain sense, work of themselves, and may be contemplated apart from their first source. Thus it comes to pass that there may be conflicting Fates, since there are distinct orders of beings with characteristic functions and powers. One law of life may cross another, as indeed all life is made up of antagonisms, and the issue in such a case will be the resultant of the forces which severally work their full effect. A higher fate—a wider and more comprehensive law—must keep in check that which is lower and more personal, and so in the end the will of Zeus, which includes in itself the separate action of every other will, is finally accomplished[2]. This aspect of fate is further illustrated by the corresponding relation of Zeus to Justice. From one side Zeus "holds the principle of right alone;" "he rules by laws which are of his own making." When the judge is called upon to decide as sworn to administer the right, he is reminded that "an oath is not of greater force than Zeus," if it can be shewn that his will is against human conclusions[3]. And yet, on the other hand, "he gives effect to fate by law hoary with age."

[1] Suppl. 1033.   [2] Ag. 993.
[3] Prom. 194, 411. Eum. 521.

His award is unfailingly just: he judges by the truth of things, and not by the pleadings of a skilful advocate. His will is just, and so it may be said that "in one sense he *cannot* help the wicked[1]."

While Zeus, whose simple will is law and truth, rules in unapproached majesty, other divine powers attend his court, as Prometheus scornfully says[2], and minister to the fulfilment of his counsels. Two stand out-beyond all others,—Pallas Athenè, the embodiment of Divine wisdom, and Phœbus Apollo, the representative and organ of Divine revelation[3]. But both derive their authority from Zeus alone. "I trust in Zeus," "Zeus gave me wisdom," are the springs from which Pallas draws her arguments to soothe the Furies; and nowhere has an ancient poet drawn a nobler figure than that in which the goddess is presented in the "Eumenides,"—spotlessly pure, and yet tender to the guilty; confident in right and strength, and yet gentle and conciliatory to her angry antagonists; trusted by all, and in the end blest by all, for "her sire regards those sheltered by her wings[4]." The

[1] Supp. 657, 396. Ag. 786. Ch. 945.

[2] Prom. 121.

[3] Mr Gladstone has pointed out at considerable length (*Homeric Studies*, ii. 139 *et seq*.) the similar position which these deities occupy in the Homeric Olympus; but the supposition that they embody "the disintegrated elements of a primitive tradition" is opposed equally to all probability and to the actual history of revelation.

[4] Eum. 790, 812, 952, &c.

character of Apollo is more complex, but as he appears in the "Orestea," where his character is most fully drawn, he is the voice of his father's counsels (Loxias). Thus it was that he charged Orestes with his terrible mission, and, when he looks back upon the sorrow wrought by its enforced accomplishment, and addresses those to whom the final judgment upon the righteousness of the deed was confided, pleads, as if he could of himself go no further nor pronounce an opinion upon it,—

> "I never spake, in my prophetic seat,
> Of man, of woman, or of state one word
> Save what Zeus bade, sire of the gods above.
> How strong this plea I straitly bid you learn,
> And follow trustfully the Father's will.
> An oath is not of greater force than Zeus[1]."

And when he has said this he commits to Divine wisdom (Pallas) the justification of the Divine word.

Zeus the Saviour, Pallas, and Loxias (Apollo) thus combine to represent Providence active for man, guiding him amidst the conflict of duties, and delivering him in the last extremity of need. To them one other deity must be added, Hermes, the messenger between the realms of light and darkness, between the gods of heaven (Olympian) and the gods of earth (Chthonian). For though the Titanic earthborn powers were subdued by Zeus, they were not destroyed. The inexorable requirements of natural law

---

[1] Eum. 586. Comp. Eum. 19; Fragm. 79 (Dindf.).

were modified but not removed by the sovereignty of supreme intelligence. The antagonism between the tyranny of material forces and the counsels of divine mercy and benevolence was still necessarily unchanged, even when the question of supremacy was decided; and Æschylus delights to represent the gradual process by which the antagonism itself was reduced to the separate exertion of distinct and complementary prerogatives, by powers which consciously or unconsciously wrought out one end. Thus, in a passage of deep significance, he traces the successive steps in the history of revelation, as it passed from the Chthonian to the Olympian powers. Earth herself was the first prophet. In the simplest phenomena of nature she first spoke to men of the Divine character and will. As time went on she gave place to Right (Themis), a daughter who was born to her; for the teaching of society and life carries us forward in the knowledge of God. Right in turn gave place to a (younger) sister Phœbe, the embodiment of light, the symbol of spiritual intelligence. With her ministry the office of the earthly powers was fulfilled, and she transferred her charge, not by claim of succession but as a voluntary offering, to the bright God of heaven, Phœbus, who himself adopted her name for his own[1]. The transition from the higher to the

[1] "First in my prayer I honour of the gods.
The Earth, first prophetess; and Themis next,
Who second sat upon her mother's throne
Of prophecy, as legends tell; and third,

lower powers and forms of thought, which is unmistakable in this pregnant passage, may be seen also in the Æschylean view of Prometheus and of the Erinyes. The struggle of finite reason (Prometheus) against the supreme will is necessarily grand and tragic. In what exact mode the contest was brought to an issue we cannot now tell. The end alone is clear. Prometheus gained his deliverance, through a suffering son of Zeus, and ministered to the power which he had defied. The Titans, according to the poetic imagery, were no longer crushed and tortured, but placed in the islands of the happy in the enjoyment of perfect earthly bliss[1]. Under the completed sway of Zeus the once rebellious powers of nature become genial and beneficent. The reconciliation of the Erinyes to the "new gods[2]" is the subject of the close of the "Eumenides," and Pallas is naturally the deity by whom it is effected. Their divine power is acknowledged, and placed above the questionings of men. In part they are established as the representatives of conscience, in part as the fulfillers of material law. It is by the voice of divine wisdom only that a limit

> By her good will, and not by violence,
> Another Titaness, Earth's daughter, came,
> Phœbe, who gave the power a birthday gift
> To Phœbus, who bears Phœbe's name new-formed."
>
> *Eum.* 1 *et seq.*

[1] Comp. Fragm. 177—8.

[2] The title is one which Prometheus and the Erinyes use of the Olympian dynasty, by which their power was subdued. (Prom. 154, 412. Eum. 156, 748.)

ÆSCHYLUS. 75

is placed to their vengeance and their working. For the rest, they are recognised as having an inevitable power over the prosperity of men; they are honoured in all the crises of life; they are received as companions of Pallas herself. The immortals (Olympian gods) admit their influence[1]. Terrible and loathsome though they are, children of the night and dwellers in subterranean gloom, they yet obtain the reverence and offerings and even the love of men[2]. In human worship the awful goddesses of inexorable retribution are seated beside the Zeus-born goddess of wisdom.

But none the less the nether world remains terrible and dark, "untrodden by Apollo, and sunless," tenanted by empty shades and dread curses, ready to take shape and torment the living[3]. Hermes alone of the Olympians is in office a Chthonian deity also, "herald of gods above and gods below[4]," the conductor of the dead, the furtherer of righteous vengeance, the guide of the victim of the Erinyes[5]. For the rest, the realms of light and gloom are wholly separate. It is on earth that their powers meet, and in the fortunes of man that the nature of the Chthonian gods is best seen[6].

[1] Eum. 762, 798, 855, 876, 910.

[2] *Ibid.* 861.

[3] S. c. Th. 853. Ch. 397. Eum. 395. Comp. S. c. Th. 69 *et seq.* Ch. 467.

[4] Ch. 1, 117.   [5] *Ibid.* 611, 796. Eum. 89.

[6] Yet it must be noticed that the offerings to the Chthonian powers—milk and honey, and wine and olives, and "woven

IV.

The picture which Prometheus draws of the condition of men at the close of the Titanic rule is that of helpless savages. Zeus, he says, proposed to destroy them and give birth to a new race, when he ordered his kingdom. This plan, however, was not carried out. By the gifts of hope and fire, and the common arts of life, Prometheus rescued them from their impending fate, and Zeus himself deigned to sanction the working of the blessings among men while he punished their author for his disloyalty. Yet it is remarkable that the highest endowments of man, which spring from the development of his moral and spiritual powers, are in no degree assigned to Prometheus. These appear to have been derived directly from Zeus, who, in course of time, sought fellowship with the children of earth. Such intercourse was for the moment full of suffering to its immediate object, for the divine can only be apprehended by mortals with toil and pain; but so heroes were born, and with them heroic virtues became part of the human heritage. In virtue of that old companionship, the wise "held their place hard by the side of Zeus." They could face their destiny in memory of those from whom they were sprung,—

flowers, children of fruitful Earth"—bear witness to a time when they were worshipped as the spontaneous givers of plenty, and not the inexorable ministers of law (Pers. 611).

"Men close akin to gods, men near to Zeus;...
Men from whose veins the blood of deities
Was not yet wholly drained."

And such are the men whom Æschylus represents. The presence of a divine capacity and power in his characters is never wholly hidden by wilfulness and sin. The passions and temptations with which he deals are of overwhelming magnitude; the situations which he plans are of terrible grandeur; the persons whom he exhibits are gigantic: but yet there are present everywhere the two conflicting elements of fate and will, out of which all action rises. The scale of representation is magnified, but the moral, when reduced to its simplest principles, is that of common experience. The life is human life, though the actors are heroes.

It is commonly said, that the key to the moral understanding of the tragedies of Æschylus is the recognition of an inflexible fate, by which families are doomed to destruction, without regard to the guilt or innocence of the victims. If this were true their highest value would be lost. But in fact the statement is as false to Æschylus as it is to life. All life includes the element of fate and circumstance as well as the element of will and choice. The traditions and beliefs in which we are reared, the memories which we inherit, the tendencies and impulses which go to form our character, the reputation in which we are held for the deeds of others who belong to us, all lie out of our power. If we allow our thoughts to rest on these only, we can conclude that we are mere puppets, whose conduct is determined by the action of forces wholly external. But if we look within, there is the consciousness of responsibility, the sense of victory and defeat, the energy of opposition, which by its elasticity and continuance bears witness at least to the possibility of success,—in a word, the intuition of personality, which supplies a power not less strong than circumstance, by which we know that our life is a struggle and not an evolution of consequences, that if its purpose fails *we* are overcome. And thus it is that Æschylus paints life. He sets fate by the side of will, and lets them work. Before our own eyes, fate, or as we say circumstance, constantly prevails over infirmity of will,—more rarely, an heroic will recognises its work and achieves it. A first sin is swelled by neglect to reckless infatuation; an inheritance of sorrow crushes the selfish sufferer who rejects the discipline of woe; a noble soul trustfully obeys the voice of divine warning, and wisdom is justified in the issue. This is the teaching of Æschylus, and the teaching of natural experience. For us indeed the area of life is widened; the faint lights of an earthly government of God grow into the brightness of a kingdom of heaven; the strength of man is perfected by fellowship with a divine Redeemer; but none the less we can see in the Greek poet the outlines of the never-ending conflict of man with evil, and marvel at the invincible constancy with which he holds his faith in the sure supremacy of good, even when he looked upon the region beyond the grave as shrouded in dismal gloom, and felt the littleness of each single life.

Personal will then is, according to Æschylus, the spring of the first sin, and the occasion of the after manifestation of its malignant consequences. "Self-willed arrogance,"—the source of crime and ruin,—

> "is in very truth
> The child of godlessness; but wealth, which all
> Love and pursue with many a prayer, takes birth
> From a sound, honest heart[1]."

When the Erinyes, the appointed ministers of just vengeance, chant the dismal strain which declares their power among men, they say,—

> "We boast to be unswerving from the right:
> No wrath from us assails with silent stroke
> The man who holds to view unstainèd hands,
> And free from harm he spends his term of years.
> But to the man who after dread offence
> Would fain conceal from sight hands red with gore,
> Rendering an upright witness to the dead,
> We shew ourselves exacting blood for blood,
> Till the full debt be paid[2]."

It had been said in old time that simple prosperity left a disastrous progeny of woe behind: the poet adds,—

> "But I think otherwise, though all alone.
> It is the impious deed which leaves behind

[1] Eum. 506. [2] Eum. 303.

A numerous brood, like to the parent stock;
For aye the lot of righteous homes lives on
In noble issues."

Elsewhere arrogance is said to breed arrogance worse than itself, and the pride of full prosperity and unholy daring. But meanwhile justice sheds her light in smoky cottages, where content dwells, and leaves with averted eyes the gilded palaces of the wicked, and guides everything to its end[1].

"He shall not be unblest who of free will,
Without constraint, is just; nor could he be
O'erthrown in utter ruin[2]."

The language is clear. Victorious evil implies personal guilt. An appeal to fate is no justification of a crime[3].

There is, however, another aspect of evil. The evil which has been once evoked works on. There is, so to speak, a conservation of moral forces. The law of equal retribution for men and states is inexorable, "That he who did should suffer is an immemorial proverb[4]." The guilty house must bear its own burden, and find its remedy within[5]. The nation must receive the exact measure of its evil deeds[6]. There is no sure rest till the whole debt is paid. While the trace of guilt remains, the Erinyes call Havoc to the work of vengeance. A hideous revel band occupies the

[1] Ag. 727.   [2] Eum. 521.   [3] Ch. 896.
[4] *Ibid.* 305. Ag. 1540. Comp. Fragm. 267; Eum. 935.
[5] Ch. 462.   [6] Persæ, 809. Comp. Suppl. 427.

polluted house. Drunk with blood, and not with wine, they refuse to go from beneath its roof; and instead of the joyous song they chant the sad story of the primal woe[1].

For the guardianship of the laws of retribution is committed to appointed ministers. These are necessarily Chthonian powers, for, as has been seen, it is in them that we must look for the enforcement of natural laws, which, indeed, they symbolized. Till they are evoked, these have no power; but when once aroused, they are irresistible till their work is done. Nor, on the other hand, can they refuse their aid against the wrong-doer. At one time the impious deed alone arms them with power[2]; at another time they are called to action by the curse of him who has been wronged. Thus the curse of Thyestes first roused the evil genius of the house of Agamemnon, and the curse of Œdipus gave occasion to the death of his sons. In one aspect the Erinys itself is a personification of the curse,—the will for vengeance embodied, as it were, at once by the expression of it, —and so it is even identified with the phantom of the dead. When the Chorus looks upon "the trophy of calamity" raised over Eteocles and Polynices, its refrain of lamentation is simply,—

"O Fate, giver of woe,
Woe fraught, O awful shade of Œdipus,
Thou dark Erinys, mighty is thy power[3]."

[1] Ch. 391. Ag. 1157.   [2] Suppl. 634.
[3] S. c. Th. 972, 988. Comp. 70, 720.

But more frequently the Erinys has a distinct existence. It is like a foul bird defiling the roof on which it sits. It rends with its claw the victim consigned to its power. It perches on the body of the dead, and sings exultingly its strain of victory. Or with a more terrible significance, it is described as incorporate in the person of a guilty avenger, and working thus the requital of the past[1].

But none the less the power of evil prevails only according to the personal character of him against whom it is directed. It is finally triumphant only over those whose sin is mortal. In every instance where Æschylus describes ruin, he distinctly marks the special guilt which merited it, whether the offenders were nations or men. Xerxes prepared the way for his disaster by neglecting the limits which Providence had fixed for his rule: the Persians were condemned for their desecration of the Greek sanctuaries. Paris had violated the sacred laws of hospitality: the Trojans had made his sin their own. Agamemnon, in spite of divine warnings, had preferred his schemes of selfish ambition and glory to the sacred duties of family: the Greeks were involved in guilt by their reckless and impious vengeance on the conquered city[2]. Thrice Apollo had warned Laius to save the State by dying childless. Clytemnestra was stained by an unholy passion before she sought retribution

---

[1] Suppl. 636. Ag. 1639 ($\chi\eta\lambda\bar{\eta}$). 1448, 1475.
[2] Pers. 102, 803. Ag. 353, 685. *Ibid.* 205, 510 (comp. 329).

for her daughter's death. But nowhere is the great truth so clearly brought out as in the contrasted fates of Eteocles and Orestes. Both receive a terrible inheritance; both are placed in a position of unnatural horror; both slay their nearest kin: but Eteocles dies, and Orestes is restored to his ancestral throne. Yet the catastrophe in each case is prepared from the beginning. Eteocles accepts his fate with a hard and proud indifference. He asks for no relief, no guidance. For the State he prays half-scornfully, and the State is saved; but for himself he offers no prayer. He rejects the entreaties of the Chorus to seek help from Heaven:—

"The gods long since have left us to our fate:
 One gift alone they prize from us—our death....
 Nay, since Heaven hastens on the deed amain,
 Let the whole Laian race, which Phœbus hates,
 Before the wind speed down the stream of woe. ...
 For my dear father's bitter, fatal curse,
 Sits ever o'er my dry and tearless eyes,
 Warning me death is better soon than late."

He surrenders himself to a mad pride, and finally regards the prospect of fratricide as a last hope of triumph[1]. Orestes, on the other hand, feels the full terror of the task before him, and shrinks from fulfilling it. Again and again he assures himself of the reality of the divine message by which it was imposed. At each crisis of action he wavers till the voice of Phœ-

[1] S. c. Th. 76, 264, 686, 692, 699, 716.

bus makes itself heard. Before the fatal moment, Pylades, his mute companion, speaks once, and this once only, to renew the divine sanction of the deed, being by birth marked out as a minister of the god[1]: "Hold all to be thy foes before the gods," for their counsels in the end will be justified. And when the paroxysms of grief had come, and the Erinyes had wrought their worst, he still reposes in faithful trust in the wisdom of the counsel of Phœbus: "So far I am contented with my lot." Before the judges he has but one plea, the command of Apollo; and when he is set free, his deliverance is acknowledged as the work of Pallas and Loxias and Zeus the Saviour. Death comes where rebellious wilfulness goes before; but for the obedient and believing, the gods bring light, even from the thickest gloom[2].

A sin, then, according to Æschylus, when once admitted, must bear to the full its bitter fruit, though the power of individual will modifies its action. No sooner is the crime committed than fate prepares an instrument for retribution, forged ready beforehand for justice to use when the time shall come[3]. But the ways of divine Providence are mysterious, though the end is reached in time, it may be in the broad light of day, or in the evening twilight, or in the night[4]. And herein lies a terrible irony of justice.

[1] As Müller well remarks, § 47.
[2] Ch. 261, 545, 886. Eum. 566, 581, 727.
[3] Ag. 1513. Ch. 634. Comp. Ag. 1400; Ch. 997.
[4] Ch. 53.

ÆSCHYLUS. 85

A man may become callous to the teachings of sorrow, and the last punishment is that he is left to himself[1]. An unholy boldness prompts him to new crimes, and with irresistible violence he is carried along with the presumptuous confidence of impunity. Then it is that—

> "Evil comes swift-footed in its course,
> And sin to him who violates the right:"

Then it is that—

> "Pollution, like a cloud, hangs o'er a man,
> And folly hides the knowledge of his fall:"

Then it is that—

> "Heaven begets occasion to mankind,
> When it will wholly 'whelm a house in woe[2]."

At last the storm breaks, and in the wreck of his fortunes the miserable victim calls on those who do not hear. For the deity laughs over the headstrong man when he is exhausted by helpless woes, in spite of his arrogant boasting, and he perishes for ever, unwept and unremembered[3].

---

[1] Some acts also are inexpiable but by death: Ag. 387. S. c. Th. 677. Comp. Ch. 41, 58.

[2] Fragm. 268. Eum. 355. Fragm. 151. The last passage is quoted by Plato (Resp. ii. 380 A) with great disapprobation, but it is undoubtedly to be interpreted of Providence furnishing the wilful man with the occasion of self-destruction, and not of the predestined destruction of the innocent.

[3] Ag. 215, 376. Eum. 523.

By these signal examples the gods shew the fatal issues of indulged selfishness; but commonly the discipline of life holds men back from the last fall. As retribution comes from crime, so learning comes from suffering. Nor can the weakness of human nature dispense with the salutary discipline of fear:—

"There is a time when awe must sit enthroned
And watch our thoughts. 'Tis well for men to learn
Self-conquest in the school of suffering."

Without this solemn dread, neither citizen nor State would regard justice as they do[1]. By experience justice brings to the guilty a knowledge of their fault; and thus the lesson of suffering opens the source from which it springs, and averts its bitterest end. He who has felt the anger of avenging powers knows whence the blows of life come, and by timely submission escapes the heaviest fall. For else the sins of former times consign him in his pride to the ministers of death, and he perishes in silent ruin[2]. In part, this fruitfulness of sorrow is the natural result of law, springing up as the necessary sequence of enforced reflection; but still more it is due to the wise counsels of Zeus, who tempers the affliction to its end, and, by merciful constraint, compels mortals to think. For he it is who—

"Guides men to wise thought,
And makes and clothes with sovereign power the law,

[1] Eum. 491.   [2] *Ibid.* 890.

'By suffering learning.' Drop by drop in sleep
Remembered sorrows trickle by the heart,
And men against their will learn self-control.
For 'tis in truth a grace the gods bestow,
Throned on their awful seats with power to force[1]."

V.

Stern and severely just as this view of human life is, with retribution ever dogging sin, and sleepless avengers exacting its uttermost penalty; with deceitful prosperity hurrying the guilty to helpless ruin, and suffering alone raising the penitent to wisdom and mastery of self, it has no relief from the opening prospect of a life beyond the grave. Æschylus has not one word of true hope for a future state, not one image of another field of labour, where the character trained by sorrow here shall find exercise for its chastened power. It is scarcely too much to say, that for him the other world, and the powers by which it is governed, exist only for the guilty. There remains an awful and just punishment for all who sinned in life against God, or strangers, or parents:—

"For Hades is a stern inquisitor
Of men beneath the earth, and views their deeds,
And writes them in the tablets of his mind....
The lewd offender shall not, when he dies,
Escape arraignment in the shades below.

[1] Ag. 170.

Even there, another Zeus, as legends tell,
Gives final judgment on the crimes of men."

And so it comes to pass that the retribution is completed there which the Erinyes had begun on earth[1].

Before this final judgment, the injured dead themselves have some power to bring about their own satisfaction. The resentment of the dead outlives the funeral pyre, and shews itself in after time[2]. The "awful shade of Œdipus" is placed in closest parallelism with the Erinys which works his curse on earth[3]. The anger of Agamemnon, revealed in portentous dreams, opens the ways to the vengeance of Orestes. The shade of Clytemnestra, pointing to her wounded breast, rouses the Erinyes to their office of torture. Orestes himself, when he assures the Athenians of the alliance of Argos through all time, in gratitude for his deliverance, threatens that

"he will make
Those who transgress the tenor of his oath,
Though at that time a tenant of the grave,
Repent them of their toil by ill-success,
Disheartening marches, and disastrous ways[4]."

But even so, the power of the dead depends, in a great measure, upon the sympathy of the living. The impunity of Orestes upon earth was disgrace and

---

[1] Eum. 258. Suppl. 226. Eum. 320, 166.
[2] Ch. 315. [3] S. c. Th. 974. [4] Eum. 737.

dishonour to Clytemnestra. His unceasing punishment was to her "a matter of life or death[1]." The neglect of those above moved Agamemnon to express his discontent. Offerings and prayers gladdened and strengthened the shadowy phantoms which alone survived[2]. But only the voice of loud and constant lamentation could reach their dulled ear and darkened mind[3]; and from one passage it appears that some fellow-feeling with the suppliant was required to touch the dead with sense[4].

Apart from this prerogative of retribution, which the dead derive directly from their connection with the Chthonian powers, their whole state is cold and dreary. Death is said to be freed from woes, but only so far as it is void of all feeling; "the dead have lost the very wish ever to rise again[5]." They sleep "in light which is not light, but darkness visible[6]." The semblance of ancient dignities remains, but their joy and vigour is gone. Darius was a king below; but though a king, he charged his suppliants who had evoked him, to reap pleasure while it was yet day, "for the dead are shrouded in thick gloom, where wealth avails not[7]." Agamemnon, on the other hand, by being unavenged, had lost his royal place, to which, if he had fallen in battle, his earthly kingship would have entitled him[8]. For so it was that neglect

[1] Eum. 114.
[2] Cr. 475.
[3] Ch. 367, 151, 485.
[4] *Ibid.* 508.
[5] Ag. 551.
[6] Ch. 311.
[7] Pers. 687, 835.
[8] Ag. 337 *et seq.*

could neutralize the claims of sovereign descent. The shadow of his former state followed a man to the grave, but the disregard of his survivors could obscure or obliterate it. His after-being was quickened and nourished from earth; and, still more than this, his true immortality not only depended on the living, but was in the living. A positivist could hardly express the idea more clearly than Electra, when she addresses her father's shade for the last time; for the sense of his personal existence below is absorbed in his existence in his descendants above:—

"O hear, my father, this my latest cry. . . .
And wipe not out the seed of Pelops' line;
For thus thou art not dead, though thou hast died;
For children are a voice which saves a man
After his death: as corks lift up a net,
And save its flaxen thread from out the deep.
Listen: for thee I utter such laments;
For thou art saved if thou regard'st my words."

VI.

At first sight, this sad and shadowy aspect of the world to come must appear strange and even discordant with the nobler and clearer views which Æschylus gives of the action of Providence on earth. Few who look at the outside of life can feel satisfied that virtue receives its full reward here; and yet Æschylus practically limits the recompence of the future to a full discharge of the arrears of punishment unpaid on earth. We might be tempted to think that the exigencies of composition had confined him to this side of the subject; that, dealing with crime and suffering here, he limited himself to the exhibition of its consequences hereafter; that his view of the life to come is tragic, just as his view of this life is tragic. But it is evident that this explanation will not hold good. The "divine counsellor," the "guileless" Darius, a "prince among the dead," comes forth from the nether world, oppressed by no guilt, obscured by no neglect, and his figure answers to the image which is suggested by the whole tenor of Æschylus' teaching about the dead. The Danaïdes, in the extremity of their distress, when they prepare to appeal to the Zeus of the dead if the Olympian gods fail to help them, look for vengeance on their persecutors, and for themselves seek simple release; but no brighter vision of Elysian fields and active joy cheers them. Under all circumstances, the view of the condition of the dead, which Æschylus brings out into the clearest light in describing the condition of the guilty, is consistent. The fulness of human life is on earth. The part of man, in all his energy and capacity for passion and action, is played out here; and when the curtain falls, there remains unbroken rest, or a faint reflection of the past, or suffering wrought by the ministers of inexorable justice. The beauty and the power of life, the manifold ministers of sense, are gone. They can be regretted, but they cannot be replaced. Sorrow is possible, but not joy.

However different this teaching may be from that of the Myths of Plato, and the vague popular belief which they witnessed to and fostered; however different, again, even from that of Pindar, with which Æschylus cannot have been unacquainted[1], it is pre-eminently Greek. Plato clothed in a Greek dress the common instincts of humanity; Æschylus works out a characteristically Greek view of life. Thus it is that his doctrine is most clearly Homeric[2]. As a Greek he feels, like Homer, the nobility of our present powers, the grandeur of strength and wealth, the manifold delights of our complex being; and what was "the close-packed urn of ashes which survived the funeral pyre" compared with the heroes whom it represented[3]? That "tear-stained dust" was the witness that man—the whole man—could not live again[4]. The poet, then, was constrained to work out a scheme of divine justice upon earth, and this Æschylus did, though its record is a strain of sorrow.

---

[1] As, for example, in the fragments of his "Threni."

[2] The well-known answer of Achilles to Odysseus, who had sought to give him comfort by reminding him of his power among the dead, may serve to prove this:—

"Scoff not at death," he answered, "noble chief!
　Rather would I in the sun's warmth divine
Serve a poor churl who drags his days in grief,
　Than the whole lordship of the dead were mine."
　　　　　　　　　　　　Odys. xi. 488 (Worsley).

[3] Ag. 422.　　　　　　[4] Comp. Ag. 987; Eum. 617.

The thrice-repeated voice of the Chorus in the "Agamemnon" is the burden of his tragedies,—

"Sing woe, sing woe, but let the good prevail."

In this respect, it is impossible to overlook the relation in which Æschylus stands to the Bible. He appears as the interpreter of a divine law, just and inevitable; and he is content to rest in the working of it upon earth. Just so, the first form in which revelation was clothed, was that of a law stern and temporal. The claims of "the Law" to obedience are peremptory, its condemnation of transgression inexorable. The sanctions of a future life form no part of its system, though the fact of a future life is implied in the idea of a covenant between God and man. In both respects, the parallel between the spiritual ideas expressed by the poet, and those enforced by the inspired Lawgiver, holds good; but the difference between the mode of their expression is not less remarkable. Æschylus was, so to speak, an intellectual witness; his appointed task was to address himself to individual reflection, and not to discipline the faith of a people; the truths which he taught were left in words, often dark and mysterious, and not embodied in a traditional and public ceremonial; they might be fruitful here and there in some devout soul, but they contained no message which could shape the common thoughts of a nation, or form the solid basis for a development of religious life. None the less, his teaching has still an office for us. It is often said, and even taken for granted, that the severer aspects of the Christian creed are due to some peculiarity of the "Semitic" mind; that they are foreign to the more genial constitution of the "Japhetic" type; that here at least the instinct which revelation satisfies is partial and not universal. Against such assumptions, the tragedies of Æschylus remain a solemn protest. The voice of law addresses us even from Athens. There is a stern and dark side to the Greek view of life. The "Prometheus," the "Seven against Thebes," and the "Orestea," contain a "natural testimony of the soul" to the reality of sin and the inevitable penalty which it carries in itself, and to the need which man has of a Divine deliverer, to check and control the consequences of violated law. And the testimony comes with the greater force because it is given by the poet who had witnessed the most glorious triumphs of Greek power. It is an utterance of outward strength, and not of exhaustion; it springs out of the fresh vigour of Greece, and not from the despairing weakness of her decline. It is indeed partial and incomplete, but its instructiveness lies in the fact that, though partial and incomplete, it was devoutly held, in virtue of the truth which was in it. It was, in some degree, taken up into later systems and variously supplemented, but for us its chief significance lies in its simplicity. If Plato tells us what are the aspirations of man, Æschylus tells us what are the requirements of the law of God. The one is, in some sense, a preparation for the other.

The law comes first, and lays bare the powerlessness of man in the full pride of his strength; and when this is once recognised, faith becomes possible,—though national hopes have faded away,—and with it a deeper insight into spiritual truth.

EURIPIDES AS A RELIGIOUS TEACHER.

AMONG the services which Browning has rendered to literature, not the least conspicuous is his interpretation of Euripides. In "Balaustion's Adventure" and "Aristophanes' Apology," he has not only given a poet's rendering of two characteristic plays, the "Alcestis" and the "Phrensied Hercules," but he has given the student sympathetic guidance to their deeper meaning. He has enabled English readers to estimate at their true worth the criticism of A. W. Schlegel, and at the same time he has opened a striking view of speculations and desires which found a place in the mind of a great Athenian when Athens was greatest. Euripides is indeed the true representative of democratic Athens. He was of honourable descent, and had enjoyed the discipline of most varied culture. Gymnast, artist, and student, he had made trial of all that the city had to teach; and as holding a sacred office in the service of Apollo he had an inheritance from older religious feeling. It may almost be said that Euripides lived and died with the Athens which has moved the world. His lifetime included the highest development of Athenian art and literature, the rise and the fall of Athenian supremacy. He was born on the day of Salamis (480 B.C.). He produced his "Medea" in the first year of the Peloponnesian War (431 B.C.). His "Trojan Women" was exhibited in the year of the expedition to Sicily and the recall of Alcibiades (415 B.C.). He died in 406 B.C., the year before Ægospotamos. He belonged wholly to the new order which is represented by the age of Pericles. Though he was only a generation younger than Æschylus, his works, when compared with those of his predecessor, represent the results of a revolution both in art and in thought.

But however different Æschylus and Euripides are in their views of existence, and in their treatment of life upon the stage, they are alike interesting to the student of the history of religious thought. Both speak with deep personal feeling. Both offer a partial interpretation of mysteries which fill them with an overwhelming awe. For both life with its infinite sorrows is greater than art. In this respect they differ from Sophocles, by whom they are naturally separated. Sophocles is not the poet as prophet, but the poet as artist. For him all that is most solemn, or terrible, or beautiful in human experience becomes simply an element in his work. He shews the perfection of calm, conscious mastery over the subjects with which he deals, but he does not speak to us himself. He has no message, no questionings, no convictions, beyond such utterances as harmoniously complete the consummate symmetry of his poems. It is otherwise with Æschylus and Euripides. Both are deeply moved and shew that they are deeply moved, by religious feeling, as a spiritual and not an æsthetic force. But the feeling in the two cases is widely different.

Æschylus is the exponent of the old faith of Greece—stern, simple, resolute, strong in self-restraint. Euripides, on the other hand, has to take account of all the novel influences under which he had grown up; the speculations of Ionian philosophy, the larger relations of national intercourse, the force of a new domestic life. Once again Asia had touched Europe and quickened there new powers. Greece had conquered Persia only that she might better receive from the East the inspiration of a wider energy.

At the same time the political circumstances under which Euripides wrote helped to intensify the thoughts which were stirred by the teachings of Heraclitus and Anaxagoras. The glorious struggle of the Persian war, in which Æschylus had taken part, with its apparently plain and decisive issue, was followed by results widely different from that final triumph; and Euripides had to witness the long horrors of civil conflict, the shaking of the popular creed under unexpected disasters, paroxysms of popular fanaticism, the moral dissolution of the plague. He felt the grievous

EURIPIDES AS A RELIGIOUS TEACHER. 99

turmoil of opinion and action, and he reflected it. His constitution fitted him for his work. He was by nature inclined to ponder the problems of life and not to enter upon affairs. He was a student of men in books as well as in society; and the popular tradition which assigns to Anaxagoras a decisive influence over his view of the world may certainly be accepted as true; though nothing is less likely than that he was diverted from philosophy to the stage by the fate of his master. For Euripides is essentially a poet, and not a speculator. He deals with the mysteries of being from the side of feeling rather than of thought. A passionate fulness of human interest is the characteristic mark of his writings, and the secret of his power. He touched the common heart because he recognised the different phases of its ordinary sorrows and temptations and strivings.

The brusque lines of Philemon are a unique testimony to his personal attractiveness:—

> "If, as some say, men still in very truth
> Had life and feeling after they are dead,
> I had hanged myself to see Euripides."

His verses had a still wider persuasiveness. After the disaster at Syracuse, prisoners found relief and even freedom if they were able to recite passages from his poems; and a chorus from the "Electra" is said to have saved Athens from destruction when it was taken by Lysander.

The significance of Euripides as a religious teacher

7—2

springs directly from his position and his character. He looks from the midst of Athenian society, a society brilliant, restless, sanguine, superstitious, at the popular mythology, at life, at the future, with the keenest insight into all that belongs to man, and what he sees is a prospect on which we may well dwell[1].

I.

In order to understand the treatment of the popular mythology by Euripides, we must bear in mind the place which was occupied by the Homeric poems in contemporary Greek education. It is not too much to say that these were (if the phrase may be allowed) a kind of Greek Bible. Every Athenian was familiar with their contents; they furnished the general view of the relations of gods and men, of the seen and the unseen, which formed a fixed back-

[1] Though it is impossible to use isolated expressions of the characters of a dramatist as evidence of his own belief, the general convergence of their opinions may be fairly taken as giving his judgment from various points of sight. In the endeavour to obtain a just view of the teaching of Euripides on the line of subjects mentioned above, I wrote out every passage in his extant plays and fragments which seemed to bear upon them, and the reader will judge how far they combine to give an intelligible result.

The references are given throughout to the edition of Nauck in Teubner's "Bibliotheca." The translations are sufficiently close, I hope, to enable the scholar to recall the original words at once, and at the same time, to convey the meaning faithfully to the English reader.

ground to the common prospect of life. This being so they produced the impression that the divine forces corresponded with human forces, differing only in intensity and range. The gods were held to be of like passions with men, but stronger and wiser, with the vigour of undecaying energy. Such a conception affords an adequate basis for the ordinary duties of worship, and was not superficially at variance with morality. But more careful reflection shewed that the beings of the Homeric Olympus failed to satisfy the ideal of spiritual sovereigns; that a mere increase in the scale of human qualities could not supply a stable foundation for reverence; that the worshipper must look beyond this crowd of conflicting deities if he was to find an object on which he could rest with supreme trust.

Such difficulties had not received a clear expression in the time of Æschylus, nor would he have been disposed to deal with them. The wants and sorrows of men vanish in his sight before the awful majesty of an inscrutable divine purpose. With Euripides the case was different : Man, and not Destiny, was the central subject of his art. His Orestes, for example, is not the instrument of a divine will, prompted, tortured, delivered by external powers, but a son racked with Hamlet-like misgivings, and finding within himself the justification and the punishment of his deed. Euripides, in other words, regarded the human and the divine as factors in life, alike real and permanent. He aimed at dealing with the whole sum of our present experience. He was therefore constrained to bring the popular creed in some way into harmony with absolute right and truth; to give a moral interpretation to current legends; to show that life, even as we see it, offers ground for calm trust on which man may at least venture to rest. Plato banished poets from his ideal republic on account of the moral difficulties raised by their representations of divine things. Euripides endeavoured to find a more practical remedy for an evil which he could not but feel: he sought to penetrate through the words and figures of the traditional teaching which the poets adopted to the truths which lay beneath, and so to preserve the symbols of primitive belief without doing violence to moral instinct.

In attempting to fulfil this work, Euripides frankly acknowledges its difficulty. All investigation of the divine is, he lays down, necessarily beset by difficulty. This difficulty is increased by a superficial view of the course of human affairs. It is made insoluble by the literal acceptance of the details of mythology.

Under various circumstances Euripides makes his characters affirm the mysteriousness of the questions involved in theology. They may not either be dealt with or set aside lightly. The poet refuses to acquiesce in those perfunctory utterances of professional diviners in which many found relief;

"Why do ye, seated at oracular shrines,
Swear that ye know the secrets of the gods?

Men have no power to fashion such replies:
For he that boasts he knows about the gods,
Knows only this, the art to win belief[1]."

There is a complexity, a manifoldness, in the vicissitudes of providential government which at once arrests human attention and baffles it:

"What mortal dares to say that he has found
By searching what is GOD, or what is not,
Or what between—the utmost bound of thought—
When he regards the work of Providence
Moving with rapid course, now here, now there,
Then elsewhere, with a sudden change of fate,
Conflicting, unexpected[2]?"

This first difficulty is inherent in all religious speculations; and the burden of ignorance may be borne with patience as belonging to man's nature. But a greater difficulty lies behind. The appearance of injustice is harder to endure than darkness, and Euripides dwells with sorrowful persistence on the moral inequalities of life. He finds in this the sorest trial of faith. The passionate exclamation of Bellerophon:

"'Tis said by some that there are gods in heaven.
There are not, are not; if men will not still,
Bound by their folly, use the old wives' tale.
Nay, look yourselves[3],"

finds frequent echoes in his plays. So it is that

[1] Philoct. fr. 793. [2] Hel. 1137, ff. Comp. Hel. 711.
[3] Beller. fr. 288. Comp. fr. 892, 893; Scyr. fr. 185. Contrast, fr. 981.

the herald Talthybius, looking at the prostrate form of Hecuba, exclaims:

"Zeus, shall I say that thou regardest men?
Or that we hold in vain this false belief,
Thinking there is indeed a race of gods,
While fortune sways all human destinies[1]?"

And this apparent miscarriage of justice is as great negatively as positively. The failure of virtue to gain recognition is not less perplexing than undeserved suffering. For—

"If the gods, to man's degree,
Had wit and wisdom, they would bring
Mankind a twofold youth, to be
Their virtue's sign-mark, all should see,
In those with whom life's winter thus grew spring.
For when they died, into the sun once more,
Would they have traversed twice life's racecourse o'er;
While ignobility had simply run
Existence through, nor second life begun[2]."

A final difficulty lies in the letter of the divine legends. According to these, the gods act as no good man would act. Euripides meets the difficulty boldly. He affirms consistently that the legends about the gods, which tend to confuse human intuitions of right and wrong, of truth and duty, are not literally true. When Heracles recovered from his phrensy, and looked upon his murdered wife and children in bitterest sorrow and shame, Theseus sought to bring

---

[1] Hec. 488.   [2] Herc. Fur. 635 (Browning).

him comfort by recalling facts from the popular mythology; but Heracles rejects the consolation and replies:—

"I neither fancy gods love lawless beds,
  Nor, that with chains they bind each other's hands,
  Have I judged worthy faith, at any time;
  Nor shall I be persuaded one is born
  His fellow's master! since GOD stands in need—
  If he is really GOD—of nought at all.
  These are the poet's pitiful conceits[1]."

Elsewhere Euripides refers to the legends of the birth of Helen and the banquet of Thyestes, only to reject them[2]. The ground is given by Iphigenia—

"I think no Deity can be unjust."

And Bellerophon expresses the thought still more decidedly—

"If gods do aught that's base they are not gods[3]."

Following out this principle, Euripides ventures to openly condemn the gods for the actions attributed to them. At the close of the "Electra" the Dioscuri, addressing Orestes, who stands awestricken by the side of Clytemnestra, so pass judgment:—

"Just is her punishment, but not thy deed;
  And Phœbus, Phœbus—well, he is my king;
  I am dumb: though wise, not wise he spake to thee[4]."

[1] Herc. Fur. 1341 (Browning). Compare Antiope, fr. 209.
[2] Hel. 21; El. 737; Iph. Taur. 389.
[3] Beller. fr. 294, 7.   [4] El. 1244. Compare 1301 ff.

And the messenger who relates the death of Neoptolemus at Delphi concludes:—

> "So did he [Apollo] to Achilles' son,
> Who offered retribution; he the king,
> Who giveth oracles to other men,
> The judge of righteousness to all the world,
> And bore in mind, like a malicious churl,
> Old grudges; how could such a one be wise[1]!"

Here, then, Euripides is directly at issue with much of the popular faith. How, it may be asked, can such language, widely different from the reckless banterings of Aristophanes, be reconciled with due respect for the divine? The answer seems to lie in the fact that Euripides draws a clear distinction between the Olympian gods and the One Being to whom they also minister. He was inclined to treat the Olympian gods as in some sense personifications or embodiments of human attributes. It is said that Anaxagoras interpreted the Homeric stories as symbolic[2], and his scholar sought in the same line a worthy meaning for the current mythology. In this sense Hecuba, addressing Helen, gives a striking interpretation of the Judgment of Paris. It was no contest of actual deities, but of conflicting passions. Aphrodite herself, could have moved Helen and Amyclæ to Troy without leaving Heaven. But the

---

[1] Androm. 1161. Compare Ion, 444 ff.; Orest. 28, 162; Iph. Taur. 35.
[2] Diog. Laert. ii. 11.

Aphrodite who came with Paris and carried off the bride of Menelaus was the feeling which Paris stirred in Helen's breast[1].

But while Euripides here finds in the soul itself the powers which man is tempted to place wholly without, it does not follow that he denies the objective existence of beings corresponding to human passions. On the contrary, he seems to recognise a correspondence between human feelings and impulses and supernatural forces, of which the Olympian deities were representatives. The origin of that which is extraordinary is referred to divine agency. Death and Madness are real powers external to man. Strife and Ambition, Hope, Justice and Persuasion, derive their force from something without which is akin to them[2]. From time to time men move in a mysterious intercourse with spiritual beings. Hippolytus in his first joy can say to Artemis:—

"I feel thee near, and answer thee in word
Hearing thy voice, yet seeing not thy face[3]."

It is not then surprising that imperfections should be found in beings which, even when they are felt to be most present and energetic, are essentially limited and human in their characteristics. But they can bring no repose or confidence to the soul. The poet

[1] Troad. 969 ff.

[2] Hel. 1002; Antig. fr. 170; Iph. Aul. 392; Phœn. 798; 531. Compare Hel. 560. Iph. Aul. 973.

[3] Hippol. 85; compare *Ibid.* 1391.

as a religious teacher must look beyond himself, beyond the many gods—those colossal human figures, symbols or sources of man's conflicting passions—for that which gives unity to the view of existence[1]. And here it is that the "theology" of Euripides becomes of the highest interest. Philosophers had sought the principle of unity in some primal element; Euripides, though his language is naturally vague, seems rather to seek it in a vital force, which slowly differentiates and moulds all things. The force is distinct from the matter through which it is manifested. Human thought is incompetent to define it exactly or simply. Under one aspect it is revealed as law, under another as intelligence, under another as will. All are harmonised in that for which we feel. Thus Hecuba gives expression to her prayer of thanksgiving, when Menelaus declares his purpose of taking vengeance on Helen, the curse of Troy:—

"O Thou
That bearest earth, Thyself by earth upborne,
Whoe'er Thou art, hard for our powers to guess,
Or Zeus, or Nature's law, or mind of man,
To thee I pray, for all the things of earth
In right Thou guidest on Thy noiseless way[2]."

[1] The famous line with which the Melanippe originally opened obviously pointed to the Zeus of mythology, as different from the Supreme Sovereign:—

"Zeus, whosoe'er Zeus is, for by report
 I know him only." (Fragm. 483).

Compare Herc. Fur. 1263.

[2] It is interesting to contrast Euripides' view of the divine

EURIPIDES AS A RELIGIOUS TEACHER. 109

From this point of sight the whole visible world appears as a progressive revelation of the One source of life. Euripides dwells on the prospect with evident delight. Heaven (Æther) and earth symbolize for him the force and the matter through whose union all the variety of things come into existence. But he teaches that even these two were once undivided. Perhaps he thought of matter as the first self-limited expression of force. Thus, in one of his earliest dramas, "Melanippe the Wise," he says:—

"Not mine the tale: my mother taught it me,
How heaven and earth were undivided once,
And when they grew distinct with separate form,
They bore, and brought to light all things that are—
Trees, birds, and beasts, the creatures of the sea,
And race of men[1]."

This primal marriage of Heaven and Earth finds renewal in the vital processes of Nature:—

"The earth longs for the rain, when the parched land,
Fruitless through drought, lacks the life-giving shower;
The glorious heaven longs, as it swells with rain,
To fall upon the earth, with deep desire;
And when they meet commingled—earth and heaven—
They give to all, whereby the race of men
Lives and is glad, being and rich support[2]."

origin of civilization (Suppl. 201) with Critias' view of the human origin of theology in the Sisyphus (Plut. Plac. Phil. 1, 7, p. 880).

[1] Troad. 884.   [2] Melanippe, fr. 488.

110   EURIPIDES AS A RELIGIOUS TEACHER.

So things come into existence, and then in due time they are dissolved. Nothing is lost, but each element returns to its source, and enters into new combinations as the great cycle of life finds fulfilment:—

"Great earth and sky supreme are source of all;
 The sky supreme is sire of gods and men,
 And earth receiving fertilizing showers,
 Gives mortals birth, gives birth to tribes of beasts
 And that whereby they live; so she is called
 Mother of all, by just prerogative.
 Then that which springs from earth to earth returns.
 And that which draws its being from the sky,
 Rises again up to the skyey height,
 And nothing dies of all that comes to be,
 But being sundered, each first element,
 Freshly combined, displays some novel form[1]."

There is then nothing strained, when Euripides identifies the Heaven (Æther) with the One supreme sovereign power:—

"See'st thou this boundless Æther high aloft,
 Enfolding earth about with moist embrace,
 Believe that this is Zeus: hold this for GOD[2]."

For, according to his conception, it suggests at least all that is contained in the sublime description of GOD—than which he has no grander:—

"The Self-existent, who in heaven's expanse
 Holds in His large embrace all things that are;

---

[1] Fragm. 890.   Compare Æsch. Danaid, fr. 38.

[2] Chrysipp. 836.   Compare fragm. 1012; and Vitruv. viii. 1.

EURIPIDES AS A RELIGIOUS TEACHER. 111

Round whom the light, round whom in dusky shade
The chequered night and the unnumbered host
Of stars move gladly in unceasing dance[1]."

Euripides gains, in fact, from his dynamical view of Nature a vivid practical belief in the divine;—

"Wretched is he who when he looks on this
Perceives not GOD, and does not cast afar
The crooked cheats of airy speculators,
Whose baneful tongue hazards on things unseen
Words void of judgment[2]."

At the same time, the partial, fragmentary, imperfect deities are given back[3]. These, though not absolute, bring the divine near to men. Through these men may rise to that by which they also are strong. The highest instincts of humanity can look for satisfaction without. These, which are a divine manifestation—

"In each of us our reason is a god[4]."

must have a perfect fulfilment in the divine. Men may confidently attribute to the gods the consummation of that which is noblest in germ in themselves. They can trust even to the severity of righteousness. He who looks for weak forgiveness of wrong done is faithless to his own heart:—

[1] Fragm. 935. Compare fragm. 867, 911. Still, in another sense, he speaks of Æther as "the dwelling of Zeus."—Melan. fr. 491.
[2] Peirith. fr. 596.   [3] Fragm. 905.
[4] Fragm. 1007. The line is attributed to Menander.

> "So thou dost think the gods are merciful,
> When one by oath seeks for escape from death,
> Or bonds, or deeds of foeman's violence;
> Or shares his home with blood-stained criminals:
> Then truly they were less intelligent
> Than men, setting the kind before the just[1]."

And the course of life, with all its inequalities, offers such glimpses of righteous retribution as are sufficient to support faith in the final triumph of supreme justice[2].

This faith springs naturally from the underlying sense of the unity of the source of all things. The gods themselves, offspring like men of the one Being, are bound by law. They are not arbitrary, capricious powers, but subject to a sovereign right. Apollo may not rescue Alcestis from death by his divine might, though the task is open to the effort of a human champion. Artemis bows to the ordinance which limits the action of one deity towards another, though obedience costs her the life of Hippolytus[3].

> "The gods are strong, and law which ruleth them;
> For 'tis by law we have our faith in gods,
> And live with certain rules of right and wrong[4]."

Man, in other words, is born religious, and born with the faculty to recognise that which claims his devotion.

---

[1] Fragm. 1030.

[2] Œnom. fr. 581; Bacch. 1325; El. 582. Compare Herc. Fur. 347.

[3] Hec. 799. Compare *Ibid.* 847.   [4] Hipp. 799.

EURIPIDES AS A RELIGIOUS TEACHER. 113

We have seen that the many gods are in one aspect ideals answering to human powers. Viewed under another light, they present different aspects of the One to whom they are finally referred. In different circumstances men necessarily conceive of GOD differently. He may bear this title or that, and the worshipper may dimly realize the unity of characters popularly divided:—

"I bear an offering of drink and meal
To thee that rulest all, whatever name
Thou lovest, Zeus or Hades; and do thou
Receive this fireless sacrifice poured forth
Of earth's abundant fruitage at my hands.
For thou amidst the gods that dwell in heaven
Wieldest Zeus' sceptre; and o'er these beneath
Sharest the rule of Hades[1]."

Euripides, therefore, is perfectly consistent when he affirms man's dependence on the gods, while he denies the historic truth of the ancient legends:—

"No issue comes to men without the gods.
We strive for many things, led on by hope,
And toil in vain, as knowing nothing sure[2]."

"Apart from GOD no man is prosperous,
Or comes to high estate. I rate at naught
The fruits of mortal zeal without the gods[3].

"Why do they say that miserable men
Are wise, O Zeus? For we depend on thee,
And do but that which answers to thy will[4]."

[1] Fragm. 904. Compare Fragm. 938, 1011.
[2] Thyest. fr. 395.   [3] Fragm. 1014.   [4] Suppl. 734.

114 EURIPIDES AS A RELIGIOUS TEACHER.

For this is only to affirm in another form that unity of being for which he searches. Man cannot isolate himself. He is strong by sympathy. On the eve of a battle, fought for the maintenance of a common right, Theseus, the type of the true king, says—

> "One thing we need, that the gods side with those
> Who honour justice: heaven and right combined
> Give victory; but virtue profits naught
> To mortals if it have not GOD to help[1]."

Fate and the divine will are not two adverse forces, but complementary views of the same force. So the Dioscuri declare that they were forced to yield to "destiny and the gods," and counsel Electra that

> "Henceforward she must do
> What Fate and Zeus determined should be done[2]."

Such general convictions, while they destroy the root of many superstitions, give a solemn sanction to the obligations of reverence and worship.

> "He hath no reason who lays cities waste;
> Temples and tombs—shrines sacred to the dead—
> He desolates, and then is lost himself[3].

> "Three virtues thou must put in act, my son;
> Honour the gods, thy parents, and the laws,

---

[1] Suppl. 594. Compare Hec. 1029.

[2] El. 1247; Hel. 1660. For Euripides' view of Providence and Fate, see Hippol. 1102 ff.; Heracl. 608 ff.; Fragm. 149, 217, 264, 354, 494, 1167; and the common refrain with which he closes the Alcestis, Andromache, Bacchæ, Helen. and Medea.

[3] Troad. 95.

EURIPIDES AS A RELIGIOUS TEACHER. 115

> The common laws of Greece. So shalt thou win
> The victor's glorious wreath of fair renown[1]."

And Heracles in a remarkable phrase connects the success of his descent to Hades with his initiation in the Mysteries[2].

But Euripides has strong words of condemnation for the unworthy use which men had made of religious feelings. The right of sanctuary, which had been designed to protect the innocent, was unjustly turned into defence for the guilty:—

> "If a man
> Seek refuge at an altar, stained with crime,
> I will myself, regardless of the law,
> Drag him to justice, and not fear the gods:
> For evil men must bear an evil fate[3]."

Especially he dwells upon the impostures of soothsaying, by which the real voice of the gods was corrupted.

> "The oracles of Loxias are sure;
> As for man's art, I will have none of it[4]."

> "He has the true diviner's skill
> Who has the gods for friends[5]."

> "He is best soothsayer who guesses well[6]."

---

[1] Antiope, fr. 219. [2] Herc. Fur. 613.
[3] Fragm. 1036.   [4] Elect. 399.
[5] Hel. 759. Compare *Ibid.* 753.
[6] Fragm. 963. The line is also attributed to Menander. Compare Iph. Aul. 955.

It is not the form of religious service, but the spirit which is precious. Acceptable worship must be accompanied by piety and effort.

"Who offers sacrifice with pious heart
  Obtains salvation, though his gift be small[1]."

"Do what thou canst, and then invoke the gods.
  GOD helps the man who toils to help himself[2]."

From what has been already said, the profound significance of the Dionysian worship for Euripides will be at once clear. In that worship Nature found the fullest recognition as the revelation of the Divine. Man sought fellowship with GOD in the completeness of his being. The organ of knowledge was confessed to be, not the intellect, but life. Thus the *Bacchæ* is no palinode, but a gathering up in rich maturity of the poet's earlier thoughts. Man cannot, he shows with tragic earnestness, attain to communion with the divine by pure reason, a part only of his constitution. He must keep himself open to every influence, and so by welcoming the new in time prove his loyalty to the old. The aged seer Teiresias strikes the keynote of the play when he affirms the coequal supremacy of ancestral belief and present revelation. In this way the majesty of the living whole of human existence is vindicated against philosophic or ceremonial one-sidedness.

[1] Fragm. 940. Compare Dan. fr. 329.
[2] Hippol. 435. Comp. Iph. Taur. 910; El. 80.

EURIPIDES AS A RELIGIOUS TEACHER. 117

"We trust no human wit in things divine.
The faith our fathers handed down, and that
Which we have welcomed, growing with our growth,
No reasonings shall o'erthrow, even though it find
The subtlest treasures of man's loftiest thought[1]."

The fresh unfolding of the divine bounty requires, he pleads, grateful acknowledgment:

"Two powers there are 'mong men,
First before all, O youth: our mother Earth,
Demeter, call her by which name thou wilt,
Who stayeth mortals with the staff of life;
And the late-come, the son of Semele,
Who formed the rich draught of the clustered vine
And brought the gift to men[2]."

Seen in this light, the Dionysian worship is the witness to a real belief in the vitality of religion as answering to the completeness of man's nature. It does not aim at superseding that which went before, but at bringing it nearer to actual experience. Men must worship as men, feeling at once the richness and the limits of their endowments:—

"Dwelling afar in heaven the Deities,
Behold the deeds of men:
It is not wisdom to be wise
And follow thoughts too high for mortal ken[3]."

"Blest above all of human line,
Who, deep in mystic rites divine,

[1] Bacch. 200. [2] Bacch. 274.
[3] *Ibid*, 392,

118 EURIPIDES AS A RELIGIOUS TEACHER.

> Leads his hallowed life with us,
> Initiate in our Thiasus;
> And purified with holiest waters,
> Goes dancing o'er the hills with Bacchus' daughters[1]."

So in manifold and solemn strains, unsurpassed in classical literature for calm sweet strength, Euripides lays open the joy of worship. The joy of the Dionysian worship with which he begins passes into the larger joy of universal piety:—

> "'Tis but light cost in his own power sublime
>   To array the godhead, whosoe'er he be;
> And law is old, even as the oldest time,
>   Nature's own unrepealed decree[2]."

> "Hold thou fast the pious mind; so, only so shall glide
>   In peace with GOD above, in peace with men on earth,
>   Thy smooth painless life.
> I admire not, envy not, who would be over-wise:
> Mine be still the glory, mine be still the prize,
>   By night and day·
> To live of the immortal gods in awe:
>   Who fears them not
> Is but the outcast of all law[3]."

II.

The theology of Euripides takes its shape from his conviction that all Nature and all Life is a manifestation of one Divine Power. His view of human life

---

[1] Bacch. 72 (Milman).
[2] *Ibid.* 893 (Milman); comp. Heracl. 902.
[3] *Ibid.* 1002 (Milman).

corresponds with this conviction, and his view of being is concentrated in his view of humanity. All that is human claims his sympathy; and it may be said conversely that all that claims his sympathy is seen in its connexion with man. He practically anticipates Browning's judgment that "little else is worth study than the incidents in the development of a soul."

This largeness of sympathy with all that is human is shown by the great range of his characters. Heroes, Greeks, barbarians, peasants, slaves, women, children, play a part, and a noble part, in his dramas. It was a reproach against him that he made all utter great thoughts alike. The charge is so far true that he strives to give to each the voice of a common humanity. He admits no exclusive prerogative of race, or sex, or birth. The yeoman in the "Electra" is as chivalrous as Achilles in the "Aulic Iphigenia."

Euripides thus deals frankly and gladly with all the elements of life, and he deals with actual life as he saw it. There is much that is mean and frivolous, and even repulsive, in the portraiture, but still the picture never ceases to be true to experience. His characters are not ideal, but the strangely mixed beings who are fashioned in the turmoil of passion and interest. It is perhaps for this reason that his women are both better and worse than his men. Through them Nature is revealed more directly; and it is a singular injustice of traditional criticism that the poet should be represented as a woman-hater who

120   EURIPIDES AS A RELIGIOUS TEACHER.

has left more types of female self-devotion than any other dramatist. The plays which exhibit the spontaneous intuitive sacrifice of Macaria; the thoughtful, reasoned resolution of Iphigenia; the tender, wifely dutifulness of Alcestis; the romantic love of Evadne, show the strength of woman in the most varied phases of its characteristic beauty.

Not less striking are the sketches of children which Euripides has given. Eumelus in the "Alcestis," Molossus in the "Andromeda," the sons of the father chiefs in the "Suppliants," add characteristic touches to the action; and the appeal of Iphigenia to the infant Orestes to plead for her life with silent tears, is conceived with pathetic tenderness[1].

Generally, indeed, the stress which Euripides lays on domestic life is worthy of study. The scene between Menelaus and Helena is a unique example in Greek tragedy of the love of husband and wife[2]. Again and again the affection of parents for children, and of children for parents, is presented as full of supreme joy: "Children are men's souls," "A Heaven-sent charm of awful power[3]."

"Lady, this splendour of the sun is dear,
 And fair the broad calm of the watery plain,
 But nothing is so bright or fair to see
 As to the childless, stung with long desire,
 The light of new-born children in the home[4]."

[1] Iph. Aul. 1124.
[2] Hel. 622 ff.
[3] Andr. 417; Alcm. fr. 104.
[4] Danae, fr., 318.

EURIPIDES AS A RELIGIOUS TEACHER. 121

"Wretched the child
Who serves not those that bare him with the meed
Of noblest toil. One gives and gains again
From his own children what he gave himself[1]."

The relations of the family lead up to the relations of the State, and when the claims of the family and State come into conflict the latter must prevail; for all life has a social destination and duty. In the "Erechtheus" the queen offers her daughter willingly for the deliverance of Athens. "Children," she says, "are born to us

"That we may save our altars and our land.
We may call the city one, and many find
Their home there: how can I then ruin these
When I may give one life to ransom all[2]?"

But Euripides had a keen sense of the perils of public life[3], and there can be no doubt that he describes his own ideal in the lines:—

"Happy the man whose lot it is to know
The secrets of the earth. He hastens not
To work his fellow's hurt by unjust deeds,
But with rapt admiration contemplates
Immortal Nature's ageless harmony,
And how and when her order came to be.
Such spirits have no place for thoughts of shame[4]."

---

[1] Suppl. 361. Comp. Fragm. 848.
[2] Erechth. fr., 362, 14.
[3] Ion, 595, ff.; Med. 294, ff.; Hec. 254, ff.
[4] Fragm. 902.

122   EURIPIDES AS A RELIGIOUS TEACHER.

And again in a lighter, more joyous strain:—

> "Well! I am not to pause
> Mingling together—wine and wine in cup—
> The Graces with the Muses up—
> Most dulcet marriage; loosed from Muses' law,
> No life for me!
> But where the wreaths abound, there ever may I be[1]!"

Thus Euripides takes account of the manifold fulness of human existence, but the whole effect of life, as he sees it, is, in its external aspect at least, clouded with great sorrow. There is no music to charm its grief[2]. At the best it is chequered, like the face of the earth, with storm and sunshine—

> "I say the heaven men call so, as time rolls,
> Shows in a parable the fate of men.
> It flashes forth bright light in summer-time;
> And deepens winter's gloom with gathered clouds;
> And makes flowers bloom and fade and live and die.
> So too the race of men with happy calm
> Is bright and glad, and then is clouded o'er.
> Some live in woe, some, prosperous for a while,
> Fade like the changes of the changeful year[3]."

> "Such is the life of miserable men,
> Not wholly happy, nor yet wholly sad,
> Blest for a while, and then again unblest[4]."

For the most part, however, pain outweighs pleasure. The consciousness of the instability of joy disturbs

---

[1] Herc. Fur. 673 (Browning).   [2] Med. 195.
[3] Daval. fr. 332.   [4] Antiope, fr. 196.

present delight with the prospect of inevitable change. There is no prerogative of immunity from suffering:—

"He must not think that he will ever find
Unaltered fortune who has had no fall;
For God, I ween, if God He must be called,
Wearies of dwelling always with the same.
A mortal's joy is mortal. They who make
The present bind the future in their pride
Prove when they suffer what man's fortune is[1]."

Death is the one certain limit of suffering[2], and, therefore, it is not strange that to men in some moods it should seem "better not to have been born[3];" or, as it is expressed at length,—

"'Twere well that men in solemn conclave met,
Should mourn each birth as prelude to great woes:
And bear the dead forth from their homes with joy
And thanksgiving, as free at last from toils[4]."

"Life is called life, but it is truly pain[5]."

"Not to be born is one, I say, with death;
And death is better than a piteous life[6]."

Nevertheless, those who are born to suffering cling to life—

"Mortals are sad
In bearing earth to earth: yet it must be.
Life must be reaped, like the ripe golden grain,
One is and one is not[7]."

[1] Fragm. 1058. Comp. Andromeda, fr. 152; Alex. fr. 63; Auge. fr. 275; Œd. fr. 558. Suppl. 331.
[2] Fragm. 908.   [3] Fragm. 900.
[4] Cresph. fr. 452.   [5] Fragm. 957.
[6] Troades, 636. Contrast *ibid.* 632.   [7] Hypsip. fr. 757.

For there is, after all, a mysterious uncertainty about the future, and men shrink from that which is beyond their experience. They—

> "Long to look upon the coming day
> Bearing a burden of unnumbered woes.
> So deep in mortals lies the love of life,
> For life we know, but ignorant of death,
> Each fears alike to leave the sun's dear light[1]."

Meanwhile, man has a hard struggle to maintain, but he is able to maintain it. Whatever we may be tempted to think, Justice is a real and a present power. She does vindicate her authority, not in a remote future and on some other scene, but essentially here and now—

> "Thinkest thou
> To overcome the wisdom of the gods?
> That justice has her dwelling far from men?
> Nay, she is near: she sees, herself unseen,
> And knows whom she must punish. Thou knowest not
> When she will bring swift ruin on the base.
> 'Tis true the working of the gods is slow,
> But it is sure and strong[2]."

There is no ever-present, overwhelming weight of physical or moral necessity which crushes him. He is allowed from time to time to see that greater labours are the condition and the discipline of greater natures. And in spite of the obvious sorrows of life

[1] Phœnix, fr. 813. Comp. Hippol. 193.
[2] Bacch. 882.

he can discern that a divine purpose is being wrought out which will find accomplishment. "There is at present great confusion in the things of gods and men[1]." But the source of the disorder lies not with GOD but with man[2]. And in due time the inequalities and injustices which form the bitterest trial of the good will be righted, and that on the present scene of human conflict and failure, not by any sudden divine intervention or startling catastrophe, but by the sure working of the forces which are already in action:—

"Think you that deeds of wrong spring to the gods
 On wings, and then some one, on Zeus' book,
 Writes them, and Zeus beholding the record
 Gives judgment? Nay, the whole expanse of heaven
 Would not suffice if Zeus wrote there man's sins;
 Nor could he send to each his punishment
 From such review. Justice is on the earth,
 Is here, is by us, if men will but see[3]."

The criminal is alarmed by unreal terrors, and then comforted by an unreal security:—

"Justice will not assail thee, fear it not,
 Not thee nor any other that doth wrong,
 And pierce thy heart; but moving silently
 With lingering foot, whene'er the hour is come,
 She lays her heavy hand upon the base[4]."

---

[1] Iph. T. 572.
[2] Pel. fr. 609.
[3] Melanippe, fr. 508. Comp. Andromeda, fr. 150.
[4] Fragm. 969. Comp. Fragm. 266, 588, 646, 1030.

For it is said truly "that Justice is the child of time," of time "that looketh keenly, he that seeth all[1]." But in the end she makes herself felt:—

"The man that for the passing hour doth wrong,
And thinks the gods have failed to see the deed,
Thinks evil, and is taken in his thought.
When Justice finds a space of quiet time,
He pays full vengeance for the wrongs he did[2]."

"Slow come, but come at length,
In their majestic strength,
Faithful and true, the avenging deities;
And chastening human folly,
And the mad pride unholy
Of those who to the gods bow not their knees[3]."

The retribution which is thus indicated is often not complete at once. The sins of parents are visited on their children[4], even as a later generation gathers the ripe fruit of earlier labour. A larger field than that which is offered by a single life is necessary for the revelation of this fulfilment of a just will; and it is a characteristic of the tragedies of Euripides that he introduces gods not so much to solve immediate difficulties in his plots, as to point out how in the future a righteous result will be assured. In no less than thirteen plays divine characters disclose the future issues of the action which will vindicate the

---

[1] Antiope, fr. 223: Melanippe, fr. 509. Comp. Beller. fr. 305.
[2] Phrix. fr. 832.
[3] Bacchæ, 882 (Milman).
[4] Fragm. 970; Alcm. fr. 83.

EURIPIDES AS A RELIGIOUS TEACHER.

mysterious course of Providence. And in this wider view of life the personal fate of the individual actors finds hardly any place[1].

A wide view of life is required for the discernment of the justice of the divine government; and a wide view of life is necessary also for the fulfilment of human destiny. One chief cause of the sufferings and failures of men lies in the partial and inadequate view of the claims of being which is taken by those who are noble and good within a narrow range. This truth is brought out with impressive power in the characters of Pentheus and Hippolytus. Both are, up to a certain point, blameless and courageous, but they are unsympathetic to that which lies beyond their experience and inclination. They contemptuously cast aside warnings against self-will. They refuse to pay respect to the convictions of others, or to admit that their view of life can fall short of fulness. With tragic irony Pentheus is led to his ruin by a guilty curiosity, and Hippolytus, in the pathetic scene of his death, lays bare his overwhelming self-confidence. He can forgive his father, but he is defiant to the powers of heaven, and in the terrible line,

"Would that the curse of men might reach the gods[2]."

he reveals at once the strength and the weakness of his character.

[1] Comp. fr. 21.   [2] Hippol. 1415.

In this connexion Euripides appears to indicate one use of suffering. The discipline of life as he regards it is fitted to give to men a truer and larger sense of human powers and duties than they were inclined to form at first. This lesson comes out prominently in the "Alcestis." In one aspect the drama is the record of a soul's purification. Admetus obtains life at the price which he was ready to pay for it, and he finds that it ceases to be the blessing which he sought. He sees in his father the full image of himself, and fiercely condemns the selfishness which he has shown. Little by little he fully realizes that what he has gained by consciously sacrificing another to himself is of no avail for happiness, and he is prepared to receive, cleansed in heart, that which has been won for him by the spontaneous effort of Heracles. This contrast of the two sacrifices and the two prizes is of the deepest meaning. Man cannot simply use another at his will for his own good; but he can enjoy the fruits of another's devotion. The life which Alcestis gave for her husband at his entreaty proved to be only a discipline of sorrow; the life which was wrested from death by human labour could be imparted to one made ready to welcome it.

In Pentheus and Hippolytus, Euripides has shown the failure of partial virtues; in Heracles—the man raised to heaven through toil—he seems to have wished to show a type of the fulness of life. The hero in the "Alcestis" keenly enjoys the pleasures of the feast in the close prospect of a terrible labour;

and when he hears of his friend's loss he hastens to meet death with a kind of natural joy. He proves in act that the reward of victory is a new conflict, and with genial vigour accepts the condition of progress.

But even here there is a want. Man, as he is, cannot with impunity wrestle with Death and rob Hades of its terrors. At the moment when Heracles seems to have prevailed over the common enemy, and to have brought deliverance to his own house, Madness comes, and he works himself the ruin which he had just averted[1]. He, too, must feel his weakness. And so it is that in this last trial he rises to his greatest height. He sees the full measure of his calamity. He acknowledges that for him henceforward there is no hope. Where he looked for glory and joy, there can be only horror and pain. And feeling this, at the bidding of Theseus, he dares to live. In a fuller sense than before he has conquered death[2], and he is ready for his elevation. The conception rises to the height of spiritual grandeur, and there is no nobler picture in Greek literature than that of the broken-hearted hero leaning on the friend whom he had rescued from the shades, and patiently going to meet exile and irremediable grief[3]. Toil consecrated by self-surrender could not but lead to heaven.

[1] Herc. Fur. 922 ff. Comp. Hartung, *Eurip. restit.* ii. 29.
[2] *Ibid.* 1146.
[3] *Ibid.* 1398 ff.

III.

A hero like Heracles is raised to heaven, but what has the unseen world for common men? To this question Euripides has no clear answer. He looks, as we have seen, for the vindication of righteousness on earth. His references to another order are few and vague. In this respect he holds the common attitude of the Athenian in the presence of death[1]. There are, as Professor Gardner has pointed out, no traces of scenes of future happiness, or misery, or judgment, on early Greek funeral sculptures. The utmost that is represented is the farewell of the traveller who is bound for some unknown realm. And in the inscriptions which accompany them the future practically finds no place. The world to come is not denied so much as left out of sight. It is not a distinct object either of hope or of fear. Euripides, indeed, has recognised, twice at least, in memorable words the mystery of life and death, the powerlessness of man to attain to a true conception of being:

"Who knows if Life is Death,
And Death is counted Life by those below?
"Who knows if Life, as we speak, is but Death,
And Death is Life[2]?"

But in the latter place he seems to shrink back from

[1] Compare Professor Gardner, C.R., Dec. 1877, pp. 148 ff.
[2] Polyid. fr. 639; Phrix. fr. 830.

EURIPIDES AS A RELIGIOUS TEACHER. 131

the positive hope which he has called up into mere negation, and he continues—

> "Nay, lay the question by;
> But this at least we do know: they that live
> Are sick and suffer; they who are no more
> Nor suffer further, nor have ills to bear."

Elsewhere dim visions are given of the possibility of new modes of existence hereafter, and he suggests that the clinging love of earthly life is not more than an instinctive shrinking from the unknown:—

> "We seem possessed by an unhappy love
> Of this strange, glittering, being upon earth,
> Because we know not any other life,
> And cannot gaze upon the things below,
> But yield to idle tales[1]."

But more commonly his characters give unqualified utterance to the dread of Death:—

> "This light is very sweet to men to see,
> The realm below is naught. He raves who prays
> To die. 'Tis better to live on in woe
> Than to die nobly[2]."

> "Death, my dear child, is not all one with Life;
> For Death is nothing, but in Life Hope lives[3]."

Death, under this aspect, is presented as extinction, dissolution, in which there seems to be no room for further restoration:—

[1] Hippol. 193; comp. Ion, 1066: Iph. Aul. 1507.
[2] Iph. Aul. 1250; comp. *ibid.* 537: contrast *ibid.* 1368 ff.
[3] Troad. 632.

"He that but now was full of lusty life,
Quenched like a falling star, hath rendered back
His spirit to heaven[1]."

"Suffer the dead to be enwrapped in earth,
Suffer each element thither to return
Whence first it came; the spirit to the sky,
The body to the earth. For 'tis not ours,
But lent to us, to dwell in while life lasts,
And then the earth which formed it takes it back[2]."

"Bless thou the living: every man when dead
Is earth and shadow: nothing turns to nothing[3]."

But, of all the utterances of the future, the most pathetic in its utter hopelessness is that of Macaria. With generous and unhesitating devotion she offers herself for the deliverance of her kindred. She bids farewell to her aged guardian, Iolaus. She prays for the efficacy of her sacrifice. She asks for burial as her just recompense. And then she concludes: "This"—this salvation which I have bought, this grateful remembrance which I have gained—

"This is my treasure there,
In place of children, for my maiden death,

---

[1] Fragm. 961.   [2] Suppl. 531.

[3] Meleag. fr. 536; Comp. Suppl. 1140. This conception of the dissolution of the elements of man's being is of frequent occurrence in funeral inscriptions. It occurs on the monument to those who fell at Potidæa in 432 B.C.; though sometimes a personal continuance of the soul "in the realm of the blest" seems to be implied.—Comp. Prof. Gardner, l.c. pp. 162 ff. Lenormant, "La voie sacrée Eleusinienne," i. 51, 62 f.

EURIPIDES AS A RELIGIOUS TEACHER. 133

> If there be any life beneath the earth.
> I pray there may be none. For if there too
> We shall have cares, poor mortals doomed to die,
> I know not whither we can turn; for death
> Is held the surest medicine for woes[1]."

Once only, as far as I know, is there any reference in Euripides to future punishment. The words have been regarded as an interpolation; but the fact that they occur in the "Helena" justifies the thought that the poet may have allowed himself to adopt in part an Egyptian belief, with which he could not have been unacquainted. Theonoe, a prophetess, sister of the king Theoclymenus, who wished to marry Helen by force in violation of the laws of hospitality, promises Menelaus her help in rescuing his long-lost wife. She cannot, she admits at once, be partner in her brother's crime:—

> "Vengeance there is for this with those below,
> And those above, for all alike. The mind
> Of those that die lives not, indeed, but has
> Immortal feeling, grown incorporate
> With the immortal æther[2]."

The thought suggested by the last lines is, as far as I know, unique. The isolated life of the individual appears to be contrasted with a conscious participation in the divine life as man's final destiny. This participation is necessarily limited by Euripides to a

---
[1] Heracl. 591. Comp. Antig. fr. 176; Alc. 937.
[2] Hel. 1013.

part of man's nature; but in fashioning the thought he seems to have reached the loftiest idea accessible before the Gospel.

If, however, this be, as I believe, a true expression of the mind of Euripides, it is a solitary flash of light in the general gloom. When he speaks, as he does rarely, of the dead as still conscious, he does not conceive of them as more than the cold shadows of the Homeric Hades. Neoptolemus invites the spirit of Achilles to drink the blood of Polyxena offered in his honour[1]. Theseus, in reply to Heracles, says that in Hades he was weaker than any man[2]. Those beneath the earth have no strength, no joy[3]. At one time they are supposed to be conscious of things above, and then again to be ignorant of them. Hecuba, in the same play, speaks of Priam as ignorant of her calamity, and anticipates the protection of Hector for his son Astyanax in the realm of the dead[4]. Orestes addresses his father in Hades as he shrinks from fulfilling the terrible duty required of him, and Electra nerves his indecision with the reply:—

"All this thy father hears. 'Tis time to go[5]."

Megara, in the "Hercules Furens," appeals to her lost husband in words which perfectly express the conflict of vague hope and fear:—

[1] Hec. 536.
[2] Herc. Fur. 1415.
[3] Orest. 1084; Cresph. fr. 454.
[4] Troad. 1314; 1234.
[5] Iph. Aul. 682.

EURIPIDES AS A RELIGIOUS TEACHER. 135

"Dearest, if any mortal voice is heard
In Hades, Heracles, to thee I speak . . . .
Help, come, appear, though but a shade to me,
For coming thou wouldst be defence enough[1]."

Once, in the "Hecuba," Euripides has ventured to introduce the dead upon the stage. The Ghost of Polydorus opens the crowning tragedy of the fall of Troy. With natural inconsistency the disembodied spirit speaks now of itself, and now of the unburied body as the "I":—

"I leave
The chamber of the dead and gates of gloom.
"I lie upon the shore[2]."

Yet even here the shadowy vitality is only a transitory manifestation. The spirit, it is true, has left the body by its own act; it has obtained from the sovereign of the nether realm the power to appear. But all that it desires is burial and a tomb, the symbol of untroubled rest and posthumous remembrance[3].

This representation of the Ghost of Polydorus offers an interesting parallel to that of the Ghost of Darius in the "Persæ." Widely different as Æschylus and Euripides are in their views of man and gods, they are alike in their general conception of Hades. The Great King, as Æschylus describes him, though

[1] Herc. Fur. 490.

[2] Hec. i. 28.

[3] Comp. Hec. 319. The reference to "the third day" is remarkable.—See St John, xi., 39 note.

a joyless prince below the earth, appears in ignorance of his people's disaster. He knows the future only as men may know it—from the oracles of the gods. The lesson which he has to give, to those who can yet follow it, is to rejoice in the present blessings of life:—

"I go beneath the gloom of earth;
But you, ye elders, though in woe, be glad;
And give your souls to joy while the day lasts,
For wealth avails not to the dead below[1]."

There is one partial exception to the general darkness which Euripides allows to fall over the grave. The plot of the "Alcestis" gives greater play to hope than is allowed elsewhere. The devotion of the heroic wife and the joyous strength of Heracles in the face of trials, which grow with each victory, inspire the spectators with confidence that even the terrors of death may be overcome at last:—

"On each soul this boldness settled now,
That one who reverenced the gods so much
Would prosper yet[2]."

But the confidence, so far as it exists, rests on the unique merits of Alcestis, and not on the common destiny of man. She is addressed with a prayer as a "blessed deity[3]." Still, for her also, Hades is sunless[4]. The future which Admetus looks forward to

[1] Persae, 839.
[2] Alc. 604 (Browning).
[3] Alc. 1003.
[4] Alc. 436.

is, at best, a reflection of the present[1]. And doubt dashes the loftiest expectation:—

"If there—aye there—some touch
Of further dignity await the good,
Sharing with them, mays't thou sit throned by her,
The bride of Hades, in companionship[2]."

But Alcestis herself does not rise beyond the legendary picture of the gloomy region of Hades. She sees the two-oared boat and Charon, and the darkness of the abode of the departed, and no ray of light falls upon it from the splendour of her devotion[3].

There are, indeed, some few who are exempted from the cheerless lot of the common dead. The kindred of the gods can reach to Heaven. Thetis promises Peleus that she will hereafter make him an immortal god, and that he shall dwell with her in the palace of Nereus[4]. Heracles rises to Heaven itself[5]. Achilles and Menelaus are to live in the island of the blest[6]; and the Muse, his mother, promises Rhesus she will obtain for him life as "a human deity" though she will never see his face[7]. But in speaking of these unusual blessings Euripides keeps within the limits of the epic legend. He repeats the old traditions, but he does not extend them. With these

[1] Alc. 363.
[2] Alc. 744 (Browning).
[3] Alc. 252 ff.
[4] Andr. 1254, ff.
[5] Heracl. 9, 871, 910 ff.
[6] Andr. l.c.; Hel. 1676.
[7] Rhes. 967.

exceptions even the gods, who show in the future the triumph of righteousness, are silent as to the retribution of an unseen state. They promise no happiness, they denounce no suffering in the invisible order. The powers of the unseen world do not come within their view. This is shown most remarkably at the close of the "Hippolytus." Artemis appears in order to bring consolation to her dying worshipper. It might have seemed almost necessary that she should draw a bright picture of future unhindered companionship, of free fellowship untroubled by passion, of purity triumphant and unassailable. But of this there is not a word. All that she offers is the prospect of a pitiful vengeance and the honour of celebration upon earth.

Vitruvius mentions that the tomb of Euripides was still a place of frequent resort in his time (c. B.C. 15). It was situated, he says, just above the confluence of two streams. The waters of the one were noxious and unfit for human use; the waters of the other were pure and refreshing, and pilgrims drank of them freely[1]. The description reads like a parable of the position of the living poet, and it is completed by a tradition preserved by Plutarch. The tomb, he relates, when it was completed was touched by fire from Heaven, in token of the favour of the gods. This divine consecration was given besides only to the tomb of Lycurgus[2].

[1] Vitruv. viii. 16.   [2] Plut. Lyc., 31.

Euripides certainly suffered, and thought and wrote, at the meeting-point of conflicting currents of opinion and hope. He reflects and, to a certain extent, interprets the effects which followed from the dissolution of the old life and the old faith under the calamities of the Peloponnesian war and the influence of foreign culture. He treated the drama as Socrates treated philosophy; he brought it to the common concerns of daily experience, to the trials and the passions of simple men and women. So it is that he is the most modern of the ancient tragedians, because he is the most human.

The view of man's condition and destiny which he gives is unquestionably sombre. He has visions of lofty truth from time to time, but he does not draw from them any abiding support for trust. In his tragedies, the sorrows and failures of the good make themselves felt in their present intensity; the anticipations of ultimate retribution rest rather upon a rational conviction that it must be, than upon that sense of a divine fellowship which draws from the fulfilment of duty an inspiration of joy under every disappointment.

The religious teaching of Euripides corresponds, in a word, with that most touching and noble sentence which Plato, in this case perhaps with more than usual truth, quotes from a conversation with Socrates on the evening of his death. "In regard to the facts of a future life, a man," said Phædo, "must either learn or find out their nature; or, if he cannot do this, take at any rate the best and least assailable of human words, and, borne on this as on a raft, perform in peril the voyage of life, unless he should be able to accomplish the journey with less risk and danger on a surer vessel—some word divine[1]."

We can then study in Euripides a distinct stage in the preparation of the world for Christianity. He paints life as he found it when Greek art and Greek thought had put forth their full power. He scatters the dream which some have indulged in of the unclouded brightness of the Athenian prospect of life: and his popularity shows that he represented truly the feelings of those with whom he lived, and of those who came after him. His recognition of the mystery of being from the point of sight of the poet and not of the philosopher, his affirmation of the establishment of the sovereignty of righteousness under the conditions of earth, his feeling after a final unity in the harmonious consummation of things in the supreme existence, his vindication of the claims of the fulness of man's nature, are so many testimonies of the soul to the character of the revelation which can perfectly meet its needs. Let any one carefully ponder them, and consider whether they do not all find fulfilment in the one fact which is the message of the Gospel.

It cannot be a mere accidental coincidence that when St Paul stood on the Areopagus and unfolded

---

[1] Phæd. p. 85, c.

the meaning of his announcement of "Jesus and the Resurrection," he did in reality proclaim, as now established in the actual experience of men, the truths which Euripides felt after—the office of feeling, the oneness and end of humanity, the completeness of man's future being, the reign of righteousness, existence in God[1].

[1] Acts xvii. 23 ff.

DIONYSIUS THE AREOPAGITE.

Ἐγὼ μὲν οὐκ οἶδα πρὸς Ἕλληνας ἢ πρὸς ἑτέρους εἰπών, ἀρκεῖν οἰόμενος ἀγαθοῖς ἀνδράσιν εἰ τὸ ἀληθὲς αὐτὸ ἐφ' ἑαυτοῦ δυνήσοιντο καὶ γνῶναι καὶ εἰπεῖν ᾗ ὄντως ἔχει.

DION. AREOP. Ep. vii.

I.

IT is the fate of books even more than of men to exert a profound influence when their individual existence is forgotten. If it be true in one sense of men that the dead are sovereign over the living, the saying has a deeper application to literature. A particular phase of thought is taken up into some broader intellectual development, and works its full effect under the changed circumstances; but the writings to which it owed its origin, or in which it first found expression, are forgotten, or, if remembered, lose their true significance. The movement goes on from life to life, but the first motor remains stationary, and few are willing to make the mental effort which alone can render its primary action intelligible. And this effort necessarily becomes more

DIONYSIUS THE AREOPAGITE. 143

difficult and more distasteful in proportion as the subject to which it has to be applied is removed from our sympathies. Still, any form of speculation which has at any time powerfully influenced human thought will repay the study which is spent in understanding it, and sooner or later claim fresh regard. The variations of human nature are too limited to place any of its developments wholly beyond the pale of our interest. An oscillation in popular feeling brings back what was for a time forgotten. Old problems rise again, upon a higher level, it may be, but yet so that the old answers are not without their use; or even if we can now see a surer way of meeting them, it is none the less invigorating to know that they have been met and in some sort solved in former times.

So it is that by a partial revolution of thought in the present age Scholastic Philosophy has lately received far more attention than was held to be due to it in the last two centuries. Our own discussions have made the difficulties with which it dealt, and the methods which it employed, more capable of realisation. At the same time that which has ceased to be formidable becomes capable of a calm analysis. But while we are tolerably familiar with the good and evil of scholasticism, and not unwilling to acknowledge its permanent effects on modern habits of mind, the mysterious writings out of which it sprung, and under the shelter of whose venerable title it was first fostered, have as yet received no popular recognition. Few even among students of theology read the works of Dionysius the Areopagite, "out of which," to quote the enthusiastic words of their editor, "the Angelic Doctor drew almost the whole of his theology, so that his 'Summa' is but the hive in whose varied cells he duly stored the honey which he gathered from them."

There is, indeed, very little in the writings to attract a reader. Their style is, as a rule, monotonously turgid. The sentences are cumbrous and involved; the words are frequently uncouth and barbarous. The same thought is continually restated with a wearisome iteration; and emphasis or distinctness is sought simply by an accumulation of details. But yet, on the other hand, a greater familiarity with the works reveals in them a real earnestness of purpose and many great thoughts. Even in the exaggerations of language there remain noble signs of the wondrous flexibility of Greek; and there are here and there a few passages in which the author proves himself to have been not an unattentive student of Plato's manner. One of these may be quoted as shewing better than a description would do, the generous and loving spirit in which he engaged in his work[1].

A monk who had assailed a priest for dealing too

[1] In translating the quotations from Dionysius, I have exercised much freedom in dealing with his cumbrous and involved style. A literal rendering would be intolerable in English.

leniently, as he thought, with a penitent, had applied to Dionysius for his support. In reply, he rebuked him severely for his want of mercy, and concludes:—

"If you please I will recount a divine vision of a saintly man; and smile not at it, for it is a true story. Once upon a time when I visited Crete, I was entertained by the holy Carpus. He was a man qualified beyond all others by the purity of his soul for the vision of GOD. . . . . . . An unbeliever, so he told me, had once grieved him by leading a Christian astray to godlessness, while the days of rejoicing over his baptism were still being celebrated[1]. And so when he ought to have prayed for both in sincere charity, that by GOD's help he might convert the one and overcome the other, ... though he had never been so affected before, he allowed rancorous enmity and bitterness to sink into his heart. In this evil state he fell asleep, for it was evening; and at midnight, when it was his habit to awake to recite the divine hymns, he rose from troubled and broken slumbers, and even in the midst of his very communion with GOD was agitated by unholy sorrow and indignation, as he pleaded that it was not right that ungodly men should live, perverting the straight paths of the Lord. And so saying he prayed GOD to slay both the offenders, without pity, by a bolt from heaven. As soon as the prayer was uttered, he said that he thought that the house in which he stood was suddenly shaken with great violence and cloven in twain from the roof, and that a line of fire, exceeding bright, streamed down from heaven to the place where he was; and that heaven itself was opened, and that upon its edge was JESUS, with innumerable angels

[1] This seems to be certainly the sense of the passage. The term *Hilaria* is simply transferred to a Christian use.

in human shape standing beside him. This was what he saw above, and as he looked on it he marvelled. But when he bent downwards he said that he saw the earth rent asunder with a dark and yawning chasm, and the men whom he cursed standing before him at the edge of the chasm, trembling and piteous, and their footing was so unsteady that by reason of that alone they were on the point of falling into it; moreover snakes crawled up from the gulf below and gliding about their feet .... sought by every kind of terror and fascination .... to cast them into the pit. There were men also among the snakes who at the same time assailed the two guilty ones with violent shakings and thrusts and blows; and it seemed that they were about to fall half-willingly, half-unwillingly, as they were gradually constrained or seduced by their evil circumstances. And Carpus said that he was delighted to look down, and forgot what was above; nay, that he was indignant and dissatisfied that they had not already fallen, and vexed that his repeated efforts to this end had failed of success; and that he cursed them still. And having with difficulty lifted his eyes upward he saw heaven again, as he had seen it before, and JESUS in pity rise from His throne and descend to the wretched men and reach to them a loving hand, and the angels helping Him and supporting the men on all sides. And he thought that JESUS said to him, when his hand was now stretched out to smite, 'Smite *Me*, if you will; for I am ready to suffer again to save men anew; yea, I would gladly endure this to rescue others from sin. But see if it be well for thee to make thy abode with snakes in the pit rather than with GOD and the good angels to whom men are dear!'

"This is what I heard, and I believe that it is true[1]."

[1] Ep. viii. 6.

DIONYSIUS THE AREOPAGITE.

If the style of the dream is not wholly unlike that of Plato, the conception of it is not unworthy of Jean Paul[1]; and at the same time it reveals the tenderness with which the writer sought to fulfil his Christian mission. He had been trained, as it seems, in some heathen school, probably that of Proclus, and in leaving that teaching for a nobler faith, he had not cast aside his old love. Like Justin, he wears the robe of the philosopher when he expounds the mysteries of the Gospel. His object, as he explains it elsewhere, was not to destroy, but to construct; or rather to destroy by construction; to conquer error by the full presentment of truth[2]. His method was sound even where his applications were false. Very much in his system, as will be seen, was faulty and defective, and yet his power of sympathy made him the fitting medium through whom the last results of Greek speculation should pass into the treasury of the Church.

II.

The earliest mention of the Dionysian writings

---

[1] The double action of the power of sense to constrain and attract will remind some of Goethe's exquisite lines in "The Fisherman," which must have the same meaning:—

"Sie sprach zu ihm, sie sang zu ihm;
Da war's um ihm geschehn:
Halb zog sie ihn, halb sank er hin,
Und ward nicht mehr gesehn."

[2] See particularly the short letter, Ep. vi.

occurs in the record of the conference between the Severians (a Monophysite sect) and the orthodox at Constantinople, in A.D. 533. The Severians quoted them in defence of their views; but their adversaries rejected the evidence as of more than doubtful authenticity. "These so-called works of the Areopagite," they said, "were unknown to Cyril and Athanasius, and if no one of the ancients quoted them, how can you establish their truth?" But though their first appearance was thus suspicious and suspected, they soon won their way to popular favour. In the next century they found a zealous champion in the saintly Maximus (†662), who illustrated them by short notes. Yet even then they were not universally admitted as genuine. The first book noticed by Photius in his "Bibliotheca" (c. 845) is an essay by Theodorus, a presbyter, in defence of the "genuineness of the volume ($\beta i \beta \lambda o s$) of Saint Dionysius." The controversy was therefore probably active at that time, and Photius' note seems to indicate that he considered Theodorus' arguments not so weighty as the objections which he endeavoured to meet. The objections were fourfold, and they may be quoted here, for they sum up excellently the proof of the late origin of the treatises. Firstly, then, it is said that they are not quoted by the earlier Fathers; next, that they are not mentioned in the catalogues of writings in Eusebius; thirdly, that the growth of the Church customs was slow, and that it is "against all likelihood, or rather a mere forgery, to represent

Dionysius as discussing results which were reached a long time after his death;" lastly, that he quotes an epistle of Ignatius, which was written on his way to martyrdom, in the time of Trajan, a manifest anachronism. "These four difficulties," Photius adds, "Theodorus strives earnestly to solve, and so to establish (as far as in him lies) the genuineness of the volume." But in the eighth and ninth centuries criticism was of little avail against possession, and the Dionysian writings were accepted as the real works of the Areopagite by the greatest writers of the Greek Church, from the end of the century in which they were first brought forward, by Leontius of Byzantium (c. 590), by Sophronius of Jerusalem (c. 638), by John of Damascus (c. 730), by Simeon Metaphrastes (c. 901), and by Euthymius Zigabenus (c. 1116).

In the west the Dionysian writings were first referred to on hearsay by Gregory the Great (c. 600), and afterwards distinctly quoted by Adrian I. in a letter to Charles the Great. But the beginning of their real influence was somewhat later and more romantic. In the year 827 Michael the Stammerer sent a copy of the books to Louis I., the son of Charles. They were received in the abbey of St Denis, near Paris, by the abbot Hilduin. The Areopagite and Bishop of Athens was identified with the Apostle of France, who was supposed to be buried there. The arrival of the gift was marked by signal miracles. It came on the very vigil of the Feast of

Dionysius, and was attended by such divine grace, "that on the same night nineteen cures were wrought on well-known persons in the neighbourhood of the monastery sick of various maladies." Such marvels could not but stimulate the pious curiosity of the king, and Hilduin appears to have attempted to prepare a version of the Greek text. Probably his knowledge of Greek failed him in the task, as well it might do, and what he accomplished was soon lost. Charles the Bald, the son of Louis, was more successful in finding a scholar to execute the work. His zeal for sacred literature was rewarded by the services of Johannes Scotus, who was well versed in the Greek Fathers, and even ventured on original Greek composition. This scholar cannot have been long at the Court of Charles before he received the command to translate into Latin the works of Dionysius. His treatise "On Predestination," published about 851, is entirely built out of Dionysian teaching; but the first definite notice of his version is a letter from Pope Nicholas I. to Charles (A.D. 861), in which he complains that the work had not been sent to him, "according to the custom of the Church," to receive the sanction of his judgment. Nothing seems to have followed from the implied censure, and some years later (c. 865) Anastasius, the Librarian of the Roman See, writing also to Charles, commends the wonderful work of "the barbarian placed in the ends of the world," with generous warmth. "The man wrought through the operation of the Spirit," he says, "who quickened in him at once the fire of love and the fire of eloquence."

This praise was hardly merited by the translation itself, which is a simple rendering of words, and not of thoughts, so that "the interpretation almost always needs an interpreter;" but obscurity was not likely to deter men who believed that they had before them the doctrine of an apostolic teacher, "venerable," as Scotus says, alike "for his antiquity, for the sublimity of the heavenly mysteries with which he dealt," and for "the singular graces" which were bestowed upon him; and on this point there was unanimous consent. Scotus never expresses a doubt of the genuineness of the books, and M. Delrio is probably to be trusted when he says that Thomas de Vio alone of the schoolmen expressed the least hesitation as to their authorship.

When the text was once accessible, numerous commentaries followed; as that of Hugo of St Victor on "The Heavenly Hierarchy" (c. 1120), of Robert Grosseteste on all the books (c. 1235), of Thomas Aquinas on "The Divine Names" (c. 1255), of Albertus Magnus (c. 1260), of Dionysius Carthusianus (c. 1450); and in almost every mediæval writing on theology the authority of the Areopagite is quoted as decisive. And so it was that two other new versions were made; one by Johannes Sarracinus in the twelfth century, and another by Ambrosius Camaldulensis in the fifteenth.

At the revival of learning the reputation of the Dionysian treatises suffered rude shocks. Scholars like Theodorus Gaza and Laurentius Valla, critical theologians like Erasmus and Cardinal Cajetan, felt the absolute certainty of their late origin. From that time the final judgment was not doubtful. The ingenious labours of Delrio and Halloix in defence of the Dionysian authorship are now only instructive monuments of misplaced learning. "The scanty handful of skirmishers," to use the image of the former writer, has conquered in the judgment of all "the serried phalanx of the East and West." Every writer, I believe, of every school now admits that the title of the books is a pseudonym.

It seems equally certain, and generally admitted, that the books cannot have been written before the fifth century. Beyond this all is conjectural. But from the remarkable coincidence of thought which the Dionysian writings shew with those of Proclus[1], who was said by some enthusiastic apologists to have pillaged the thoughts of the Areopagite, it may be reasonably concluded that they were written late in the century; and their general character suggests Syria, or the far East, as their birthplace. The position which they occupy with regard to the great controversies on the Person of Christ points distinctly to this conclusion. Without being formally Monophysite, they yet exhibit most clearly the working of

[1] The coincidences with Damascius, the second in succession from Proclus and the last Platonic teacher at Athens, are even more remarkable. It is worthy of notice that Damascius was of Syrian origin.

those influences which gave rise to Monophysitism, and which, even after the condemnation of the doctrine at Chalcedon (A.D. 451), still exercised a powerful charm over the speculations of the monks of Egypt and Syria. It was, as we have seen, by Monophysites that they were first brought forward, and in later times they found among them numerous translators and commentators. It is, perhaps, possible to advance yet further towards a solution of the question of their date. The pseudo-Dionysius quotes Hierotheus as an elder contemporary and teacher; and it appears that, at the end of the fifth century, an abbot of a monastery at Edessa, Bar Sadaili, either wrote a book under that name, or found one there bearing it, by the help of which he supported his own mystic doctrines. Thus the name Hierotheus at least came into notice then. In itself the coincidence is perhaps slight, but it falls in with every other indication of place and date which the Dionysian writings contain; and the error cannot be great if it be conjectured that they were composed A.D. 480—520, either at Edessa or under the influence of the Edessene school.

But though the writings are pseudonymous, there is no reason to consider them a forgery. The historic dress is of the most meagre texture, and the writer rests his conclusions on Scripture and tradition and reason, and not on his individual authority. The references to his connexion with the apostles are most superficial, and chiefly confined to the superscriptions of his books. His Essays are addressed to "his fellow-presbyter Timotheus." Among his letters is one to "Polycarp, Bishop" [of Smyrna]; another to "Titus, Bishop" [of Crete]; and another to "John the Divine, Apostle and Evangelist, exiled in the island of Patmos." But there is no endeavour to give any appearance of naturalness to the writings by the introduction of circumstantial allusions or personal reminiscences. Two such allusions indeed occur, and they are very significant; but they are introduced for special purposes, and appear to refer to late but widespread legends. In recounting the praises of Hierotheus, the writer says that when they went with "James, the brother of the Lord (ἀδελφόθεος), and Peter the chief and noblest head of the inspired apostles (ἡ κορυφαία καὶ πρεσβυτάτη τῶν θεολόγων ἀκρότης), to gaze upon the (dead) body of her who was the beginning of life and the recipient of GOD," Hierotheus surpassed all, after the apostles, in the ecstatic hymns to which he then gave utterance[1]. And, again, he charges Polycarp to remind Apollophanes, a philosopher who was a vehement adversary of Christianity, of what had once happened to him when they were fellow-students at Heliopolis; how they had seen the sun eclipsed by the passage of the moon from opposition to conjunction, moving from east to west; and then, after the total darkness, returning from west to east, at the time, as it appeared afterwards, of the Passion. So that, when he saw this, Apollophanes said, "It is a crisis in the affairs of heaven;" and Dionysius

[1] De div. Nom. iii. 2.

DIONYSIUS THE AREOPAGITE. 155

replied, "Either the God of Nature suffers, or the fabric of the world is broken up[1]." On the other hand, nothing was more natural than that a later writer, himself deeply influenced by Greek philosophy, should adopt the one name in the New Testament which combined Greek culture with Christian faith. If Dionysius[2] was originally a student in the Athenian school of Proclus, the selection of the name had yet another recommendation. There was a real meaning even in the fiction by which an Athenian Christian was made to claim for the Faith some of the results which it had suggested to heathen teachers in his own city. The first bishop was, in a true sense, the intellectual ancestor of the last philosopher. But however this may be, the title was significant, and its adoption was not abhorrent from the literary instinct of the age. In this respect the Dionysian writings may be compared with the Clementines. The names under which both appear were representative names. They describe the spirit and object of the writers, and are not in themselves signs of wilful dishonesty.

III.

The writings which remain are but a portion of the whole collection, if any trust can be placed in the

[1] Ep. vii. 2.

[2] For the sake of convenience I shall call the unknown writer by the name which he assumed.

references which the author makes to his other works; but these form a tolerably complete whole, and no trace of the missing books is left beyond their titles[1]. The order in which they are commonly arranged gives their proper sequence:—1. *On the Heavenly Hierarchy;* 2. *On the Ecclesiastical Hierarchy;* 3. *On the Divine Names;* 4. *On Mystical Theology.* To these are added ten *Letters* of not less interest than the integral treatises. Between (2) and (3) the writer places his missing essay *On Theological Outlines;* and between (3) and (4) that *On Symbolical Theology.* Besides these he refers to essays *On the Soul, On the Just Judgment of God, On the Objects of Intellect and Sense, On Divine Hymns*[2]; of which the first three suggest topics with which the extant writings deal very unsatisfactorily. Indeed, it may be said that they mark the weak points where the Dionysian system breaks down as a complete theory of Being.

For it is nothing less than this that Dionysius claims to give. His books taken together are a

[1] The Abbé Migne's reprint of the edition of Corderius (Paris, 1857), with some additions, contains everything which a student needs for the elucidation of the text. The notes of Corderius illustrate most fully the connexion of Thomas Aquinas with Dionysius.

[2] Two other books are sometimes ascribed to him *On the Attributes and Ranks of Angels,* and *On Legal Theology.* The former title probably refers to the *Divine Hierarchy;* and the later title is obtained only by a false interpretation of the text in which it is supposed to be named.

Philosophy of Being. He starts from the Absolute, and passing through the successions of its descending manifestations rises again to the Absolute in the ecstasy of a mystic union of man with GOD. The grandeur of the problem gives a solemn dignity to the earnest effort to solve it; and popular speculations of our own time give even a present interest to the first Christian solution, however imperfect it may be, of what remains the last human mystery.

The word "Hierarchy," which expresses the Divine law of the subordination and mutual dependence of the different ranks of beings, is one of the key-words to the whole scheme. Step by step there is, according to Dionysius, a measured rise from the lowest being to the highest. Thus at each point a passage is possible to a superior level; and by a slow and progressive revelation the faithful worshipper attains a truer conception of the one supreme Being, and a closer fellowship with Him. Everything finite is a help towards the apprehension of the infinite; everything complex is a stage in the ascent to the One. The framework is necessary for human infirmity; and man himself is but one link in a magnificent whole. At the same time our view of the Divine order is necessarily a human view, and we refer its several parts to ourselves. It is to meet this infirmity that the revelation of the Divine economy is given. For us the simple is made manifold. The material discipline of earthly ordinances is the prelude to a purer knowledge. Each sight and sound, the processes of reason and the perceptions of sense, have something of a sacramental value. And this not by any afterthought, so to speak, or special grace, but by their own inherent nature and the primal law of things. Thus all was ordered from the first; and

"it is impossible that the beams of the Divine source can shine upon us unless they are shrouded in the manifold texture of sacred veils, so as to prepare our powers for a fuller vision, and adapted by a paternal providence through an appropriate and peculiar dispensation to the circumstances of our life[1]."

The other key-word is "Unity." This characterizes the origin and end of things, as "Hierarchy" describes the economy by which the interval between the production of all from the One, and the union of all with the One, is filled up. Even in the present state of transition the participation in the One, however imperfect, is the universal condition of being.

"That which is manifold in its parts is one in the whole; that which is manifold in its accidents is one in the subject; that which is manifold in number or powers is one in species; that which is manifold in species is one in genus; that which is manifold in its processions is one in its source; and there is no object in the range of being which does not in some way partake in the one, which from the first embraced in one single existence everything and every whole, even opposites, in the unity which permeates all things[2]."

[1] De Div. Hier. i. 2, 3.
[2] De Div. Nom. xiii. 2.

DIONYSIUS THE AREOPAGITE. 159

The writings, therefore, fall into two groups, those which deal mainly with the revelation of the Divine Order, and those which guide the believer to the deeper mysteries of the revelation of the Divine Being. To the former belong the *Divine* and *Ecclesiastical Hierarchies;* to the latter the essays on *The Divine Names* and *Mystical Theology.* The letters have no specially distinctive character. But though this division holds generally, there is very much common to the two groups. Both are based on the fundamental propositions that all knowledge is relative; that all human knowledge is relative to the special circumstances of man; and that none the less there is a power in him by which, through the help of the Divine guidance, he may rise, not indeed to a *knowledge* of the Absolute, but to a *fellowship* with it. Yet so it is that for the present he will remain imperfect. However swiftly he may advance, to use an old image, he will never outstrip his shadow.

Corresponding in some degree with these two objects of speculation—the Divine Order and the Divine Being—are two methods of theology, the affirmative and the negative[1]. The correspondence, indeed, lies rather in the spirit of the methods than in their application; but still they are characteristic of the lines of thought which diverged in these two directions. According to the one everything which *is* may be affirmed of GOD, because so far as it is, it

[1] Καταφατική and ἀποφατική: or more definitely, κατὰ θέσιν and κατ' ἀφαίρεσιν.—Myst. Theol. 2, 3.

exists in Him. According to the other, everything, so far as we are cognizant of it, may be denied of GOD, because our conception introduces the element of limitation which cannot be applied to Him. Thus on the one hand He is Wisdom, and Love, and Truth, and Light because the absolute ideas belonging to these words are included in His Being; and on the other hand He is *not* Wisdom, *not* Love, *not* Truth, *not* Light, because He is raised infinitely above the notions with which the words are necessarily connected by men. The latter statements are in themselves more true, but the former are better suited to the common discipline of life. And here Dionysius acutely adds that those positive affirmations are to be preferred which, while they convey a partial truth, yet convey it in such a form as to avoid any semblance of expressing a complete truth. Thus there is little danger in describing the angels under the similitude of beasts and birds, because no one could suppose that the likeness extended beyond the single point of comparison, while many may be deceived by the nobler imagery which describes "the beings of heaven as creatures of light in human form, of dazzling brightness, and exquisite beauty, arrayed in glittering robes, and flashing forth the radiance of innocuous fire." Moreover, by the use of humbler types, we are not only forced to rise above the illustration, but also reminded of another truth. For "there is not one being in the universe which is wholly deprived of participation in the good (τὸ καλόν), if it be the case, as the infallible oracles say, that *all things are very good* (καλά)[1]." Thus we may use the meanest material forms to represent heavenly objects, for "matter, as it received its original existence from the absolutely good, retains throughout the whole of its material disposition traces of its ideal (νοερός) beauty[2]."

IV.

Having laid down these introductory principles, Dionysius proceeds to develop his view of the heavenly hierarchy. "A Hierarchy is," he says, according to his use, "a sacred order, and science, and activity (ἐνέργεια), assimilated as far as possible to the godlike, and elevated to the imitation of GOD proportionately to the Divine illuminations conceded to it." Its scope is "the assimilation to and union with GOD." He is "the guide of all holy science and activity." His "loveliness is imaged in the ranks of beings" whom He has appointed. And each true member of His holy band becomes "a most clear and stainless mirror to receive the beams of the primal and sovereign light," and to reflect it in turn without stint "on all around according to the Divine ordinances." Thus it is that each becomes in his turn "a fellow-worker with GOD," purifying, illuminating, perfecting, according to his proper function[3].

The origin of this complex order is to be found in the Divine goodness. It is the characteristic of "the

[1] De Cæl. Hier. ii. 3.   [2] *Id.* ii. 4.   [3] *Id.* iii. 1, 2.

super-essential and all-efficient Godhead" to call all things "to fellowship with itself according to their proper nature." Even "things inanimate partake of this: for the being of all is the Godhead which is above being." But above all others the angels enjoy most, and most often, this Divine communion; and it was by them GOD wrought under the Old Covenant, and specially in the revelation of the mystery of the Incarnation[1].

From this ministering office the name "angel" has been commonly applied to all the orders of the heavenly host, though properly it belongs only to the lowest of the three ranks into which they are divided. In Scripture nine titles are given to them, and these fall into three equal groups. First are those beings which are ever about GOD, and most closely united with Him, the Thrones, and the many-eyed Cherubim and Seraphim. Next stand Authorities, Dominations, Powers; and last, Angels, Archangels, and Princedoms[2]. Each rank has its peculiar work, and each subordinate division contributes to the completeness with which it is accomplished. But the difference of work consists in its mode and measure, but not its object, which is always threefold and always the same, "the reception and impartment of complete purification, and Divine light, and perfecting knowledge[3];" and to this end there is one only way—participation in the relative knowledge of GOD.

[1] De Cæl. Hier. iv.   [2] *Id.* vi. 2.   [3] *Id.* vii. 2.

The first rank of the heavenly hierarchy enjoy this immediately, remaining always in the Divine presence, and drawing from that the direct revelation of His nature. Thus the Seraphim are filled with a holy and inextinguishable fire by which every meaner thought in them is consumed. Thus the Cherubim gain a power of contemplating and knowing GOD without the admixture of any material symbols. Thus the Thrones are established in a calm and immovable supremacy over all lower desires, and lie open to every Divine impression. And what they severally receive they administer in turn to the rank below them, purifying, illuminating, and perfecting them in due measure as they have themselves been purified, illuminated, and perfected by GOD[1]. Hence the Dominations, with the spirit of generous freedom, strive towards a likeness to the true dominion, regardless of all vain attractions: the Powers with masculine and unshaken courage seek to carry out every divine motion: the Authorities, with clear and well-ordered sway, to bring everything into right subjection to the source of all authority. From these the divine revelation passes to the third rank of Princedoms, Archangels, Angels, by whose intervention in the affairs of men, as guiding the destinies of nations, or bearing the messages of GOD, or ministering to the wants of individuals, the powers of heaven are brought into connexion with the beings of earth[2].

[1] De Cæl. Hier. viii. 1.   [2] *Id.* ix.

It is needless to follow Dionysius in his interpretation of passages of Scripture which deal with the operations of angels, and unfold their nature under material imagery. There are, however, two points in which these discussions of detail illustrate his general views. Though the angels are so much mightier than men, and endowed with an inheritance of transcendent light, yet their action does not overpower the human will, which may by perseverance and obstinacy resist their benevolent influences.

"For our life is not swayed by necessity, nor, again, are the divine lights of our providential illumination in themselves darkened through the absolute freedom of the acts which are foreseen; but the want of affinity in our intellectual powers of vision, either wholly hinders our reception of the overflowing light-gift of the paternal goodness, and so checks its distribution in virtue of their resistance, or modifies the fashion of our participation, making it small or great, obscure or bright, while the fontal basis in which we share is one and simple, ever the same, and universally diffused[1]."

And it is in this law, which preserves the fulness of human freedom, that the differences of national, no less than individual, fortune find their explanation. The Jews alone preserved in old time the pure knowledge of the true GOD; but it was not that they alone were the objects of His care. Michael was their prince, but "the Most High set the borders of the nations according to the number of the angels of

[1] De Cœl. Hier. ix. 3.

God[1]." The Gentiles were not given over to the dominion of strange gods.

"There was one sovereignty over all, and it was to this that the angels presiding over each nation according to the Divine order led those who followed them. . . . . The one Providence of the Most High extended equally to all, and, with a view to their salvation, assigned all men to the elevating guidance of their proper angels, but Israel almost alone, above all, turned to the light-gift and knowledge of the true Lord[2]."

Thus the first circle of the Divine Revelation is completed, and in that is seen the image of the whole. No one being is perfect in himself, or absolutely independent, except the One. All are bound together by the offices of mutual ministration : are quickened to unceasing activity by the contemplation of a purity infinitely holier, a light infinitely fuller, a perfection infinitely more complete than that to which they have attained. And as these heavenly hosts surpass all our conceptions in the energy of their service and the glory of their nature, so they exceed in multitude all the feeble and contracted powers of our material numeration[3]. They are in the sight of God, and we upon earth ; but yet we know that we are not uncared for by Him. We know that that Divine Being is—

"A unity of the Three Persons, who makes His loving providence to penetrate to all things, from super-celestial essences to the last things of earth, as being the beginning

[1] De Cæl. Hier. ix. 2. Comp. Dan. x. 13 ff.
[2] *Id.* ix. 3.   [3] *Id.* xiv.

and cause of all beings, beyond all beginning, and enfolding all things transcendentally in His infinite embrace[1]."

V.

The heavenly Hierarchy is the type of the earthly *Ecclesiastical Hierarchy*. Both have the same scope and the same essential laws of action. It is the one object of every member of every hierarchy to become god-like; to impart to those below him, according to their due, the results of his divine assimilation; to follow at once and to lead; to strive upwards under the guidance of superior natures; to raise inferior natures to loftier heights. But there is a great difference in form between the Hierarchy of Heaven and the Hierarchy of Earth.

"The beings and ranks above us are incorporeal; their Hierarchy is intellectual (νοητή) and supramundane; but ours, in due relation to ourselves, is furnished with a manifold array of sensible symbols, by which, according to the divine order, after the right measure of our powers, we are raised to GOD and divine virtue, that we may be made like Him in the one way. They, as minds, perceive truth as is allowed them; we, by sensible images, are raised, as we can be raised, to divine contemplation[2]."

But none the less this lower Hierarchy is of divine institution. Its origin is the fountain of life, the "essence of goodness, the one cause of all things, the Trinity, from which comes being and well-being

[1] De Cæl. Hier. vii. 4.   [2] De Eccles. Hier. i. 2.

to all things that are." And that through the goodness of GOD, whose "will is the rational salvation of beings on earth and above us." And salvation can only be attained by those who are saved being made divine. The thought has often occurred before, but the expression of it in this place, when it becomes practical, is singularly striking.

"To be made divine ($\dot{\eta}$ $\theta\acute{\epsilon}\omega\sigma\iota\varsigma$) is to be made like GOD, as far as may be, and to be made one with Him. This is the common end of every hierarchy, the continuous devotion of love to GOD and the things of GOD, wrought by sacred means in a godly and single fashion; and as a preliminary to this, the complete and unhesitating abandonment of all that is contrary to it, the recognition of things as they are, the sight and knowledge of sacred truth, the godly participation in the one mode of perfectioning, participation in the One Himself, as far as may be, the feast of the beatific vision which nourishes intellectually and makes divine every one who strains aloft to behold it[1]."

Such being the glorious aim and origin of the Ecclesiastical Hierarchy, "the God-given oracles are its essence," partly written, and partly oral, transferred in this latter case "from mind to mind, by the medium of speech, bodily, it is true, but yet in a less material mode than is commonly the case." For us this veil of words and symbols is necessary. We can rise only from the sensible to the intellectual. And that which is a veil of love to those who seek to pierce beneath it, is a veil of mercy to those who care

[1] De Eccles. Hier. i. 3.

not for the mysteries which it preserves. For it is so ordered by the Divine Providence that the emblems which reveal truth to the holy hide it from the profane[1].

Having thus laid down the necessity of symbolic acts for the divine training of *men*, Dionysius examines in successive chapters the symbolic acts of Christianity, Baptism (φώτισμα, *illumination*), Communion (σύναξις, *gathering*), the Consecration and Use of the Chrism, Holy Orders, the Consecration of Monks, the Rites of Burial. The three first stand on a different footing from the others, and include in themselves the triple idea which characterizes the divine assimilation of man. Baptism—

"is proved from the oracles to be a purification and illuminating revelation; communion and the consecration (τελετή) of the chrism a perfecting recognition and knowledge of the divine actions, whereby in a sacred manner the unifying elevation to the Supreme Being and most blessed fellowship with Him is completed[2]."

Each chapter contains a description of the ceremonies observed in the particular rite, and a "Contemplation" in which they are spiritually explained. The elaborateness of the ritual which is developed is in itself a complete proof of the lateness of the writings; for though some observances are not supported by any other authority, the pictures of the Christian services doubtless contain, on the whole, a fair representation of their general form in the sixth century. A single

[1] De Eccles. Hier. i. 4, 5.   [2] *Id.* v. 3.

DIONYSIUS THE AREOPAGITE. 169

illustration will be sufficient to characterize this part of the Dionysian books.

The order of Baptism then is as follows. The sacred minister (ἱεράρχης, *i.e.* bishop) proclaims to all the Gospel that GOD Himself deigned to come to us through His love, and to make like to Himself whatever is united with Him. Hereupon whoever is enamoured of this Divine fellowship finds some Christian to take him to the minister, who receives them joyfully with a mental thanksgiving and bodily prostration to the source of all good. Then he summons all the sacred body to the holy place, and after chanting a Psalm with them, and saluting the holy Table, he goes forward and asks the candidate, What he desires? According to the instruction of his sponsor he asks to "obtain by his mediation GOD and the things of GOD." And having promised to live according to the rules of Christian citizenship, he receives imposition of hands from the bishop, who seals him, and charges the priests to enrol his name with the name of his sponsor. A prayer follows, in which the whole congregation join, and afterwards the deacons unfasten the sandals of the candidate, and unclothe him. He is then turned to the west, and with gestures of abhorrence he thrice renounces Satan in a set form of words. Next he is led to the east, and instructed to declare thrice his allegiance to Christ, with eyes and hands upraised to heaven. A blessing and imposition of hands follow. Then the deacons complete the unrobing, and the priests bring the holy oil. The bishop begins the unction by a triple cross, and leaving the priests to complete it, goes "to the mother of adoption" (the font), and consecrates the water with prayers and three cross-formed affusions of the holy chrism, and bids the candidate be brought to him. His name is then called out with the name of his sponsor, and he is brought to the bishop. Again the priests declare his name with a loud voice, and the bishop thrice dips him, invoking at each immersion the three Persons of the Blessed Trinity. Then he is consigned to his sponsor, and being reclothed in a white robe, is brought back to the bishop, who seals him with the sacred chrism, and pronounces him capable of being admitted to the Eucharist.

It is impossible to quote in detail the corresponding descriptions of the other divine rites. Some few passages from the "Contemplation" on Holy Communion—"the rite of rites," "the gathering together of our divided lives into one uniform assimilation to GOD[1],"—will illustrate the method of interpretation which Dionysius follows, and the general aspect under which he regards external observances. The central idea of the sacrament is placed in unity realised in multeity, in the

"most divine and common peaceful impartment of the one and the same bread and cup, which enjoins on the partakers, as reared in the same family, a godly harmony of character, and brings them to a holy remembrance of the

[1] De Eccles. Hier. iii. 1.

most divine Supper, the primal type of the mysteries celebrated[1]."

Thus all the ceremonies which are gathered round the rite contribute to enforce this truth : an "array of riddles in which it is expressively enwrapped," beneath which "the intellectual vision pierces when filled with single and unveiled light[2]." Even the combination of lessons from the Old and New Testaments indicates the mystic unity by which the whole counsel of God is marked.

"The accomplishment which the one records assures us of the truth of the promises of the other; the divine working (θεουργία) is the consummation of the divine teaching (θεολογία)[3]."

Taken in connexion with the work of Christianity, the Communion is the remembrance of the Incarnation and not only of the Passion, for by this

"having been made one with our lowly state while yet retaining His proper nature wholly without confusion or injury, Christ gave us freely henceforth fellowship with that, as being of the same race with Him .... to be effected by our sacred assimilation with it according to our power. How, then (Dionysius asks), could the imitation of God be produced within us otherwise than by the renewing of the continual remembrance of the most sacred divine acts, by the sacred teaching and acts according to the holy order?"

[1] De Eccles. Hier. iii. 3, 1.
[2] *Id.* iii. 3, 2.   [3] *Id.* iii. 3, 5.

So it is that the priest, when he has taken the likeness of Christ at the Last Supper,

"uncovers the bread, which was before covered and undivided, and having divided it into many, and having shared among all the oneness of the cup, under a symbol multiplies and distributes unity. For that which was one and simple and hidden in Jesus, the primal Divine Word, by His incarnation among us came to the compound and visible, unchanged, through His goodness and love for man, and wrought out by His beneficent working a unifying fellowship between us and Himself, having supremely united our lowly nature with His most divine nature, if so be we are fitted with Him as members to a body, in the identity of a spotless and divine life. . . . . For we must, if we desire fellowship with Him, look upwards to His most divine life in the flesh, and by assimilation to it, ascend to the god-like and spotless habit of sacred sinlessness. . . . . This is what the bishop teaches by the sacred acts which he performs, bringing out the hidden gifts to the light, and dividing their unity into many parts, and by the supreme union of the elements distributed with those who receive them, making those who partake truly partners in them."

In a word, the elements thus united and shared are a figure of Christ, our spiritual (νοητή) life, who comes forth from the darkness of GOD, and by His incarnation, without change proceeds from His natural unity to our divided nature,

"calling the race of man to participation in Himself and His proper blessings, if so be we are united to His most divine life, by assimilation to it according to our power;

and in this way we shall truly have fellowship with GOD, and that which is of GOD[1]."

The same estimate of the predominantly subjective value of the divine ordinances prevails everywhere in the "Contemplations" on the several rites, and it is superfluous to quote additional passages. It appears in a somewhat different shape in Dionysius' scheme of the sacred ministry. The three orders mark an advancing personal relationship of the minister to GOD, as in the heavenly hierarchy; and the Christian hierarchy as a whole occupies a mid place between the legal hierarchy of the Old Covenant and the divine hierarchy of the spiritual world. To the deacons (λειτουργοί) belongs the function of purification; to the priests (ἱερεῖς) of illumination; to the Bishops (ἱεράρχαι) of perfecting[2]; and the various ceremonies by which they are ordained are shewn to have a direct bearing upon their several duties and characters. One quotation will suffice, which explains the representation of their common ministerial character:

"Bishops, priests, and deacons at their ordination are alike led to the divine altar, and bow the knee before it, and receive the imposition of the bishop's hand and the sign of the cross. . . . . The two first mark their absolute subjection of their proper life to GOD, and the offering to Him of their whole spiritual nature . . . . the imposition of hands, the divine shelter . . . . the sign of the cross the mortifying of all fleshly desires[3]."

[1] De Eccles. Hier. iii. 3, 12, 13.
[2] *Id.* v. 1, 3—7.   [3] *Id.* v. 3, 2—4.

But it is in his view of the ranks of the "initiated" that Dionysius exhibits most clearly his judgment on the subjective apprehension of Christianity. These fall into three groups, those who are being purified, those who are being illuminated, those who are being perfected. The first includes all those who are under preparation by the deacons for the participation in the sacraments from which they are as yet excluded. The second consists of "the holy people" who have been admitted "to complete purification and the vision of, and fellowship in, the most glorious rites." These are committed to the priests, and led by them to the habit and power of contemplation; and as they partake "in the most divine symbols . . . they are furnished by their elevating powers, as it were, with wings to soar to the divine desire of true knowledge of them." But the third and highest rank is that of the monks who are committed to the loftiest instruction of the bishops. These, having passed through the stages of purification and illumination, are absorbed in the "pure service and devotion to GOD, in an undivided and single life, which brings them to an absolute god-like unity and perfection by the sacred combination of the elements of their nature primarily separated and distinct[1]."

The difference which is thus established upon earth is supposed to survive death.

'If any one has lived here a godly and most holy life,

[1] De Eccles. Hier. vi. 1—3. Comp. vi. 3, 5.

so far as man can attain to the imitation of GOD, he will enjoy in the world to come a godly and blessed lot; if he has fallen short of this supreme ideal, and yet lived a holy life, he will receive a holy recompense proportioned to his state[1]."

Thus the law of the divine ascent is fulfilled. The sacred ordinances on earth are themselves progressive, and minister to progress. What we see is but a part of a vast scheme, a result at once, and a preparation. There is, so to speak, a natural connexion between the visible and the invisible life, however different may be the conditions under which the two are realized. How different they are according to Dionysius is seen from the second group of his writings, in which he endeavours to rise to a clearer vision of the Divine Nature, as in those which have been just reviewed he traced the downward passage of the Divine Revelation to man, "who originally fell in his folly from the possession of godly blessings[2]."

VI.

The treatise *On the Divine Names* is the longest and most important of the Dionysian writings. Its general scope is to gather what we may learn positively, according to our present powers, of Him who is at once Nameless and Many-named, from the titles under which He is described in Holy Scripture. In the course of this inquiry, several vast questions arise, as

[1] De Eccles. Hier. vii. 3, 1.   [2] *Id.* iii. 3, 11.

those of the distinctness of the Divine Persons, of the nature of evil, of the connexion of partial being with absolute being, of the relation of time and eternity to GOD. To do more than glance very summarily at the treatment of these topics is obviously impossible here; but the most meagre exhibition of the Dionysian thoughts will shew what a profound influence they exercised upon mediæval speculation, and how strangely they anticipate difficulties which we are tempted to believe are peculiar to our own days.

The work was, if we may believe the writer, a sequel to his "Theological Outlines." By emphasizing this arrangement, he probably means to bring out clearly that the philosophical discussion presupposes the doctrinal one; and at the same time he is freed from the necessity of adjusting his positions with the popular creed, as this is supposed to have been done already. The basis of the investigation is laid in the fundamental limitation that we cannot know GOD as He is, but only obtain a partial revelation of GOD according to our powers. One passage in which this idea is enunciated may stand for many : —

"Just as the objects of thought are incomprehensible by the power of sense......so the super-essential infinitude transcends all beings; the unity which is beyond mind transcends all minds; the one which is beyond understanding cannot be understood by any understanding; the good which is beyond word cannot be expressed by any word; for it is in fact a unit which gives unity to every unit, essence above essence, mind inconceivable, word unutterable; or rather the negation of word, and mind, and name, existing after the form of no special existence; the cause of being in all, and itself without being, as lying above being, and comprehensible only as it may please to declare of itself authoritatively, and according to our faculties of knowledge[1]."

Since this is so, we look to the rays of the divine oracles, and, guided by their beams, rise to the contemplation of the light given by them proportionately to our knowledge; and celebrate GOD as

"the life of all things that live, the being of all things that exist, the beginning and cause of all life and all being, through His goodness, whereby He calls into being the things which are, and sustains them while they are[2]."

Thus for us the manifestation of the nature of GOD is a glorious "hymn," in which we celebrate His love which "multiplies and variously moulds His simplicity, transcending nature and unconfined to form, by the manifold use of distinct symbols[3]." Yet even so our souls rise, as they may, beyond the symbols to the contemplation of the higher truth which they veil. If they cannot apprehend the One, they can see with devout faith the convergence of all lines of being towards it.

At the very outset we are met by this mystery of the one and the many. Some of the terms applied to

[1] De Div. Nom. i. 1.
[2] *Id.* i. 3. The whole passage is very noble and in the writer's best style, but it is too long to quote.
[3] *Id.* i. 4.

the Divine Being in Scripture are "conjunctive," and belong to the whole Godhead; others are "disjunctive," and belong to the separate Persons as they are revealed to us. The former belong to the ineffable and unintelligible essence of GOD, as abiding in hidden and unbroken rest (as "being," "goodness," &c.); the latter to His loving processions and manifestations (as Father, Son, &c.). Yet it must be observed that both sets of terms are equally relative to us, and not mutually exclusive. In our fellowship with GOD, the fellowship is with the whole Godhead, and not with a part of it; and

"all that pertains to GOD, and all that has been revealed to us, is known by our participations only; but the essences themselves, and their actual nature, as they are originally and abide in themselves, transcend mind, and being, and knowledge[1]."

So it is also with the combination of the human and Divine natures in Christ. We can apprehend partially the distinction, but not the absolute union. So it is with the manifold impartment of the Holy Spirit to believers. Hence

"there seems to be a division and multiplication of the One GOD, but none the less GOD, as He is transcendently from the beginning, is One GOD, undivided in the divided, united in Himself, unconfounded and unmultiplied in the many[2]."

Of all the attributes of GOD, goodness is that

[1] De Div. Nom. ii. 7.   [2] *Id.* ii. 11.

DIONYSIUS THE AREOPAGITE. 179

which is most characteristic. Just as the sun, because it is the sun, shines on all; so the love of GOD, because He is GOD, reaches to all, and called all things into being[1]. "In a word, everything which *is* is from the fair and good, and is in the fair and good, and turns to the fair and good." Nay, we do not shrink from saying that "He who is the cause of all, through excess of goodness, loves all things, works all things, accomplishes all things, sustains all things, turns all things to Himself[2]."

But it may be objected, if this be so, how is it that evil exists? whence did it spring? in what does it find its being? how can it be an object of desire? The answers to these time-long questions sound like echoes from some modern essay, and yet they are but adaptations of Neo-Platonism. Evil as such, Dionysius replies, does *not* exist:—

"All things that exist, so far as they exist, are good and spring from the good; so far as they are deprived of the good, they are neither good nor existent[3]."

That which we call evil exists not as evil, but as partaking in some measure in the good; and it is sought in virtue of this participation. It is equally clear that evil is neither in GOD nor from GOD, either simply or in time[4]; nor is it in spirit or in man as evil, but as a deficiency and want of the completeness of their proper good[5]. Nor, again, can it find a place in

---

[1] De Div. Nom. iii. 1.   [2] *Id.* iv. 10.
[3] *Id.* iv. 20.   [4] *Id.* iv. 21.   [5] *Id.* iv. 24.

brutes, or in nature generally, or in bodies, or in matter. If this were so, we should be forced to admit two original principles, which is absurd, because a first source must be one. Evil, then, is a negation relative to the peculiar character of the object in which it is said to exist,—

"a deficiency, a weakness, a want of harmony, a failure; bereft of aim, of beauty, of life, of mind, of reason, of end, of basis, of cause; without limit, issue, effect, strength, order, symmetry; infinite, dark, and essenceless; by itself, having nowhere and in no case any existence[1]."

Being such, it springs from many and partial defects, as free beings fail to realize their true ends. But "GOD knows the evil as it is good, and in His sight the causes of evil are powers which work good[2]." For, as has been already seen, nothing which exists is wholly bereft of good, and divine Providence extends to all things which exist, and nothing which exists is removed from its action. So then "Providence uses those who prove evil for a good purpose, either for their own profit or for that of others, either specially

[1] De Div. Nom. iv. 32. Mr Browning's Abt Vogler expresses this idea perfectly:—

"There shall never be one lost good! What was, shall live as before.

The evil is null, is nought, is silence implying sound;

What was good, shall be good, with, for evil, so much good more;

On the earth the broken arcs; in the heaven, a perfect round."

[2] *Id.* iv. 30.

or generally." For this reason it does not force us to be good against our will, "for it is foreign to it to destroy nature; and so as Providence preserves the nature of each being, it acts on free agents as such," and dispenses to each its gift of goodness according to the nature of the recipient.

If then evil is weakness, it may be asked how it can be visited with divine punishment? To this objection Dionysius replies that as the power was given in the first instance, then the neglect to use it was culpable. This subject, he adds, he has dealt with in his treatise "On the Just Judgment of GOD." The answer as it stands is obviously incomplete, but it shews a real appreciation of the difficulty, and indicates the direction where the practical solution must be found, since personal responsibility is claimed as an intuitive truth.

Evil having been thus deprived of all absolute essence, and reduced to a negative accident consequent upon the limited freedom of finite beings, it is easy to bring all else into harmony with GOD and immediate dependence upon Him. Whatever *is*, is only by the inherence of His presence: whatever *becomes*, becomes by the communication of His presence. No partial existence of whatever kind is independent or absolute. There is one cause above every cause, one essence above every essence, in virtue of which all things become and are, which none the less remains in itself immutable and uncircumscribed. Everything partakes in its presence, and yet it is necessarily incommunicable. The idea and the individual realization of the idea both exist from and in the one Supreme Being.

"Absolute beauty, and the effluence which produces the idea; universal beauty and partial beauty; objects beautiful as wholes, and beautiful in part; and everything else that has been and will be similarly defined, exhibit manifestations of providence and goodness shared by those things which exist, proceeding from GOD who is incommunicable, through His bounteous dispensation, that He who is the cause of all may be beyond all, and that that which transcends essence and nature may be above everything which exists according to the laws of any essence or nature soever[1]."

For GOD does not exist in any special way, but

"absolutely and infinitely, as embracing and anticipating in Himself universal being; wherefore He is called also King of the Ages, as though all being existed and subsisted in Him and around Him; and He neither was nor will be, nor becomes nor will become, nay, rather not even is; but is Himself the being in things that are; and not things themselves only, but the absolute being of things proceeded from Him who is before all ages[2]."

Thus it is that every form of life is, as it were, a more or less distant "echo of the one life." And "when this is withdrawn all life fails, and to this also those objects which have failed by lack of strength to participate in it, return, and again become living beings[3]." Nor this only, but the Divine wisdom is

---

[1] De Div. Nom. xi. 5.   [2] *Id.* v. 4.   [3] *Id.* vi. 1.

the source and cause and end of our wisdom and mind and reason: nay, even of "the mind of devils so far as that is mind[1]." But when we say this we must remember that GOD does not know things as they exist from their existence, but as existing originally in Him. He has not

"a knowledge of Himself; and a separate knowledge, which embraces all things that are; for it is not possible that the Cause of all things, if He knows Himself, should not know those things which proceed from Him, of which He is the cause[2]."

And conversely it is only through this subordinate order that we can know Him, inasmuch as it has been arranged by Him, and contains "certain images and likenesses of the Divine patterns." For it is the Divine wisdom which

"creates all things and ever fits all things together, and is the cause of the indissoluble connexion and arrangement of all things, and unites the ends of one series of phenomena with the beginnings of the subsequent series, and happily works out the one harmony and concord of the universe[3]."

Following out this idea of the divine significance of all the subjects of human knowledge, Dionysius investigates the revelation of GOD which is given in Scripture by the terms which are applied to Him, as Power, and Righteousness, or Great and Small, or King of kings, and Ancient of days, and the like.

[1] De Div. Nom. vii. 2.   [2] *Id.* l.c.   [3] *Id.* vii. 3.

The criticism is always ingenious, and at times powerful. In one place, when discussing the usage of the words time (χρόνος) and eternity (αἰών), he deals with a difference which quite lately seemed to have been forgotten :—

"Time is applied in Scripture (he says) to that which is subject to beginning, and decay, and change; and so theology teaches that we who are here bounded by the laws of time shall be partakers of eternity (αἰών) when we reach the age (αἰών) which is incorruptible and ever unchanged. Sometimes, it is true, eternity in Scripture is represented as temporal, and time as eternal, yet we know that more frequently and more properly things that *are* are described and expressed by eternity, and things which *become* by time[1]."

But of all the titles of GOD the *One* is that in which alone we can rest. Towards this all thought and speculation tend. This is the idea which finally results from faithfully interpreting the lessons of the many[2]; the centre in which all the radii of the vast circle of life converge[3]. To strive after this is the noblest work of man; and just as in universal nature the separate characteristics of each individual nature are absolutely harmonized: just as the different powers which act through our bodies are united in the one soul; so there is a unity which infinitely transcends these faint images by which it is provisionally typified to us. And starting from these it is "reasonable that we should ascend to the cause of

[1] De Div. Nom. x. 3.   [2] *Id.* xiii. 3.   [3] *Id.* v. 6.

all, and with supramundane vision contemplate all in the Cause of all, even things contrary to one another, reconciled in one supreme concord[1]."

VII.

The nearer contemplation of this sublime unity is the purpose of the *Mystic Theology*, which professes to present the esoteric teaching of Christianity. For the revelations and workings of GOD, even in the most glorious form under which they are shewn to us, are but steps by which the devout worshipper rises to higher things. At the most, he sees in these not GOD, but, like Moses, the place where GOD is. In other words, the highest and most divine manifestations which are made through sense or thought simply suggest ideas which (so to speak) underlie Him who transcends all ideas, through which His presence is indicated visiting the spiritual heights of His holiest place. And then the truly initiated is

"released from the objects and the powers of sight, and penetrates into the darkness of un-knowledge (ἀγνωσία), which is truly mystic, and lays aside all conceptions of knowledge and is absorbed in the intangible and invisible, wholly given up to that which is beyond all things, and belonging no longer to himself nor to any other finite being, but in virtue of some nobler faculty is united with that which is wholly unknowable by the absolute inoperation of all limited knowledge, and knows in a manner beyond mind by knowing nothing[2]."

[1] De Div. Nom. v. 7. [2] Myst. Theol. i. 3.

This description gives a fair notion of the object and of the method of "Mystic Theology." The object is to rise above the world of sense and thought defined by sense; the method is to lay aside everything which gives speciality to conceptions, since every distinct limitation springs out of the transitory conditions of our present state. Consequently in "Mystic Theology" the negative process is more valid than the affirmative, but yet the affirmations are not opposed to the negations, since both are applied to being which is far above both in its transcendental nature[1]. But it is only by the removal of each definite attribute, so far as it is definite, that man can arrive at any conception of the infinite. The exact knowledge of a finite being can reach only to that which is finite; and if he would rise beyond it, it must be by avoiding the definiteness which belongs to the imperfections of his nature. In this sense, unknowledge transcends knowledge, because it is the negation of limit: and gloom underlies light, because for us light is only a reflection from objects in themselves bounded[2].

Thus the final result is that man can have no absolute conception of GOD as the subject of thought, though he can be united with Him by the devotion of love. The mind can exercise itself upon its proper objects, but it cannot pass beyond them. The power by which the soul is brought into fellowship with that which transcends it, is of a loftier nature.

[1] Myst. Theol. i. 2. [2] *Id.* ii.

"This power, then, we are bound to follow in our thoughts of divine things, and not ourselves; we must wholly divest ourselves of ourselves, and give ourselves wholly to GOD; for it is better to belong to GOD than to ourselves; and so the things of GOD will be given to those who are united with Him[1]."

VIII.

It is unnecessary to dwell at length on the points of resemblance which the Dionysian system offers to that of the later Neo-Platonists. The progressive revelation of the infinite, the hierarchic triads, the conception of evil as a negation and a defect, the striving towards union with the One, the resolution of all that is partial into being which transcends all special definition, are common to both, and it is not difficult to see that Dionysius so far borrows ideas which had their source elsewhere than in the Christian Church. But while this is conceded most fully, his treatment of them nevertheless claims the merit of originality. However devotedly he may have studied Proclus or Damascius, he studied them as a Christian. He starts always from the Bible[2], and not from Plato. He endeavours to obey his own lesson, and welcomes truth wherever he finds it, but revelation is his touchstone of truth. He is, so to speak, the extreme result of the speculative school of Greek Theology; and in this aspect his writings, strangely incomplete, one-

[1] De Div. Nom. vii. 1.   [2] De Cœl. Hier. vi. 2.

sided, even dangerous as they may appear to us, are of deep interest at a crisis when it is impossible not to see the brightest hope for Christendom in a living appreciation of the spirit of the great Greek Fathers; for it is not too much to say that a work remains for Greek divinity in the nineteenth century hardly less pregnant with results than that wrought by the Greek classics in the fifteenth.

Many, perhaps, will be surprised that such a scheme of Christianity as Dionysius has sketched should even be reckoned Christian at all. Several of the cardinal dogmas of the Western Churches are either unnoticed in it, or fall into a secondary rank in the whole economy of redemption. The conception of grace is, at the least, very defective. The idea of the Atonement, where it is noticed most distinctly, is represented as the delivery of being from the negative influences of disorder and weakness and failure[1]. The characteristic doctrine of evil when it was made the groundwork of a special treatise by Johannes Erigena was at once condemned by Gallican councils. But in spite of these and other faults, which are brought out clearly by their antagonism with Latin developments or exhibitions of truth, the writings of "the divine Dionysius" have always maintained their place among the orthodox treasures of the East. Nay, more; though parts of their teaching were rejected in the West when removed from the shelter of the apostolic name, they have found even to late times apolo-

[1] De Div. Nom. viii. 9.

gists who have forced them into harmony with the Tridentine decrees.

Such a method of interpretation deprives them of their intellectual and historical significance. It must be frankly admitted that they bear the impress not only of a particular age and school, but also of a particular man, which is not wholly of a Christian type. They present the thoughts of one who lived in an age of transition, and strove to save from the wreck of ancient philosophy truths which he seemed to find coherent with the Christian faith. Indeed, under the treatment of the new teacher, many of the fancies of Neo-Platonism gain a solid consistency, which they wanted before, by being brought into connexion with a historic creed. The doctrine of an original fall, consequent upon man's free action, gives a certain standing-point for the contemplation of life as it is chequered with good and evil[1]. Holy rites, distinctly springing out of accredited facts, take the place of theurgic celebrations. An ecclesiastical organization, definite and popular, furnishes the basis for a complete hierarchical view of the universe. The mystery of the Incarnation contains the pledge of the believer's union with the One, while the Resurrection vindicates the proper unity of his whole nature and the completeness of his future hope[2].

This harmonization of Christianity and Platonism was not effected without a sacrifice. It is impossible

[1] De Eccles. Hier. iii. 3, 11.
[2] De Div. Nom. vi. 2.

not to feel in Dionysius, in spite of his pure and generous and apostolic aspirations, the lack of something which is required for the completeness of his own views. He fails indeed by neglecting to take in the whole breadth of the Gospel. The central source of his dogmatic errors lies where at first it might be least looked for. The whole view of life which he offers is essentially individual and personal and subjective; the one man is the supreme object in whose progress his interest is engaged. Though he gives a magnificent view of the mutual coherence of all the parts of the moral and physical worlds, yet he turns with the deepest satisfaction to the solitary monk, isolated and self-absorbed, as the highest type of Christian energy. Though he dwells upon the Divine order of the Sacraments, and traces the spiritual significance of each detail in their celebration, yet he looks upon them as occasions for instruction and blessing, suggested by appointed forms, and not supplied by a Divine gift. He stops short of that profounder faith which sees the unity of worlds in the harmonious and yet independent action of derivative forces; one indeed in their source, and yet regarded as separate in their operation. He is still so far overpowered by Platonism that he cannot, in speculation as well as in confession, consistently treat man's bodily powers as belonging to the perfection of his nature. The end of the discipline of life is, in his view, to help the believer to cast aside all things that belong to earth, and not to find in them gifts which may by consecration to GOD become hereafter the beginning of a nobler activity. And so it is that he is unable to see in their full beauty and strength those instincts and faculties of man, by which he is impelled towards social combination, and the divine institutions by which these instincts and faculties are sanctioned and supported.

The ecclesiastical and civil disorders of the fifth century may well have obscured the highest glories of the Church and the Empire. It was not unnatural that devout men should in such times seek repose in their cells, and the triumph of Mohammedanism was the penalty of their despair. But yet the writings of Dionysius are a witness to the higher conceptions of the Divine order which lingered among the immediate successors of Cyril. Even now they take their place among the speculations of to-day, and though in a dialect partially antiquated, record the judgment which ancient thinkers passed upon problems which, at each time of their recurrence, seem to offer a new and strange trial to faith. No reasoner can argue more resolutely than Dionysius for the Divine Presence in all things which are, and yet no one can be further removed from identifying the Divine Being with the manifestations of Him in creation. It would be impossible to affirm more distinctly than he does the absolute incapacity of man to have knowledge of anything beyond phenomena, and yet at the same time he recognises that there is a sphere beyond knowledge, to which he must look up with devout and patient adoration. Above his pantheism there is the intense belief in one God: above his positivism there is the trustful aspiration of faith.

One passage, in which he deals with the mystery of prayer, will illustrate what has been just said, and is not unworthy of consideration in itself :—

"The glorious Trinity, the source of all good, is present to all things, but all things are not present to It. But, then, when we invoke It with holy prayers, and unsullied soul, and that frame of mind which is adapted for divine union, then are we also present to It; for It has no local presence so that It can be anywhere absent, or pass from place to place."

Thus the action of prayer is as though there were "a chain of light let down from the heights of heaven and reaching to earth, and as we grasp it, first with the one hand and then with the other, we seem to draw it to us, while really we are raised by it to the loftier splendours of the light. Or as though we were on shipboard and strained at a rope fastened to a rock and thrown out to help us; we do not draw the rock to ourselves, but ourselves and the ship to the rock. And, conversely, if one stands on the vessel and thrusts the rock from him, the rock will remain firm and unmoved, but he will separate himself from it, and the distance between them will be proportioned to his effort. And so before everything, and especially in theology, we must make a solemn beginning to all acts with prayer, not as drawing to us the power which is present at once everywhere and nowhere, but as placing ourselves in His hands, and uniting ourselves with Him by remembering Him, and calling upon His name[1]."

[1] De div. Nom. iii. 1.

The words are old words, but yet new, and though they do not express more than half the truth, they will bear comparison with the splendid passage in which a living poet has expressed kindred, and yet converse, thoughts strangely in the spirit of Dionysius :—

"It seemed, it was certain, to match man's birth,
Nature in turn conceived, obeying an impulse as I;
And the emulous heaven yearned down, made effort to reach the earth,
As the earth had done her best, in my passion, to scale the sky :
Novel splendours burst forth, grew familiar and dwelt with mine,
Not a point nor peak but found and fixed its wandering star;
Meteor-moons, balls of blaze : and they did not pale nor pine,
For earth had attained to heaven, there was no more near nor far."

ORIGEN AND THE BEGINNINGS OF CHRISTIAN PHILOSOPHY.

I.

THE progress of Christianity can best be represented as a series of victories. But when we speak of victories we imply resistance, suffering, loss: the triumph of a great cause, but the triumph through effort and sacrifice. Such, in fact, has been the history of the Faith: a sad and yet a glorious succession of battles, often hardly fought, and sometimes indecisive, between the new life and the old life. We know that the struggle can never be ended in this visible order; but we know also that more of the total powers of humanity, and more of the fulness of the individual man are brought from age to age within the domain of the truth. Each age has to sustain its own part in the conflict, and the retrospect of earlier successes gives to those who have to face new antagonists and to occupy new positions, patience and the certainty of hope.

In this respect the history of the first three centuries—the first complete period, and that a period of spontaneous evolution in the Christian body—is an epitome or a figure of the whole work of the Faith. It is the history of a three-fold contest between Christianity and the Powers of the Old World, closed by a three-fold victory. The Church and the Empire started from the same point and advanced side by side. They met in the market and the house; they met in the discussions of the Schools; they met in the institutions of political government; and in each place the Church was triumphant. In this way Christianity asserted, once for all, its sovereign power among men by the victory of common life, by the victory of thought, by the victory of civil organisation. These first victories contain the promise of all that later ages have to reap.

The object of this and a following paper is to indicate some features in the second of these victories, the victory of thought. And, before going further, I would ask the reader to observe that this victory of thought is the second, and not the first, in order of accomplishment. The succession involves a principle. The Christian victory of common life was wrought out in silence and patience and nameless agonies. It was the victory of the soldiers and not of the captains of Christ's army. But in due time another conflict had to be sustained, not by the masses, but by great men, the consequence and the completion of that which had gone before.

It is with the society as with the individual. The discipline of action precedes the effort of reason. The work of the many prepares the medium for the subtler operations of the few. So it came to pass that the period during which this second conflict of the Faith was waged was, roughly speaking, from the middle of the second to the middle of the third century.

This period, from the accession of Marcus Aurelius (A.D. 161) to the accession of Valerian (A.D. 253) was for the Gentile world a period of unrest and exhaustion, of ferment and of indecision. The time of great hopes and creative minds was gone. The most conspicuous men were, with few exceptions, busied with the past. There is not among them a single writer who can be called a poet. They were lawyers, or antiquarians, or commentators, or grammarians, or rhetoricians. One indeed, the greatest of all, Galen, would be ranked, perhaps, in modern times, as a "positivist." Latin literature had almost ceased to exist: even the meditations of an Emperor were in Greek. The fact is full of meaning. Greek was the language not of a people, but of the world. Local beliefs had lost their power. Even old Rome ceased to exercise an unquestioned moral supremacy. Men strove to be cosmopolitan. They strove vaguely after a unity in which the scattered elements of ancient experience should be harmonized. The effect can be seen both in the policy of statesmen and in the speculations of philosophers, in Marcus Aurelius,

CHRISTIAN PHILOSOPHY. 197

or Alexander Severus, or Decius, no less than in Plotinus or Porphyry. As a necessary consequence, the teaching of the Bible accessible in Greek began to attract serious attention among the heathen. The assailants of Christianity, even if they affected contempt, shewed that they were deeply moved by its doctrines. The memorable saying of Numenius, "What is Plato but Moses speaking in the language of Athens?" shews at once the feeling after spiritual sympathy which began to be entertained, and the want of spiritual insight in the representatives of Gentile thought. Though there is no evidence that Numenius studied or taught at Alexandria, his words express the form of feeling which prevailed there. Nowhere else were the characteristic tendencies of the age more marked than in that marvellous city. Alexandria had been from its foundation a meeting-place of the East and West—of old and new—the home of learning, of criticism, of syncretism. It presented a unique example in the Old World of that mixture of races which forms one of the most important features of modern society. Indians, Jews, Greeks, Romans, met there on common ground. Their characteristic ideas were discussed, exchanged, combined. The extremes of luxury and asceticism existed side by side. Over all the excitement and turmoil of the recent city rested the solemn shadow of Egypt. The thoughtful Alexandrine inherited in the history of countless ages, sympathy with a vast life. For him, as for the priest who is said to have rebuked the pride of Solon, the annals of other nations were but episodes in a greater drama in which he played his part with a full consciousness of its grandeur. The pyramids and the tombs repeated to him the reproof of isolated assumption often quoted from Plato by Christian apologists[1]: "You Greeks are always children; you have no doctrine hoary with age." While it was so with the thoughtful Alexandrines, others found in restless scepticism or fitful superstition or fanatical passion, frequent occasions for violence. All alike are eager for movement, sympathising with change, easily impressed and bold in giving utterance to their feelings, confident in their resources and trusting to the future.

We have a picture of the people from an imperial pen. The Emperor Hadrian, who himself entered the lists with the professors at the Museum[2], has left in a private letter a vivid account of the impression which the Alexandrines produced upon him as he saw them from the outside. "There is" [at Alexandria], he writes[3], "no ruler of the synagogue among the Jews, no Samaritan, no Christian, who is not also an astrologer, a soothsayer, a trainer. . . . . . The inhabitants are most seditious, inconstant, insolent: the city is wealthy and productive, seeing that no one lives there in idleness. Some make glass, others

[1] Comp. Potter, Clem. Alex. Strom. i. 15, p. 356.
[2] Spartianus, Hadr. p. 10.
[3] Vopiscus, Saturn. c. 8.

make paper. . . . . . The lame have their occupation; the blind follow a craft; even the crippled lead a busy life. Money is their god. Christians, Jews, and Gentiles combine unanimously in the worship of this deity. . . . ."

One element in this confusion, indicated by Hadrian, is too remarkable to be passed over without remark. The practice of magic, which gained an evil prominence in the later Alexandrine schools, was already coming into vogue. Celsus compared the miracles of the Lord with "the feats of those who have been taught by Egyptians[1]." Such a passion, even in its grosser forms, is never without some moral, we may perhaps say, some spiritual, importance. Its spread at this crisis can hardly be misinterpreted. There was a longing among men for some sensible revelation of the unseen; and a conviction that such a revelation was possible. Even Origen appears to admit the statement that demons were vanquished by the use of certain names which lost their virtue if translated[2], and he mentions one interesting symptom of the general excitement which belongs to the better side of the feeling. "Many," he says, "embraced Christianity, as it were, against their will. Some spirit turned their mind (τὸ ἡγεμονικόν) suddenly from hating the Word to being ready to die for it, and shewed them visions either waking or sleeping[3]." One who is reckoned among the

[1] Orig. c. Cels. i. 68.   [2] *Ibid.* v. 45.   [3] *Ibid.* i. 46.

martyrs whom Origen himself trained furnishes an example[1]. Basilides, a young soldier, shielded a Christian maiden from insult on her way to death. She promised to recompense him. A few days after he confessed himself a Christian. He said that Potamiæna, such was the maiden's name, had appeared to him three days after her martyrdom, and placed a crown upon his head, and assured him that he, in answer to her prayers, would shortly share her victory. So then it was that argumentative scepticism and stern dogmatism, spiritualism, as it would be called at the present day, and materialistic pantheism, each in its measure a symptom of instability and spiritual unrest, existed side by side at Alexandria in the second century, just as may be the case in one of our cities now, where the many streams of life converge. But in all this variety there was a point of agreement, as there is, I believe, among ourselves. Speculation was being turned more and more in a theological direction. Philosophers were learning to concentrate their thoughts on questions which lie at the basis of religion. In very different schools they were listening for the voice, as Plato said, "of some divine Word."

It is easy to see what was the natural office of Christianity in such a society. Alexandria offered an epitome of that Old World which the Faith had to quicken in all its parts. The work had been

[1] Euseb. H. E. vi. 5.

already recognised. Early in the second century manifold attempts were made there to shape a Christian solution of the enigmas of life which thought and experience had brought into a definite form. The result was seen in the various systems of Gnosticism, which present in a strange and repellent dialect many anticipations of the Transcendentalism of the last generation. Such speculations were premature and ended in failure; but they rendered an important service to Christian philosophy. They fixed attention upon those final problems of life, of which a religion which claims to be universal must take account. How did rational creatures come into being? how, that is, can we reconcile the co-existence of the Absolute and the finite? And again: How did rational creatures fall? how, that is, can we conceive of the origin of evil? Or, indeed, are not both these questions in the end one? and is not limitation itself evil? To some perhaps such questions may appear to be wholly foreign to true human work, but they were the questions which were uppermost in men's minds at the time of which we speak; and for the sake of clearness it will be well to distinguish at once the three different types of answers which are rendered to them, two partial and tentative, answering respectively to the East and West, the Gnostic and Neo-Platonic: the third provisionally complete for man, the Christian. The differences will be most clearly seen if we refer the other answers to the Christian as a standard of comparison. As against the Gnostic, then, the Christian maintained that the universe was created, not by any subordinate or rival power, but by an act of love of the One Infinite God, and that evil therefore is not inherent in matter but due to the will of responsible creatures. As against the Neo-Platonist, he maintained the separate, personal existence of God as One to be approached and worshipped, Who thinks and loves; the reality of a redemption consequent on the Incarnation; the historical progress of the sum of life to an appointed end. As against both, he maintained that God is immanent in the world, and separate though not alien from it: that the world was originally and essentially good: that it has been and is disturbed by unseen forces: that man is the crown and end of creation.

And yet further: Gnostic and Platonist despaired of the world and of the mass of men. Both placed safety in flight: they knew of no salvation for the multitude. The Christian, on the other hand, spoke, argued, lived, with the spirit of a conqueror who possessed the power of transfiguring to nobler service what he was charged to subdue. Others sought for an abstraction which was beyond and above all comprehension and all worship, an abstraction which ever escaped from them: he had been found by One who came down to earth and became flesh[1]. Others laboriously framed systems designed to meet the

[1] Comp. Kingsley, *The Schools of Alexandria*, p. 100.

wants and the intelligence of the few : he appealed to all in virtue of a common divine faculty and a common GOD-given freedom, of a universal message and a universal fact. Others looked forward for peace, to the advent of what they called "The Great Ignorance," when each creature should obtain perfect repose by knowing nothing better than itself: he had already begun to know the calmness of joy in absolute surrender to One infinitely great.

The development and co-ordination of these conceptions, of these realities, was, or rather is, necessarily gradual. But it is of importance to notice that from the moment when philosophers expressed their difficulties, Christian teachers undertook to meet them on their own lines. Christian teachers did not lay aside the philosopher's mantle in virtue of their office, but rather assumed it. At Alexandria, a Christian "School"—the well-known Catechetical School—arose by the side of the Museum. In its constitution no less than in its work this School bore a striking if partial resemblance to the "schools of the prophets" under the old Dispensation. It was not ecclesiastical in its organization. Its teachers were not necessarily, or always in fact, priests. Its aim was not to perpetuate a system, but to gain fresh conquests. From obscure beginnings the work went on. Great thoughts, great principles found utterance ; and then a master was raised up not unworthy to combine and quicken them.

The first famous names which occur in connexion

with the School, those of Pantænus and Clement, might well detain us[1]. Both men were led to the Faith through the study of Philosophy. Both continued the study as Christians. They had learnt the needs of men by their own experience, and by that they interpreted what they had found.

The scanty notices of Pantænus which have been preserved suggest the idea of a man of originality and vigour, who combined action with thought. Clement again is perhaps in intuitive power the greatest in the line of Catechists. It would be easy to collect from his writings a series of pregnant passages containing, with some significant exceptions, an outline of the system of Origen; but he had himself no sense of a system. The last book in his Trilogy is fitly called "Miscellanies." He appears also to have wanted practical energy, and even if this assertion seems to be a paradox, I believe that this defect accounts for his intellectual failure. His successor, Origen, supplied that which was wanting. He did not stop at writing Miscellanies. He was filled with the conception of a vast moral unity; of necessity, therefore, he felt that the truths by which this unity was established must form a unity also. It is then to him rather than to his predecessors, or perhaps it may be more true to say to his predecessors in him, that we must look if we wish to gain a right notion of typical Christian thought

---

[1] Comp. Alexander ap. Euseb. H. E. vi. 14.

at Alexandria, a right notion of the beginnings of Christian philosophy.

Origen was of Christian parentage. The son of a martyr, he earned himself a truer martyr's crown through the continuous labours of seventy years. In his case no sharp struggle, no violent change, no slow process wrought the conviction of faith. He did not, like Justin Martyr, or his immediate predecessors, Pantænus and Clement, find in Christianity after painful wanderings that rest which he had sought vainly in the schools of Greek wisdom. He did not, like Tertullian, follow the bent of an uncontrollable and impetuous nature, and close in open schism a life of courageous toil. He did not, like Augustine, come to the truth through heresy, and bear even to the last the marks of the chains by which he had been weighed down. His whole life, from first to last, was fashioned on the same type. It was according to his own grand ideal "one unbroken prayer" (μία προσευχὴ συνεχομένη), one ceaseless effort after closer fellowship with the Unseen and the Eternal. No distractions diverted him from the pursuit of divine wisdom. No persecution checked for more than the briefest space the energy of his efforts. He endured "a double martyrdom," perils and sufferings from the heathen, reproaches and wrongs from Christians; and the retrospect of what he had borne only stirred within him a humbler sense of his shortcomings.

In Origen we have the first glimpse of a Christian

boy. He was conspicuous, "even from his cradle:" "a great man from his childhood[1]," in the judgment of his bitterest enemy. From the first the range of his training was complete. His father Leonidas, after providing carefully for his general education, himself instructed him in Holy Scripture. The boy's nature answered to the demands which were made upon him. His eagerness to penetrate to the deeper meaning of the written Word gave early promise of his characteristic power; and it is said that Leonidas often uncovered his son's breast—his breast, and not his brow—*pectus facit theologum*—as he lay asleep and kissed it, as though it were already a dwelling-place of the Holy Spirit.

When Origen had reached his seventeenth year the persecution under Severus broke out. Leonidas was thrown into prison. Origen was only hindered by the loving device of his mother from sharing his fate. As it was, he wrote to strengthen his father with the simple words: "Take heed! let no thought for us alter your purpose." Leonidas was martyred; his property was confiscated; and the young student at once entered on the career of independent labour which closed only with his life.

At first Origen supported himself by teaching grammar, the customary subjects of a literary education. But immediately a richer field was opened to

[1] Euseb. H. E. vi. 2; Hieron. Ep. 84, 58 (*ad Pammach. et Ocean.*).

CHRISTIAN PHILOSOPHY. 207

him. The Catechetical School in which he had worked under Pantænus and Clement was left without a head, owing to the fierceness of the persecution. For a time Origen gave instruction in Christianity privately to those heathen who wished to learn. His success was such that before he was eighteen he was appointed to fill the vacant post of honour and danger. Martyrs—Eusebius enumerates seven—passed from his class to death. His own escape seemed to be the work of Providence. Marked and pursued, he still evaded his enemies. His influence grew with his self-devotion, and further experience of his new work stirred him to larger sacrifices. He had collected in earlier times a library of classical authors. This he now sold for an annuity of four obols—sixpence—a day, that he might need no assistance from the scholars, who were grieved that they might not help him[1]. So he lived for more than five-and-twenty years, labouring almost day and night, and offering such an example of absolute self-denial as won many to the faith of which he shewed the power in his own person.

While Origen was thus engaged, his principles were put to a severe test. Ammonius Saccas, the founder of Neo-Platonism, began to lecture at Alexandria. His success shewed that he had some neglected forms of truth to make known; and Origen became one of his hearers. The situation was remarkable, and full of interest. The master of Christ-

[1] Euseb. H. E. vi. 3.

ianity was a learner in the school of Greeks. There can be no doubt that Origen was deeply influenced by the new philosophy, which seemed to him to unveil fresh depths in the Bible; and it is not unlikely that this connexion, which lasted for a considerable time, gave occasion to those suspicions and jealousies on the part of some members of the Church at Alexandria, which at no long interval bore bitter fruit. Origen, however, was clear and steadfast as to his purpose, and he found at least some sympathy. For when in later years he was assailed for giving his attention to the opinions of heretics and gentiles, he defended himself not only by the example of Pantænus, but also by that of Heraclas, his fellow-student in the school of Ammonius, who "while now," he writes, "a presbyter at Alexandria, still wears the dress of a philosopher, and studies with all diligence the writings of the Greeks[1]."

An anecdote which is told of the time of his early work may seem in this respect as a symbol of his life[2]. A heathen mob seized him one day and placed him on the steps of the Temple of Serapis, forcing him to offer palm-branches in honour of the god to those who came to worship. He took the palms, and cried out, "Come, take the palm, not the palm of the idol, but the palm of Christ."

The way of Greek wisdom was not the only

[1] Epist. ap. Euseb. H. E. vi. 19.
[2] Epiph. Hær. 64, 1, p. 524.

CHRISTIAN PHILOSOPHY. 209

unusual direction in which Origen sought help for that study of Scripture to which he had consecrated his life. He turned to the Jews also[1], and learnt Hebrew, a task which overcame the spirit of Erasmus, as he tells us[2], even in the excitement of the Renaissance. About the same time, when he was now fully equipped for work, he found assistance and impulse from the friendship of Ambrose, a wealthy Alexandrine whom he had won from heresy to the Truth. Origen draws a lively picture of the activity and importunity of his friend. Meals, rest, exercise, sleep, all had to be sacrificed to his zeal, which may be measured by the fact that he furnished Origen with seven clerks to write at his dictation[3].

This period of happy and incessant labour was at last rudely interrupted. After working publicly at Alexandria for twenty-eight years, with short intervals of absence on foreign missions, Origen was driven from the city to which he was bound by every sacred tie, and never visited it again. There is no need to attempt to unravel the circumstances which led to the catastrophe. It is enough to notice that no word of anger escaped from the great master when he shewed afterwards how keenly he felt the blow. Thenceforth the scene, but not the character, of his work was changed; and he was enabled to carry on at Cæsarea for twenty years longer, with undiminished

[1] From Hier. *Ep.* 39 (22) § 1, it may be not unreasonably inferred that his mother was of Jewish descent.
[2] Epist. 95.   [3] Euseb. H. E. vi. 23.

influence, all the tasks which he had begun. Ambrose was still with him, and his reputation even attracted Porphyry for a brief visit.

At length the end came. In the persecution of Decius he was imprisoned, tortured, threatened with the stake. From the midst of his sufferings he wrote words of encouragement to his fellow-confessors. His persecutors denied him the visible glory of the martyr's death, but already exhausted by age and toil he sank, three years afterwards, under the effects of what he had suffered (A.D. 253).

He was buried at Tyre[1]; and his tomb was honoured as long as the city survived. When a cathedral named after the Holy Sepulchre was built there, his body is said to have occupied the place of greatest honour, being enclosed in the wall behind the High Altar[2]. The same church received in a later age (A.D. 1190) the remains of Barbarossa; but the name of the great theologian prevailed over the name of the great warrior. Burchard, who visited Tyre in the last quarter of the thirteenth century (c. 1283), saw the inscription in Origen's memory in a building which was amazing for its splendour[3].

---

[1] William of Tyre (c. 1180), Hist. xiii. 1: haec (Tyrus) et Origenis corpus occultat, sicut oculata fide etiam hodie licet inspicere.

[2] Cotovicus (1598), Itin. Hier. p. 121: pone altare maximum magni Origenis corpus conditum ferunt.

[3] Burchardus, Descript. Terræ Sanctæ, p. 25 (ed. Laurent): Origenis ibidem in ecclesia Sancti Sepulcri requiescit in muro

CHRISTIAN PHILOSOPHY. 211

Before the close of the century the city was wasted by the Saracens; but if we may trust the words of a traveller at the beginning of the sixteenth century (c. 1520), the inscription was still preserved on "a marble column, sumptuously adorned with gold and jewels[1]." Not long after, at the end of the sixteenth century, the place where Origen lay was only known by tradition. The tradition, however, still lingers about the ruins of the city; for it is said that the natives, to the present time, point out the spot where "Oriunus" lies under a vault, the relic of an ancient church, now covered by their huts[2].

Origen's writings are commensurate in range and number with the intense activity of his life. They were, it is said, measured by thousands, and yet, as he argued, they were all one, one in purpose and in spirit; and it is almost amusing to observe the way in which he writes to Ambrose, who urged him to

conclusus. Cujus titulum ibidem uidi (the edition of 1587 adds *et legi*). Sunt ibi columpnae marmoreae et aliorum lapidum tam magnae, quod stupor est uidere.

[1] Bart. de Saligniaco, Itin. Hier. ix. 10: In templo Sancti Sepulcri, Origenis doctoris ossa magno in honore servantur, quorum titulus est in columna marmorea magno sumptu gemmarum et auri. It is not unlikely, I fear, that this statement is a false rendering of Burchard's notice. Burchard's book was very widely known in the sixteenth century. The statements of Adrichonius (Theatr. T. S. Tr. Aser, 84), which are repeated by Huet and others, have no independent value whatever.

[2] Prutz, *Aus Phönicien*, 219, 306, quoted by Piper, *Ztschr. für Krchgsch.* 1876, p. 208.

14—2

fresh labours, pleading that he has already broken, in the letter, the command of Solomon to "avoid making many books[1]." But, he goes on to argue, multitude really lies in contradiction and inconsistency. A few books which are charged with errors are many. Many books which are alike inspired by the truth are one. "If, then," he concludes, "I set forth anything as the truth which is not the truth, then I shall transgress. Now, while I strive by all means to counteract false teaching, I obey the spirit of the precept which seems at first to condemn me."

This claim which Origen makes to an essential unity—a unity of purpose and spirit—in all his works is fully justified by their character. Commentaries, homilies, essays, tracts, letters, are alike animated by the same free and lofty strivings towards a due sense of the Divine Majesty, and the same profound devotion to the teaching of Scripture. It is no less remarkable that in all these different departments of literature his influence was decisive and permanent. In this respect his reputation, however great, falls below the truth. Those parts of his teaching which failed to find general acceptance were brought into prominence by the animosity of Jerome, who himself often silently appropriated the other parts as belonging to the common heritage of the Church. Origen, in a word, first laid down the lines of a systematic study of the Bible. Both in criticism and in interpretation his labours marked

[1] In Joh. v. Præf.

CHRISTIAN PHILOSOPHY.

an epoch. There were homilies before his, but he fixed the type of a popular exposition. His Hexapla was the greatest textual enterprise of ancient times. His treatise on First Principles was the earliest attempt at a systematic view of the Christian faith.

But we must not linger over his writings. Writings are but one element of the teacher. A method is often more characteristic and more influential than doctrine. It was so with Origen; and, in his case, we fortunately possess a vivid and detailed description of the plan of study which he pursued and enforced. Gregory, surnamed Thaumaturgus, the wonder-worker, from his marvellous labours in Pontus, after working under him for five years at Cæsarea, at a later time delivered a farewell address in his presence (c. 239 A.D.[1]). In this the scholar records with touching devotion the course along which he had been guided by the man to whom he felt that he owed his spiritual life. He had come to Syria to study Roman law in the school of Berytus, but on his way there he met with Origen, and at once felt that he had found in him the wisdom for which he was seeking. The day of that meeting was to him, in his own words, the dawn of a new being; his soul clave to the master whom he recognised, and he surrendered himself gladly to his guidance. As Origen spoke he kindled within the

[1] In the following paragraphs I have endeavoured to give shortly the substance of Gregory's description in his *Oratio Panegyrica.*

young advocate's breast a love for the Holy Word, the most lovely of all objects, and for himself, the Word's herald. "That love," Gregory adds, "induced me to give up country and friends, the aims which I had proposed to myself, the study of law of which I was proud. I had but one passion—philosophy—and the godlike man who directed me in the pursuit of it[1]."

Origen's first care, so his scholar Gregory tells us, was to make the character of a pupil his special study. In this he followed the example of Clement[2]. He ascertained with delicate and patient attention the capacities, the faults, the tendencies, of him whom he had to teach. Rank growths of opinion were cleared away; weaknesses were laid open; every effort was used to develop endurance, firmness, patience, thoroughness. "In true Socratic fashion he sometimes overthrew us by argument," Gregory writes; "if he saw us restive and starting out of the course. . . . . The process was at first disagreeable to us, and painful; but so he purified us . . . . and . . . . prepared us for the reception of the words of truth . . . ," "by probing us and questioning us, and offering problems for our solution[3]." In this way Origen taught his scholars to regard language as designed not to furnish materials for display, but to express truth with the most exact accuracy and

[1] Paneg. c. 5.
[2] Comp. Strom. i. 1, 8, p. 320.
[3] Paneg. c. 7.

logic; as powerful, not to secure a plausible success but, to test beliefs with the strictest rigour.

This was the first stage of intellectual discipline, the accurate preparation of the instruments of thought. In the next place, Origen led his pupils to apply them, first, to the "lofty and divine, and most lovely" study of external Nature. Here he stood where we stand still, for he made geometry the sure and immovable foundation of his teaching, and from this rose step by step to the heights of heaven and the most sublime mysteries of the universe. Gregory's language implies that Origen was himself a student of physics; as, in some degree, the true theologian must be. Such investigations served to shew man in his just relation to the world[1]. A rational feeling for the vast grandeur of the external order, "the sacred economy of the universe," as Gregory calls it, was substituted for the ignorant and senseless wonder with which it is commonly regarded. The lessons of others, he writes, or his own observation, enabled him to explain the connexion, the differences, the changes of the objects of sense.

But physics were naturally treated by Origen as a preparation and not as an end. Moral science came next; and here he laid the greatest stress upon the method of experiment. His aim was not merely to analyse and to define and to classify feelings and motives, though he did this, but to form a character. For him, ethics were a life and not only a theory.

[1] Paneg. c. 8.

The four cardinal virtues of Plato—practical wisdom, self-control, righteousness, courage—seemed to him to require for their maturing careful and diligent introspection and culture. And here he gave a commentary upon his teaching. His discipline lay even more in action than in precept. His own conduct was, in his scholars' minds, a more influential persuasion than his arguments[1].

So it was that Origen was the first teacher who really led Gregory to the pursuit of Greek philosophy, by bringing speculation into a vital union with practice[2]. Gregory saw in him the inspiring example of one at once wise and holy. The noble phrase of older masters gained a distinct meaning for the Christian disciple. In failure and weakness he was enabled to perceive that the end of all was "to become like to GOD with a pure mind, and to draw near to Him and to abide in Him."

Guarded and guided by this conviction, Origen encouraged his scholars in theology to look for help in all the works of human genius. They were to examine the writings of philosophers and poets of every nation—the dogmatic atheists alone excepted —with faithful candour and wise catholicity. For them there was to be no sect, no party. And in their arduous work they had ever at hand in their master a friend who knew the difficulties of the ground to be traversed. If they were bewildered in the tangled mazes of conflicting opinions, he was

[1] Paneg. c. 8.   [2] *Id.* cc. 11, 12.

ready to lead them with a firm hand. If they were in danger of being swallowed up in the quicksands of shifting error, he was near to lift them up to the sure resting-place which he had himself found[1].

Even yet the end was not reached. The hierarchy of sciences was not completed till Theology, with her own proper gifts, crowned the succession which we have followed hitherto, logic, physics, ethics. New data corresponded with the highest philosophy; and Origen found in the Holy Scriptures and the teaching of the Spirit the final and absolute spring of Divine Truth. It was in this region that Gregory felt his master's power to be supreme. Origen's sovereign command of the mysteries of "the oracles of GOD," gave him perfect boldness in dealing with all other writings. "Therefore," Gregory adds, "there was no subject forbidden to us; nothing hidden or inaccessible. We were allowed to become acquainted with every doctrine, barbarian or Greek, on things spiritual or civil, divine and human, traversing with all freedom, and investigating the whole circuit of knowledge, and satisfying ourselves with the full enjoyment of all the pleasures of the soul. . . [2]."

Such, in meagre outline, was, as Gregory tells us, the method of Origen. He describes what he knew, and what his hearers knew. I know no parallel to the picture in ancient times. And when every allowance has been made for the partial enthusiasm of a pupil, the view which it offers of a system of

[1] Paneg. c. 14.   [2] *Id*. c. 15.

Christian training actually realised exhibits a type which we cannot hope to surpass. May we not say that the ideal of Christian education and the ideal of Christian philosophy were fashioned together? And can we wonder that, under that comprehensive and loving discipline, Gregory, already trained in heathen schools, first learnt, step by step, according to his own testimony, what the pursuit of philosophy truly was, and came to know the solemn duty of forming opinions which were to be, not the amusement of a moment, but the solid foundations of lifelong work? Have we yet, perhaps we ask, mastered the lessons?

The method of Origen, such as Gregory has described it, in all its breadth and freedom was forced upon him by what he held to be the deepest law of human nature. It may be true (and he admitted it) that we are, in our present state, but poorly furnished for the pursuit of knowledge; but he was never weary of proclaiming that we are at least born to engage in the endless search. If we see some admirable work of man's art, he says[1], we are at once eager to investigate the nature, the manner, the end of its production; and the contemplation of the works of GOD stirs us with an incomparably greater longing to learn the principles, the method, the purpose of creation. "This desire, this passion, has without doubt," he continues, "been implanted in us by GOD. And as the eye seeks the

[1] De Princ. ii. 4, p. 105.

light, as our body craves food, so our mind is impressed with the characteristic and natural desire of knowing the truth of GOD and the causes of what we observe." Such a desire, since it is a divine endowment, carries with it the promise of future satisfaction. In our present life we may not be able to do more by the utmost toil than obtain some small fragments from the infinite treasures of divine knowledge, still the concentration of our souls upon the lovely vision of Truth, the occupation of our various faculties in lofty inquiries, the very ambition with which we rise above our actual powers, is in itself fruitful in blessing, and fits us better for the reception of wisdom hereafter at some later stage of existence. Now we draw at the best a faint outline, a preparatory sketch of the features of Truth; the true and living colours will be added *then*. Perhaps, he concludes most characteristically, that is the meaning of the words " to every one that hath shall be given;" by which we are assured that he who has gained in this life some faint outline of truth and knowledge, will have it completed in the age to come with the beauty of the perfect image.

Such words, thrilling alike by their humility and by their confidence, noble in the confession of the actual weakness of man, and invigorating by the assertion of his magnificent destiny, can never grow old. They live by the inspiration of spiritual genius, and through them Origen comes into vital contact with ourselves. He was himself greater than his actions, than his writings, than his method. The philosopher was greater than his system. He possessed the highest endowment of a teacher. He was able to give to the innumerable crowd of doctors, confessors, martyrs, who gathered round him, not merely a tabulated series of formulas, but a living energy of faith. He stirred, quickened, kindled, as Gregory says, those who approached him. He communicated not his words, but himself; not opinions so much as a fire of love. Even Erasmus found in this the secret of his charm. "He loved," he says[1], "that of which he spoke, and we speak with delight of the things which we love." In the face of this purifying passion, Origen's errors, however we may judge of them, are details which cannot finally affect our judgment of the man.

During his lifetime there was undoubtedly a strong party opposed to him. His enemies represented a principle—hierarchical supremacy—and not only a personal antipathy. Their bitterness was a proof of his influence. But even after his condemnation at Alexandria his spiritual supremacy was undisturbed. Dionysius carried his spirit to the patriarchal throne. Pamphilus, the martyr, solaced his imprisonment by writing his defence. Even Jerome, before personal feelings had warped his judgment, styled him one "confessed by all competent to judge to be the Master of the Churches after the Apostles." "I could wish," he says, "to

[1] Praef. in Orig. Opp.

CHRISTIAN PHILOSOPHY. 221

have his knowledge of the Scriptures, even if I had to bear the ill-will which attaches to his name."

So long as he was remembered as a living power he was honoured by the admiration of the leaders of Christian thought. But as time went on, the fashion of the Church changed. The freedom of speculation was confined, perhaps necessarily confined, within narrower limits. The men who professed to follow Origen misinterpreted and misrepresented him. For others he was the personification of opinions which had been pronounced heretical by those who had authority. Here and there, however, a bold voice was still raised in his defence. "I do not choose," said a bishop, when appealed to to join in the condemnation of his writings[1], "to do outrage to a man who has long since fallen to sleep in honour; nor am I bold enough to undertake a calumnious task in condemning what those before us did not reject. . . . ." The historian (a layman) who has preserved the anecdote, pauses for a moment to point its moral. "Men," he writes, "of slender ability, who are unable to come to the light by their own fame, wished to gain distinction by blaming their betters. . . . . Such men's accusations contribute, I maintain, to establish his reputation. . . . . And they who revile Origen forget that they calumniate Athanasius who praised him. . . . ."[2].

But no individual devotion could turn the tide of

[1] Theotimus, 'the bishop of Scythia.' Socr. H. E. vi. 12.
[2] *Id.* vi. 13.

opinion which had set in against Origen before the close of the fifth century. It corresponded with an intellectual revolution. For three centuries or more Platonic idealism had been supreme. Aristotelian realism was now on the point of displacing it. The signs of the change can be noticed in theology and in politics. In one sense it was necessary as a condition for the development of mediævalism. The institutions of the past, which carried with them the noblest memories and symbolized the old order, were now emptied of their true life, and therefore not unmeet to fall by the hands of an alien Emperor. It was the singular and significant fortune of Justinian to strike a threefold blow at the past—to close the Schools of Athens, to abolish the Consulship at Rome, to procure a formal condemnation of Origen. By a happy coincidence he warred in each case with the dead, and he was not unworthy to wage such a conflict which could bring no fruit and no glory. It would be idle to suppose that such a man could either sympathise with or understand the difficulties or the thoughts of Origen. For good and for evil he was wholly cast in the mould of formulas. He knew nothing higher than an edict. With less knowledge than Henry VIII., he aspired to be a defender of the Faith, and ended by compromising his reputation for orthodoxy. The spectacle is for a moment one of unspeakable sadness, Origen condemned on the impeachment of Justinian. But the life of the martyr triumphed over the anathemas of

CHRISTIAN PHILOSOPHY. 223

the persecutor. Justinian could flatter himself that he killed again that which had no life because it was false; but Origen—the preacher of humility and patience and reverence and hope and absolute devotion to the Divine Word—slept on calmly in the tomb; and when "Greece rose from the dead," as it has been finely expressed, "with the New Testament in her hand," he rose too to disclose once again fresh springs of Truth. "I have read," writes Erasmus to our own Colet in 1504, "a great part of the works of Origen; and under his teaching I think that I have made good progress; for he opens, so to speak, the fountains of Theology, and indicates the methods of the science."

Even while Origen was still held to be under the ban of the Church, he exercised a strange fascination by the memories of his name. His salvation was a question of the Schools, and was said to have been the subject of revelations. An abbot, so the story ran, saw him in eternal torment with the chief hæresiarchs, Arius and Nestorius. On the other hand, it was alleged that it had been made known to St Mechtildis[1] that "the fate of Samson, Solomon, and Origen was kept hidden in the divine counsels, in order that the strongest, the wisest, and the most learned might be filled with salutary fear." Picus of Mirandula maintained in the face of violent opposition, that it was "more reasonable to believe in his salvation than not." A learned Jesuit has com-

[1] See Bayle, *Dict. Origène*, Note D.

posed an imaginary account of his trial before the Court of Heaven, with witnesses, advocates, and accusers, in which he finally gives him the benefit of the doubt. "There is a perplexed controversy," writes a German chronicler of the fifteenth century, "in which sundry people engage about Samson, Solomon, Trajan, and Origen, whether they were saved or not. That I leave to the Lord."

Such notices serve for more than a momentary surprise. They shew that Origen, though practically unknown, still kept his hold on the interests of men; that he was still an object of personal love; that there is in the fact of a life of humble self-sacrifice something too majestic, too divine, to be overthrown by the measured sentence of an ecclesiastical synod.

II.

In the last paper I endeavoured to indicate some characteristic features in the position, the life, the works, the method, the influence of Origen. I wish now to give a general idea of his chief philosophic work—the treatise *On First Principles*—of its contents and of its spirit, in connexion with the history of Christian thought. Origen was in the full course of his work at Alexandria when the work on First Principles was written. He was probably at the time not much more than thirty years old, and still a layman; but there is no reason to think that he modified in any important respects the opinions which he has expressed in it. It must, however, be remembered that the book was not written for simple believers, but for scholars—for those who were familiar with the teaching of Gnosticism and Platonism; and with a view to questions which then first become urgent when men have risen to a wide view of Nature and life. Non-Christian philosophies moved in a region of sublime abstractions, "ideas." Origen felt that Christianity converts these abstractions into realities, the personal facts of a complete life; and he strove to express what he felt in the modes of thought and language of his age. He aimed at presenting the higher "knowledge" ($\gamma\nu\hat{\omega}\sigma\iota\varsigma$) as an objective system. But in doing this he had no intention of fashioning two Christianities —a Christianity for the learned and a Christianity for the simple. The Faith was one, one essentially and unalterably, but infinite in fulness, so that the trained eye could see more of its harmonies, as it necessarily looked for more. Fresh wants made fresh truths visible. He who found much had nothing over; he who found little had no lack.

The book is, as has been already said, the earliest attempt to form a system of Christian doctrine, or rather a philosophy of the Christian faith. In this respect it marks an epoch in Christian thought, but no change in the contents of the Christian creed. The elements of the dogmatic basis are assumed on the authority of the Church. The author's object is, as he says, to shew how they can be arranged as a whole, by the help either of the statements of Scripture or of the methods of exact reasoning. And, however strange or startling the teaching of Origen may seem to us, it is necessary to bear in mind that this is the account which he gives of it. He takes for granted that all that he brings forward is in harmony with received teaching. He professes to accept as final the same authorities as ourselves[1].

The treatise consists of four books. It has been preserved for the most part only in an inexact Latin translation, but sufficient evidence remains to shew that the translation gives the main thoughts correctly. The composition is not strictly methodical. Digressions and repetitions interfere with the symmetry of the plan. But, to speak generally, the first book deals with GOD and Creation (religious statics, if I may use the phrase); the second and third books with Creation and Providence, with Man and Redemption (religious dynamics); and the fourth book with Holy Scripture. Or, to put the facts somewhat differently, the first three books contain the exposition of a Christian philosophy, gathered round the three ideas of GOD, the world, and the rational soul; and the last gives the basis of it. Even in the repetitions (as on "the restoration of things") it is not difficult to see that each successive treatment corresponds with a new point of sight.

Bearing these broad divisions in mind, we can

[1] De Princ. Præf.

CHRISTIAN PHILOSOPHY. 227

enter a little further into detail. In the first book, then, Origen brings before us the final elements of all religious philosophy—GOD, the world, rational creatures. After dwelling on the essential nature of GOD as incorporeal, invisible, incomprehensible, and on the characteristic relations of the Persons of the Holy Trinity to man, as the Authors of being and reason and holiness, he gives a summary view of the end of human life; for the elements of a problem cannot be really understood until we have comprehended its scope. The end of life, then, according to Origen, is the progressive assimilation of man to GOD by the voluntary appropriation of His gifts. Gentile philosophers had proposed to themselves the idea of assimilation to GOD, but Origen adds the means. "By the unceasing action of the Father, Son, and Holy Spirit towards us, renewed at each successive stage of our advance, we shall be able," he says, "with difficulty perchance at some future time to look on the holy and blessed life; and, when once we have been enabled to reach that, after many struggles, we ought so to continue in it that no weariness may take hold on us. Each fresh enjoyment of that bliss ought to enlarge or deepen our desire for it; while we are ever receiving or holding with more ardent love and larger grasp the Father and the Son and the Holy Spirit[1]."

But it will be said that this condition of progress, effort, assimilation, involves the possibility of declen-

[1] De Princ. i. 3. 8.

sion, indolence, the obliteration of the Divine image. If man can go forward he can go backward. Origen accepts the consequence, and finds in it an explanation of the actual state of men and angels. The present position of each rational being corresponds, in his judgment, with the use which he has hitherto made of the revelations and gifts of GOD. No beings were created originally immutable in character. Some by diligent obedience have been raised to the loftiest places in the celestial hierarchy; others by perverse selfwill and rebellion have sunk into the condition of demons. Others occupy an intermediate place, and are capable of being raised again to their first state, and so upwards, if they avail themselves of the helps which are provided by the love of GOD. "Of these," he adds, "I think, as far as I can form an opinion, that this order of the human race was formed, which in the future age, or in the ages which succeed, when there shall be a new heaven and a new earth, shall be restored to that unity which the Lord promises in His intercessory prayer." "Meanwhile," he continues, "both in the ages which are seen and temporal, and in those which are not seen and eternal, all rational beings who have fallen are dealt with according to the order, the character, the measure of their deserts. Some in the first, others in the second, some again even in the last times, through greater and heavier sufferings, borne through many ages, reformed by sharper discipline, and restored .... stage by stage .... reach that which is invisible and eternal. . . . .[1]" Only one kind of change is impossible. There is no such transmigration of souls as Plato pictured after the fashion of the Hindus in the legend of "Er the son of Armenius." No rational being can sink into the nature of a brute[2].

The progress of this discussion is interrupted by one singular episode, which is characteristic of the time. How, Origen asks, are we to regard the heavenly bodies—the sun and moon and stars? Are they animated and rational? Are they the temporary abodes of souls which shall hereafter be released from them? Are they finally to be brought into the great unity, when "God shall be all in all?" The questions, he admits, are bold; but he answers all in the affirmative, on what he holds to be the authority of Scripture[3].

In the second book Origen pursues at greater length that view of the visible world as a place of discipline and preparation, which has been already indicated. He follows out as a movement what he had before regarded as a condition. The endless variety in the situations of men, the inequality of their material and moral circumstances, their critical spiritual differences, all tend to shew, so he argues, that the position of each has been determined in accordance with previous conduct. And God in His ineffable wisdom has united all together with abso-

[1] De Princ. i. 6. 2, f.   [2] *Id.* i. 8. 4.
[3] *Id.* i. 7; cf. c. Cels. v. 10, 11.

lute justice, so that all these creatures, most diverse in themselves, combine to work out His purpose, while "their very variety tends to the one end of perfection." All things were made for the sake of man and rational beings[1]. It is through man therefore that this world, as GOD's work, becomes complete and perfect. The individual is never isolated, though he is never irresponsible. At every moment he is acting and acted upon, adding something to the sum of the moral forces of the world, furnishing that out of which GOD is fulfilling His purpose. The difficulties of life, as Origen regards them, give scope for heroic effort and loving service. The fruits of a moral victory become more permanent as they are gained through harder toil. The obstacles and hindrances by which man is hemmed in are incentives to exertion. His body is not a "prison" in the sense of a place of punishment only; it is a beneficent provision for the discipline of beings to whom it furnishes such salutary restraints as are best fitted to further their moral growth[2].

This view of the dependence of the present on the past—to use the forms of human speech—seemed to Origen to remove a difficulty which weighed heavily upon thoughtful men in the first age as it has weighed heavily upon thoughtful men in our own generation. Very many said then, what one of the most influential and rigorous philosophers of modern times said not long ago with a voice from

---

[1] De Princ. ii. 1; cf. c. Cels. iv. 99. [2] *Id.* ii. 2.

the grave, that the sufferings and disparities of life, the contrasts of the Law and the Gospel, point to the action of rival spiritual powers or to a Creator limited by something external to Himself. Not so, was Origen's reply: they simply reveal that what we see is a fragment of a vast system in which we can do no more than trace tendencies, convergences, signs, and rest upon the historic fact of the Incarnation. In this respect he ventured to regard the entire range of being as "one thought" answering to the absolutely perfect will of GOD, while "we that are not all, as parts can see but parts—now this, now that[1]."

And this seems to me to be the true meaning of his famous assertion that the power of GOD in creation was finite, and not infinite. It would, that is, be inconsistent with our ideas of perfect order, and therefore with our idea of the Divine Being, that the sum of finite existence should not form one whole. "GOD made all things in number and measure." The Omnipotence of GOD is defined (as we are forced to conceive) by the absolute Perfections of His Nature. "He cannot deny Himself[2]."

But it may be objected more definitely that our difficulties do not lie only in the circumstances of the present: that the issues of the present, so far as we can see them, bring difficulties no less overwhelming: that even if we allow that this world is fitted to be a place of discipline for fallen beings who

[1] De Princ. ii. 5; 9. 5.   [2] *Id.* ii. 9. 1; iv. 35.

are capable of recovery, it is only too evident that the discipline does not always work amendment. Origen admits the fact, and draws from it the conclusion that other systems of penal purification and moral advance follow. According to him, world grows out of world, so to speak, till the consummation is reached. What is the nature, or position, or constitution of the world to come he does not attempt to define. It is enough to believe that from first to last the will of Him who is most righteous and most loving is fulfilled; and that each loftier region gained is the entrance to some still more glorious abode above, so that all being becomes, as it were, in the highest sense a journey of the saints from mansion to mansion up to the very throne of GOD[1].

In order to give clearness to this view, Origen follows out in imagination the normal course of the progressive training, purifying, and illumination of men in the future. He pictures them passing from sphere to sphere, and resting in each so as to receive such revelations of the providence of GOD as they can grasp; lower phenomena are successively explained to them, and higher phenomena are indicated. As they look backward old mysteries are illuminated; as they look forward unimagined mysteries stir their souls with divine desire. Everywhere their Lord is with them, and they advance from strength to strength, through the perpetual supply of spiritual food. This food, he says, is the contemplation and

[1] De Princ. ii. 10.

understanding of GOD, according to its proper measure in each case and as suits a nature which is made and created. And this measure—this due harmony and proportion between aim and power (would that we could remember the truth!)—it is right that every one should regard even now who is beginning to see GOD, that is, to understand Him in purity of heart[1].

But while Origen opens this infinite prospect of scene upon scene to faith, or hope, or imagination—call it as we may—he goes on to shew that Scripture concentrates our attention upon the next scene, summed up in the words, Resurrection, Judgment, Retribution. Nowhere is he more studiously anxious to keep to the teaching of the Word than in dealing with these cardinal ideas. For him the Resurrection is not the reproduction of any particular organism, but the preservation of complete identity of person, an identity maintained under new conditions, which he presents under the Apostolic figure of the growth of the plant from the seed: the seed is committed to the earth and perishes, and yet the vital power which it contains gathers a new frame answering to its proper nature. Judgment is no limited and local act, but the unimpeded execution of the absolute divine law by which the man is made to feel what he is and what he has become, and to bear the inexorable consequences of the revelation. Punishment is no vengeance, but the just severity of a righteous King by which the soul is placed at least on the

[1] De Princ. ii. 11. 6 f.

way of purification. Blessedness is no sensuous joy or indolent repose, but the opening vision of the divine glory, the growing insight into the mysteries of the fulfilment of the divine counsels[1].

In the third book Origen discusses the moral basis of his system. This lies in the recognition of free-will as the inalienable endowment of rational beings. But this free-will does not carry with it the power of independent action, but only the power of receiving the help which is extended to each according to his capacity and needs, and therefore just responsibility for the consequences of action. Such free-will offers a sufficient explanation, in Origen's judgment, for what we see, and gives a stable foundation for what we hope. It places sin definitely within the man himself, and not without him. It preserves the possibility of restoration while it enforces the penalty of failure. "God said," so he writes, "'Let us make man in our image, after our likeness.' Then the sacred writer adds, 'And God made man: in the image of God made he him.' This therefore that he says, 'In the image of God made he him,' while he is silent as to the likeness, has no other meaning than this, that man received the dignity of the image at his first creation; while the perfection of this likeness is kept in the consummation (of all things); that is, that he should himself gain it by the efforts of his own endeavour, since the possibility of perfection had been given him at the first. . . . .[2]"

[1] De Princ. ii. 10.   [2] *Id.* iii. 6. 1.

Such a doctrine, he shews, gives a deep solemnity to the moral conflicts of life. We cannot even to the last plead that we are the victims of circumstances or of the evil spirits. The decision in each case, this way or that, rests with ourselves, yet so that all we have and are truly is the gift of GOD. Each soul obtains from the object of its love the power to fulfil His will. "It draws and takes to itself," he says, "the Word of GOD in proportion to its capacity and faith. And when souls have drawn to themselves the Word of GOD, and have let Him penetrate their senses and their understandings, and have perceived the sweetness of His fragrance, ... filled with vigour and cheerfulness, they speed after Him. . . . . .[1]" Nor can I forbear to add that such a doctrine, so far from tending to Pelagianism, is the very refutation of it. It lays down that the essence of freedom is absolute self-surrender; that the power of right action is nothing but the power of GOD. Every act of man is the act of a free being, but not an exercise of freedom; if done without dependence upon GOD, it is done in despite of freedom, responsibly indeed, but under adverse constraint.

The decision from moment to moment, Origen maintains, rests with us, but not the end. That is determined from the first, though the conduct of creatures can delay through untold ages the consummation of all things. The gift of being, once given, abides for ever. The rational creature is

[1] In Cant. i., t. iii. p. 41 R.

capable of change, of better and worse, but it can never cease to be. What mysteries, however, lie behind, what is the nature of the spiritual body in which we shall be clothed, whether all that is finite shall be gathered up in some unspeakable way into the Absolute, that Origen holds to be beyond our minds to conceive[1].

As the third book deals with the moral basis of Origen's system, so the fourth and last deals with its dogmatic basis. This order of succession in the treatise is unusual, and yet it is intelligible. It moves from the universal to the special; from that which is most abstract to that which is most concrete; from the heights of speculation to the rule of authority. "In investigating such great subjects as these," Origen writes, "we are not content with common ideas, and the clear evidence of what we see, but we take testimonies to prove what we state, even those which are drawn from the Scriptures, which we believe to be Divine[2]." Therefore, in conclusion, he examines with a reverence, an insight, a humility, a grandeur of feeling never surpassed, the questions of the inspiration and the interpretation of the Bible. The intellectual value of the work may best be characterised by one fact: a single sentence taken from it was quoted by Butler as containing the germ of his "Analogy."

Such is the main outline, as far as I am able to trace it, of Origen's philosophical work. It will be

[1] De Princ. iii. 6.   [2] *Id.* iv. 1 init.

CHRISTIAN PHILOSOPHY. 237

obvious at first sight how widely it differs from mediæval and modern expositions of the "first principles" of the Christian Faith. It contains very little technical teaching. It is silent as to the Sacraments. It contains no theory of the Atonement; no teaching on Justification. Yet it does deal with questions which are felt to be momentous, and which everything at present tends to bring again into prominence.

In this aspect there are several points of great interest in the sketch which can hardly fail to have been noticed. But before touching on these it will be well to mark once again the answers which Origen gave to the questions which (as we have seen) were uppermost in the contemporary Schools as to the origin of finite existences and of evil.

"In the beginning," he writes, "when GOD created what He pleased to create—that is, rational natures —He had no other cause of creation beside Himself —that is, His own goodness[1]." And the rational creatures which He made were all alike, for there was no cause for difference, but they were inalienably endowed with freedom of will; and this freedom of will led either to their advance through imitation of GOD or to their declension through neglect of Him; and hence came the present order, which in all its diversities is still guided by Infinite Righteousness[2].

Evil, it follows, is negative, the loss of good which was attainable: the shadow which marks the absence,

[1] De Princ. ii. 9. 6; comp. iv. 35.   [2] Id. ii. 9. 6.

or rather the exclusion, of light. The creation of finite rational beings by the free act of GOD involved the creation of a medium through which they could give expression to their character. Such a medium is matter in its boundless subtle modifications. While, therefore, the expression of character will be dependent upon matter within certain limits, yet man, for example, is still capable of receiving and giving utterance to a divine revelation as a spiritual being, in accordance with the laws of his present organisation.

Briefly, therefore, Origen aims at giving shape to two great thoughts—(1) that the whole world is a manifestation of the goodness and righteousness of GOD in every detail; and (2) that the moral determination of each individual is a decisive element in the working out of the divine counsel.

This compound conception of the sum of finite being as a unity, consistent with, or rather dependent upon, the free and responsible action of each individual, is evidently of the utmost significance. There can be none greater. Nor does it lose in grandeur when we go on to consider some particular points in Origen's treatment of it.

The first which I desire to mark is the stress which Origen lays upon the moral end of philosophy, and of religion as the supreme philosophy. No teacher of the present day could insist with greater earnestness upon the importance of conduct than he does. There is absolutely nothing in which he does

CHRISTIAN PHILOSOPHY. 239

not see ethical influences. His thought wearies itself in following out the effects of action. Without perpetuating the associations of the present he strives to give definiteness to our conceptions of the continuity of the spiritual life. He carries the sense of responsibility up to the highest orders of finite existence. His system is a system of absolute idealism, but of idealism as a spring for action. "GOD cares," he says[1], "not only for the whole, as Celsus thinks, but beyond the whole in an especial manner for each rational being." Thus in his doctrine of the reincorporation of souls there is nothing accidental, nothing capricious, as in Plato's famous Myth. The belief, according to him, represents to human apprehension a judgment of Infinite Righteousness executed by Infinite Love. It is an embodiment, if I may so express it, of two principles which he assumes as axioms—the first that every gift of GOD is perfect, and the second that GOD's gift to His rational creatures was not virtue, which it could not be by the nature of the case, but the capacity for virtue.

In the next place, Origen distinctly claims for Christianity that it is a philosophy, that it has for its domain every human interest and power, that it is capable of co-ordinating all thought and all experience. Faith is the foundation of knowledge. The fact that our results on earth will be to the last fragmentary and tentative, does not interfere with the reality of the spirit which quickens the Gospel.

[1] c. Cels. iv. 99.

"*Now*," he says, "we seek for a while, *then* we shall see clearly[1]." But both in the search and in the fruition the object is the same. The fulness of Truth, which is finally nothing less than a manifold revelation of GOD leading up to absolute fellowship with Him, is that towards which the believer is led by the Spirit alike through thought and feeling and action.

As a necessary consequence he insists, in the third place, on the new data which are given by revelation for the solution of the problems of philosophy. Again and again he points out the insufficiency of reason, of the independent faculties of man, to attain to that towards which it is turned. Reason enables man to recognise GOD when He makes Himself known, to receive a revelation from Him in virtue of his affinity with the Divine Word, but it does not enable the creature to derive from within the knowledge for which it longs. It follows that the capacity for knowing GOD belongs to man as man, and not to man as a philosopher. Origen therefore acknowledges the nobility of Plato's words when he said that "it is a hard matter to find out the Maker and Father of the universe, and impossible for one who has found Him to declare Him to all men[2]." But he adds that Plato affirms too much and too little. As Christians "we declare that human nature is not in itself competent in any way to seek GOD and find Him purely without the help

[1] De Princ. ii. 11. 5.   [2] c. Cels. vii. 43.

CHRISTIAN PHILOSOPHY. 241

of Him who is sought, nay, of Him who is found by those who confess, after they have done all in their power, that they have yet need of Him. . . . ."

The Platonic passage here quoted was indeed one in which the Christian Apologist rightly felt that an essential contrast between Gentile and Christian philosophy was expressed[1]; and I cannot but add Clement's comment on the words. "Well said, Plato: you have touched the truth; but do not faint in thy efforts: join with me in the search for the good; for in all men absolutely, and in a special way in those who occupy themselves with the discussion of great questions ($\pi\epsilon\rho\grave{\iota}$ $\lambda\acute{o}\gamma o\upsilon s$), a divine effluence hath been instilled. . . ." "Philosophy," he says elsewhere, "seeks for the truth and the nature of things; and this is the Truth, of which the Lord said, I am the Truth[2]."

Such is the true position of the Christian philosopher. He accepts gladly all the consequences which can be deduced from the intellectual constitution of man, and from man's observation of nature; but he affirms beside that GOD has made known something of Himself. And in this affirmation there is nothing at variance with the principles of philosophy. If it be true that there are three ultimate existences of which the reality is equally incapable of proof and disproof,—self, the world, and GOD,— we may expect that we shall gain knowledge as to

[1] Clem. Alex. Cohort. § 68, p. 59.
[2] Clem. Alex. Strom. i. 5, p. 335.

each, not in the same way, but in different and corresponding ways. It is just as much in harmony with the spiritual faculty that man should be able to receive communications from GOD, as it is in harmony with his sensuous faculties that he should receive impressions from the world without. "The soul has its sense no less than the body." And if this be so, the sense of the soul must be trained that it may receive right impressions from the objects to which it is directed. Aristotle spoke of "an eye of experience," which is sharpened by the practical conduct of affairs. Origen may be said to require "an eye of holiness" for the vision of the purest Truth.

This characteristic of Origen's teaching places his views on conduct in a new light. Right action is not only a necessity for the moulding of the character after the Divine likeness; it is also a necessity for the progressive reception of the Divine revelation. Morality, in the largest sense of the word, is bound to Theology as a condition of knowledge. "The pure in heart see GOD," and see Him with a clearness answering to their growth in purity[1].

A fourth point in Origen's treatise is the intense reality with which he invests the spiritual world. He already lives and moves in it. External objects, peoples, cities, are to him veils and symbols of invisible things. Phenomena are shadows, and he looks upon the substances by which they are cast.

[1] Comp. c. Cels. iv. 30; v. 43; vi. 2.

He cheerfully admits every hindrance which besets us now, but reaches out to the state when they will exist no longer. Hence comes the earnestness with which he combats every tendency to unite indissolubly present conditions with the future, or to trust to deductions drawn from the temporal and local limitations of human observation. The grossness of Millenarianism filled him with alarm. And those who are familiar with the writings and influence of Tertullian will know that Origen's opposition to materialism in every form was called for by pressing dangers. Perhaps we have even yet hardly realised what a heavy burden of materialistic conceptions we have ourselves inherited from African theology which Origen set aside by anticipation.

But while Origen affirms with the utmost force the spirituality of the unseen world, and contends against the popular transference of the thoughts which belong to this order of being to another, he affirms with equal distinctness that we have to do there with a world of persons and not of abstractions. Where he is in one sense most Platonic, he is in another sense most opposed to Plato and the Neo-Platonists. He preserves and intensifies every moral relation in that loftier sphere. Nothing is lost there, but all is ennobled. A single illustration will shew the wisdom of his judgment.

No one of his opinions was more vehemently assailed than his teaching on the Resurrection. Even his early and later apologists were perplexed in their defence of him. Yet there is no point on which his insight was more conspicuous. By keeping strictly to the Apostolic language he anticipated results which we have hardly yet secured. He saw that it is "the spirit" which moulds the frame through which it is manifested: that the body is the same, not by any material continuity, but by the permanence of that which gives the law, the "ratio" as he calls it, of its constitution[1]. Our opponents say now that this idea is a late refinement of doctrine forced upon us by the exigencies of controversy. The answer is that no exigencies of controversy brought Origen to his conclusion. It was, in his judgment, the clear teaching of St Paul.

I will notice only one point more. He held, as we have just seen, that age is linked with age under the laws of a divine growth. As a necessary consequence the secular periods which he imagines are not like the "great ages" of the Stoics, fated periods of recurrence, in which the old drama of existence is played out again[2]; or the still stranger repetitions of the past in a reversed order, such as Plato imagined in his "Politicus[3];" but stages in a majestic progress. This vast movement, this magnificent and sure growth, seemed to him not only to be consistent with, but to answer to, the action of Providence, and the fact of freedom in every particular life. "GOD cares for each," he says, to continue a passage which

[1] Comp. Fragm. de Resurr. lib. ii. t. i. p. 34 R.
[2] c. Cels. v. 20, f.   [3] See p. 16.

CHRISTIAN PHILOSOPHY. 245

I began to quote before, "nor will He ever abandon the whole. For even if it should become worse through the sin of rational beings, who are a part of it, He administers it so as to purify it; and after a time to turn it to Himself[1]." Such a unity, which he cannot distinctly shape, extends, as he believed, to the whole man, to the whole world, to the whole order of finite beings. "The end," he says, "is always like the beginning. . . . From one beginning arose many differences and varieties, which again, through the goodness of GOD, and subjection to Christ and unity of the Holy Spirit, are recalled to one end. . . .[2]" That beginning and that end can be, he allows, apprehended by no created nature, neither by man nor by angels. Yet he yearns towards the thought which cannot be made distinct. And when difficulties crowd in upon him which he cannot solve, he falls back upon the words of St Paul, which appear to him to crown hope with the assurance of a fulfilment : "GOD shall be all in all."

Those who have followed so far the opinions which I have tried to summarise, will have felt, I believe, that if there is much in them to startle, there is much also in them to move and to humble and to elevate. It does not fall within my scope to discuss the opinions or to point out the inconsistencies and want of proportion which mar the treatise from which they have been drawn. I cannot

[1] c. Cels. iv. 99; cf. De Princ. ii. 1. 2; i. 6. 2.
[2] De Princ. i. 6. 2.

even touch, as I could have wished to do, on Origen's central error of excessive Transcendentalism; but such errors are not likely to be underrated at present. It seems to me that we have more to learn than to fear from the study of Origen's writings. With all his faults and shortcomings, he is the greatest representative of a type of Greek Christian thought which has not yet done its work in the West. By his sympathy with all effort, by his largeness of view, by his combination of a noble morality with a deep mysticism, he indicates, if he does not bring, the true remedy for the evils of that Africanism which has been dominant in Europe since the time of Augustine.

No fact, I think, is sadder in the history of religious thought than that Augustine had no real knowledge of Greek. He remarks in his "Confessions" that he can hardly tell why he shrank from the study of the language[1]. The reason probably was in the very constitution of his nature. Augustine was a Latin thinker, and more than a Latin—an African. He looked at everything from the side of law and not of freedom; from the side of GOD, as an irresponsible Sovereign, and not of man, as a loving servant. In spite of his admiration for Plato he was driven by a passion for system to fix, to externalise, to freeze every idea into a rigid shape. In spite of his genius he could not shake off the influence of a legal and rhetorical training, which

[1] Lib. i. 14.

controversy called into active exercise. The successive forms of his belief were a manifestation of his essential character. To the last he bore within him that which once had made him a Manichæan. The argument by which he trusted to win men for the Church was a coarse representation of future rewards and punishments. The centre of his whole dogmatic theory is sin. In his greatest work he writes "Of the City of GOD," and he draws at the same time the portraiture of a rival "city of the devil," equally stable and enduring.

Few contrasts indeed can be more striking than that offered by the two philosophies of Christianity (as they may be called) of Origen and Augustine, of the East and West, of Alexandria and Hippo. The treatise "On First Principles," and the treatise "On the City of GOD," were both written by men of commanding power and of unquestioning faith. Both reach back to an ideal beginning which expresses a conception of the innermost law of the present order, and forward to an ideal end which expresses the fulness of hope. Both extend over the whole range of history. Both claim the authority of Scripture for their foundation. But here the resemblance ends. The two are profoundly different in form and in spirit. The treatise of Origen deals with truths so that they are in danger of being lost in thoughts: the treatise of Augustine deals with truths so that they are bound by the limiting form of facts. There awe prevails, and here assertion. Over the one there hangs a strange mystery, half light and half darkness; and sight is lost in the endeavour to follow the long-drawn vista of successive scenes faintly indicated before and behind. In the other every image is fixed with a firm, sharp pencil; the picture is bounded on this side and that: the divine symbolism of Genesis and of the Apocalypse is converted into a most literal description of that which has been and that which shall be. In Origen there is a feeling, not very clearly defined, that the history both "of the nations" and of "the people" is charged with moral lessons of permanent meaning[1]; that there is carried forward from age to age an education of the world for eternity. In Augustine history is a mere succession of external events; the Divine teaching through heathendom lies in the utterances of the Sibyls and not in the course of Empires. For Origen, in spite of his idealism, life has a moral significance of incalculable value: for Augustine, in spite of his realism, life is a mere show, in which actors fulfil the parts irrevocably assigned to them. The Alexandrine cannot rest without looking forward to a final unity which still he confesses more than once that he is unable to grasp: the African acquiesces without a difficulty in an abiding dualism in the future, which must seem to other minds not less oppressive to the moral sense than the absolute dualism of Mani.

In indicating these contrasts, I am far from

[1] Cf. c. Cels. v. 30.

wishing to exalt Origen at the cost of Augustine. In spite of popular judgment I cannot think that the book "On the City of GOD" presents Augustine under his noblest aspect. Isolated passages of singular beauty seem to me to be insufficient to counteract the general want of sympathy which it displays for the progress and the destiny of mankind. On the other hand, the very grandeur of the hope which inspires Origen's essay "On First Principles" perhaps blinds the reader to the errors which accompany it. And in judging the works of the two great Fathers we must not forget the positions which they occupied. They were the representatives of two ages, of two crises.

Origen, standing in the meeting-place of struggling thoughts, knew that he had that to speak which could harmonize and satisfy every spiritual aspiration of man: an answer to the despair of the West, which saw in man's good an unattainable ideal; an answer to the despair of the East, which saw in man's way a vain delusion. Augustine, under the cruel pressure of barbarian invasion, was called upon to pronounce sentence on the old world, and to vindicate Christianity from the charge of social disorganisation. The one was the interpreter of a universal hope; the other was the interpreter of a secular overthrow.

We may go further, and venture to say that the Africanism of Augustine was, in the order of Providence, a salutary preparation for the discipline of the Middle Ages. It was fitted by its partial truths to deal effectively with the problems which then came to the front. But it is partial, and its defects lie in those regions of physical and moral speculation which now attract the most devout minds. Over the questions with which we have now to deal Augustine can no longer hold dominion, and the shadow of his power is perilous to the growth of Truth. But in saying this I am too sensible of the faults of Origen to wish to raise him to the vacant throne. None the less it will be well for us to remember what he found in the Bible, and how he interpreted the message of the Faith, when as yet there was no pressure from the forces which bear most heavily upon ourselves. In this respect both as a theologian and as a philosopher he has still a work to do.

I do not, however, as I said before, dwell upon his opinions. I desire to insist upon his principles and his spirit. To this end, we must regard his teaching as not so much a system as an aspiration. Welcomed as an aspiration, it can, I believe, do us good service. We are inclined to underrate the practical effect of wide thoughts and of great ideals. But life is impoverished and action is enfeebled for the lack of them. And I can hardly imagine that any one can picture to himself what Origen meant when he offered his spectacle of the moral continuity and destination of being; when he imaged the spiritual antitypes of outward things; when he interpreted the sorrows and sadnesses of the world as part of a vast scheme of purificatory chastisement;

CHRISTIAN PHILOSOPHY.   251

when he concentrated every line of study upon the interpretation of the Divine oracles; when he reckoned the fuller insight into the mysteries of Nature as one of the joys of a future state; when he made the love of truth, in all its amplitude and in all its depth, the last passion of rational creatures, and affirmed that the instinct could not for ever want its satisfaction; without feeling that there is in worship a personal Divine communion, which he fails too often to realise; that there is in the Bible a significance which he is apt to overlook; that there is in life a majesty and a promise which he cannot see till he rises above the confused turmoil of the day.

The end of Philosophy is Truth; not in one region but in all; Truth apprehended, if it may be, in its highest unity. The name of Christianity is Truth; and I think that I have shewn that the first great writer who endeavoured to face the question affirmed, with unquestioning belief, that Christianity is the fulfilment of Philosophy[1]. Human wisdom, he says, is the school of the soul: Divine wisdom is the end. Faith, knowledge, wisdom—that, in his judgment, is the order of spiritual growth. The immediate issue was not in the direction to which he pointed. But he expressed and preserved the thoughts of an age which was to pass away under new forces. We now seem to be entering again upon the controversy which he supported. We are his heirs. He has left us the duty of maintaining his

[1] c. Cels. vi. 13.

conclusions in a later age, and with richer materials at our command. He has left us also the example of a life great, I will dare to say, by unsurpassed self-sacrifice. He has left us the encouragement of a faith which carried him through a life of martyrdom —a faith that all things are ours, because all things are Christ's.

Origen may have erred, I think he did err, on many points; but he never lost sight of the true ground and method and end of the Christian revelation, and so of Christian thought. His view of life was imperfect, but not his view of the relation of religion to life. He strove, with however many failures, to recognise all the facts of reflection and experience, and to present in an intelligible union man, the world, and GOD. In an age of conflict and weariness he was animated by the strain of unremitting labour, and the consciousness of an approaching victory. His faith was catholic, and therefore he welcomed every kind of knowledge as tributary to its fulness. His faith was living, and therefore he was assured that no age could seal any expression of doctrine as complete. From his time the best thought and the best literature of the West has been Christian, or profoundly influenced by Christianity. And still, after sixteen hundred years, we have not yet made good the positions which he marked out as belonging to the domain of Christian philosophy.

ON SOME POINTS IN BROWNING'S VIEW OF LIFE.

IN my undergraduate days, if I remember rightly, I came across the description of a poet which speaks of him as one "who sees the infinite in things." The thought has been to me from that time forward a great help in studying the noblest poetry. The true poet does, I believe, of necessity, see the infinite in his subject; and he so presents his vision to his readers that they too, if their eyes are open, are enabled in some degree to share in its lessons.

The same gift belongs in a certain degree to the artist. But the range of the poet is unlimited; while the artist's choice of subject is conditioned by the requirement that its treatment shall come within the domain of the beautiful. The ground of this difference obviously lies in the different means which the poet and the artist use to express what they see with the eyes of the soul. The mode in which words and the melody of words (not to speak now of music) affect us is different in kind from the action of form and colour.

All life, all nature, is therefore the legitimate field of the poet, as prophet. There is an infinite, an eternal, meaning in all, and it is his office to make this intelligible to his students. No modern poet has more boldly claimed the fulness of his heritage of life than Browning. He has dared to look on the darkest and meanest forms of action and passion, from which we commonly and rightly turn our eyes, and he has brought back for us from this universal survey a conviction of hope. He has laid bare what there is in man of sordid, selfish, impure, corrupt, brutish, and he proclaims in spite of every disappointment and every wound, that he still finds a spiritual power in him, answering to a spiritual power without him, which restores assurance as to the destiny of creation.

Such a survey and such a conviction command careful study; and I wish to indicate a few points in Browning's view of human life which have especially struck me—we can each see only a little of the poet's teaching—but before doing this it is necessary to emphasise this fact, that it is personal human life with which he characteristically deals by deliberate choice. "Little else," he tells us, "is worth study (than the development of a soul); I, at least, always thought so[1]." He recognises rarely, and, as it were, at a distance, the larger life of humanity[2]; but the

[1] Dedication to *Sordello*.
[2] *By the Fireside*, 50:
"Each of the many helps to recruit
The life of the race by a general plan;
Each living his own, to boot."
This thought lives in *The Boy and the Angel*.

single soul in its discipline, its progress, its aspirations, its failures, is the main object of his study, analysis, and portraiture. It has been so from first to last, in *Paracelsus*, in *Sordello*, and in the latest Dramatic Idylls.

By this choice, as has been well pointed out[1], Browning occupies a position complementary to that of Wordsworth. He looks for the revelation of the Divine as coming through the spiritual struggles of man and not through Nature. Both poets, however, agree in this, that they assert the sovereignty of feeling over knowledge, of that within us which they hold to have affinity with the heavenly and eternal, over that which must be earthly and temporal[2]. But Browning justifies the position with the fullest detail of illustration, as was natural from the current of contemporary thought which he has encountered. He never wearies of dwelling on the relativity of physical knowledge, on its inadequacy to satisfy man, on its subordinate action in the crises of moral growth. The key-note of his teaching, in a word, is not knowledge, but love.

A single passage in which he lays down the relation of love to life will serve as an introduction to the thoughts which follow:

... Life, with all it yields of joy and woe,
And hope and fear, ...

[1] Particularly in a paper by M. A. Lewis in *Macmillan* for June, 1882.

[2] *The Ring and Book, The Pope*, 1003 ff.

> Is just our chance o' the prize of learning love
> How love might be, hath been indeed, and is[1].

This learning of love, this acquisition of the power of self-sacrifice, involves a long and painful discipline:

> Life is probation, and this earth no goal,
> But starting-point of man....
> * * * * *
> To try man's foot, if it will creep or climb,
> 'Mid obstacles in seeming, points that prove
> Advantage for who vaults from low to high,
> And makes the stumbling-block a stepping-stone.
> * * * * *
> Why comes temptation but for man to meet
> And master, and make crouch beneath his foot,
> And so be pedestalled in triumph[2]?

As Browning presents the great drama of the soul, thus significantly foreshadowed, several truths seem to me to come into prominence, which I may call briefly the unity of life, the discipline of life, the continuity of life, the assurance of life. In other words, the poet teaches that life now must be treated as a whole; that learning comes through suffering; that every failure felt to be failure points to final achievement; that the visible present is but one scene in an illimitable growth. These then are the points to which I wish to call attention.

[1] *A Death in the Desert*, p. 101.
[2] *The Pope*, 1435 f.; 409 ff.; 1184 ff.

I.

Our present life is to be taken in its entirety. The discipline of man is to be fulfilled, the progress of man is to be secured, under the conditions of our complex earthly being. These lets and limitations are not to be disparaged or overborne, but accepted and used in due order. No attempt must be made either to retain that which has been or to anticipate that which will be. Each element in human nature is to be allowed its proper office. Each season brings its own work and its own means. This conception is wrought out in many-sided completeness in *Rabbi Ben Ezra,* which is, in epitome, a philosophy of life. To quote a few lines is to do injury to the perfect structure of the whole; but at least they will attract not only to the reading but to the study of it. Here are the lessons of advancing years:

> Let us not always say,
> "Spite of this flesh to-day,
> I strove, made head, gained ground upon the whole!"
> As the bird wings and sings,
> Let us cry, "All good things
> Are ours, nor soul helps flesh more now, than flesh helps soul!"

* * * * *

> Grow old along with me!
> The best is yet to be,
> The last of life, for which the first was made:
> Our times are in His hand
> Who saith, "A whole I planned,
> Youth shows but half; trust God; see all, nor be afraid."

* * * * *
> So take and use thy work!
> Amend what flaws may lurk,
> What strain o' the stuff, what warpings past the aim!
> My times be in Thy hand!
> Perfect the cup as planned!
> Let age approve of youth, and death complete the same[1].

The capacity for moral progress, thus recognised in the law of outward growth and decay, is indeed laid down by Browning to be the essential characteristic of man:

> ... Man ...
> Creeps ever on from fancies to the fact,
> And in this striving ...
> Finds progress, man's distinctive mark alone,
> Not God's, and not the beasts': God is, they are,
> Man partly is and wholly hopes to be.
> * * * * *
> Getting increase of knowledge, since he learns
> Because he lives, which is to be a man,
> Set to instruct himself by his past self[2].

Hence the mutability of things may become a help to his growth:

> Rejoice that man is hurled
> From change to change unceasingly,
> His soul's wings never furled.
> * * * * *
> There's life's pact,
> Perhaps probation—do *I* know?
> God does: endure His act![3]

[1] *Rabbi Ben Ezra*, 12, 1, 32.
[2] *A Death in the Desert*, p. 115.
[3] *James Lee*, vi. 14 f.

The very infirmities of later years, incapacity to receive new impressions, dulness of sight by which far and near are blended together, have their peculiar office in revealing the lessons of life. Thus the weird visitor, who has laid before the Duchess the trials and triumphs of the life to which she invites her, a life wholly given up that it may be received again in richer fulness, concludes:

> So at the last shall come old age,
> Decrepit as befits that stage;
> How else would'st thou retire apart
> With the hoarded memories of thy heart,
> And gather all to the very least
> Of the fragments of life's earlier feast,
> Let fall thro' eagerness to find
> The crowning dainties yet behind?
> Ponder on the entire Past
> Laid together thus at last,
> When the twilight helps to fuse
> The first fresh with the faded hues,
> And the outline of the whole,
> As round eve's shades their framework roll,
> Grandly fronts for once thy soul.
> And then as, 'mid the dark, a gleam
> Of yet another morning breaks,
> And like the hand which ends a dream,
> Death, with the might of his sunbeam,
> Touches the flesh and the soul awakes,
> Then——[1]

The true human life will therefore present a just

[1] *The flight of the Duchess*, i. 270 (compare *Transcendentalism*, i. p. 322).

balance of powers in the course of its varied progress. To make this truth more impressive by contrast, Browning has worked it out in two pairs of characters, each stamped with a real nobility and yet seen to be essentially imperfect, Aprile and Paracelsus, Lazarus and Cleon.

The complementary aspirations and failures of Aprile and Paracelsus—the absorbing undisciplined desire to love, on the one hand, and to know, on the other—are plainly and fully portrayed by the poet himself, and it is sufficient to refer to the poem of *Paracelsus*. The correspondences between Lazarus and Cleon are less obvious.

In the strangely fascinating *Epistle of Karshish* Browning has drawn the portraiture of one to whom the eternal is sensibly present, whose spirit has gained prematurely absolute predominance:

> Heaven opened to a soul while yet on earth,
> Earth forced on a soul's use while seeing Heaven[1]:

and the result is not a man but a sign; a being

> Professedly the faultier that he knows
> God's secret, while he holds the thread of life[2].

Lazarus therefore, while he moves in the world, has lost all sense of proportion in things about him, all measure of and faculty of dealing with that which sways his fellows. He has no power or will to win them to his faith, but he simply stands among men

[1] *An Epistle*, i. 337.   [2] *Id.* 339.

as a patient witness of the overwhelming reality of
the divine; a witness whose authority is confessed,
even against his inclination, by the student of nature,
who turns again and again to the phenomenon which
he affects to disparage.

In this crucial example Browning shews how the
exclusive dominance of the spirit destroys the fulness
of human life, its uses and powers, while it leaves a
passive life, crowned with an unearthly beauty. On
the other hand, he shews in his study of Cleon that
the richest results of earth in art and speculation,
and pleasure and power, are unable to remove from
life the desolation of final gloom. Thus, over against
the picture of Lazarus is placed that of the poet, who
by happy circumstance has been enabled to gather to
himself all that is highest in the civilisation of
Greece. Cleon enjoys every prize of present success,
the homage of king and fisherman, the glory of artist
and philosopher; and over all there is the oppressive
shadow of an inevitable loss. Writing "to Protus in
his tyranny," his judgment is, that he dare not accept
the view

> That imperfection means perfection hid,
> Reserved in part, to grace the after-time[1].

The wealth of man's endowment, which is understood
too late for use, seems to him to be rather a curse
than a blessing, nourishing vain hopes, and shewing
what joy man is capable of feeling, and never can

[1] *Cleon*, i. p. 417.

feel,

> The consummation coming past escape,
> When [he] shall know most and yet least enjoy[1].

The contrast is of the deepest significance. The Jewish peasant endures earth, being in possession of heaven: the Greek poet, in possession of earth, feels that heaven, some future state

> Unlimited in capability
> For joy, as this is in desire for joy,

is a necessity for man; but no,

> Zeus has not yet revealed it; and alas,
> He must have done so, were it possible!

But we must not pause to follow out the contrast into details. It is enough to see broadly that flesh and spirit each claim recognition in connexion with their proper spheres, in order that the present life may bear its true result.

We must then, in other words, that we may live human lives, loyally yield ourselves to, and yet master, the circumstances in which we are placed. This is an arduous task, but it is fruitful: "when pain ends gain ends too[2]." And the principle holds good not only in regard to the physical, but also in regard to the intellectual difficulties by which we are beset. For doubt, rightly understood, is just that vivid, personal, questioning of phenomena, which

---

[1] *Cleon*, i. p. 422.
[2] *A Death in the Desert*, p. 99.

breaks "the torpor of assurance[1]," and gives a living value to decision. In this sense, and not as if doubt were an absolution from the duty of endeavour, we can each say,

> I prize the doubt,
> Low kinds exist without,
> Finished and finite clods, untroubled by a spark[2].

Nor is it difficult to understand that the circumstances which make doubt possible answer to the necessities of our nature:

> Sun-suffused
> A cloud may soothe the eye made blind by blaze—
> Better the very clarity of heaven:
> The soft streaks are the beautiful and dear.
> What but the weakness in a faith supplies
> The incentive to humanity, no strength
> Absolute, irresistible, comports?
> How can man love but what he yearns to help?[3]

II.

In such a view of life, as is thus outlined, no room is left for indifference or neutrality. There is no surrender to an idle optimism. A part must be taken and maintained. The spirit in which Luther said *pecca fortiter* finds a powerful expression in *The*

[1] *The Pope*, 1853.
[2] *Rabbi Ben Ezra*, 3; compare *Bp. Blougram's Apology*, pp. 381, 397; *Paracelsus*, iii. p. 143; *Easter Day*, § iv.
[3] *The Pope*, 1644 ff.

Statue and the Bust:

> Let a man contend to the uttermost
> For his life's set prize, be it what it will!
> * * * * *
> And the sin I impute to each frustrate ghost
> Is, the unlit lamp and the ungirt loin[1].

And again in the concentrated and moving pathos of *The Lost Leader:*

> Best fight on well, for we taught him—strike gallantly,
> Menace our heart ere we master his own;
> Then let him receive the new knowledge and wait us,
> Pardoned in heaven, the first by the throne[2].

The erring but generous adversary of the truth must be struck down sooner or later; and he who has chosen the right side will not escape the severity of reverses. Such an one sums up his experience shortly:

> (And so) I live (you see),
> Go through the world, try, prove, reject,
> Prefer, still struggling to effect
> My warfare; happy that I can
> Be crossed and thwarted as a man,
> Not left in God's contempt apart,
> With ghastly smooth life, dead at heart[3].

Thus, in the midst of strenuous endeavour or of patient suffering, the lesson of life, the lesson of love, is brought within man's reach. It is finally taught perhaps by a sudden appeal of distress (*Caponsacchi*);

---

[1] i. p. 309.   [2] i. p. 5.
[3] *Easter Day*, xxxiii.

or by human companionship (*By the Fireside*); or by a message felt to be divine (*Easter Day*).

There are also sharper ways of enforcing the lesson. One illustration I cannot forbear quoting, for it brings out the basis of Browning's hopefulness, and combines two passages which in different ways, for grandeur of imagery and for spiritual insight, are unsurpassed in Browning—I will venture to say in literature.

I need not recall the character of Guido, which Browning has analysed with exceptional power and evidently with the deepest interest. This, at last, is the judgment which the Pope pronounces on him:

For the main criminal I have no hope
Except in such a suddenness of fate.
I stood at Naples once, a night so dark
I could have scarce conjectured there was earth
Anywhere, sky, or sea, or world at all;
But the night's black was burst through by a blaze,
Thunder struck blow on blow, earth groaned and bore
Through her whole length of mountain visible:
There lay the city thick and plain with spires,
And, like a ghost dis-shrouded, white the sea.
So may the truth be flashed out by one blow,
And Guido see, one instant, and be saved[1].

Degraded and debased, Guido is discerned to be not past hope by the true spiritual eye. And what is the issue? Up to the last, with fresh kindled passion, the great criminal reasserts his hate. He gathers his

[1] *The Pope*, 2116 ff.

strength to repeat his crime in will. I grow, he says, one gorge

> To loathingly reject Pompilia's pale
> Poison my hasty hunger took for food.

So the end comes. The ministers of death claim him. In his agony he summons every helper whom he has known or heard of—

> Abate, Cardinal, Christ, Maria, God—

and then the light breaks through the blackest gloom:

> Pompilia, will you let them murder me[1]?

In this supreme moment he has known what love is, and, knowing it, has begun to feel it. The cry, like the intercession of the rich man in Hades for his five brethren, is a promise of a far-off deliverance.

In this case the poet shews how we may take heart again in looking on the tragedies of guilt. But there are wider and more general sorrows in life. There is the failure, the falling from our ideal, of which we are all conscious; there is the incompleteness of opportunity, which leaves noblest powers unused. Browning states the facts without reserve or palliation:

> All labour, yet no less
> Bear up beneath their unsuccess.
> Look at the end of work, contrast
> The petty Done, the Undone vast,

---

[1] *Guido* (2), 2425 f.

> This Present of theirs with the hopeful Past!
> What hand and brain went ever paired?
> What heart alike conceived and dared?
> What act proved all its thought had been?
> What will but felt the fleshy screen?[1]

> In this world, who can do a thing will not;
> And who would do it, cannot, I perceive:
> Yet the will's somewhat—somewhat, too, the power—
> And thus we half-men struggle[2].

In dealing with the difficulties which are thus raised, Browning offers what appears to me to be his most striking message. Acknowledged failure is, he teaches, a promise of future attainment; unfruitful preparation is the sign of the continuity of life. And these two principles rest upon another: imperfection is the condition of growth:

> Let the mere star-fish in his vault
>   Crawl in a wash of weed, indeed,
> Rose-jacynth to the finger-tips:
>   He, whole in body and soul, outstrips
> Man, found with either in default.
> But what's whole can increase no more,
>   Is dwarfed and dies, since here's its sphere[3].

And hence comes (as may be noticed parenthetically) the contrast between works of art and living men:

> They are perfect—how else? they shall never change:
> We are faulty—why not? we have time in store.

---

[1] *The Last Ride together*, v. vi.

[2] *Andrea del Sarto*, i. p. 364.

[3] *Dis aliter visum*, 28 f.

The artificer's hand is not arrested
  With us—we are rough-hewn, nowise polished:
They stand for our copy, and once invested
  With all they can teach, we shall see them abolished.
'Tis a life-long toil till our lump be leaven;
  The better! what's come to perfection perishes[1].

Perhaps we can all readily acquiesce in the fact of imperfection; but the consideration of failure is more complicated. Failure, as Browning treats it, may come in two ways. It may come from what he does not scruple to call "the corruption of man's heart[2]," or it may come from the want of necessary external help. The first form of failure is in various degrees universal. But as long as effort is directed to the highest, that aim, though it is out of reach, is the standard of hope. The existence of a capacity, cherished and quickened, is a pledge that it will find scope. The punishment of the man who has fixed all his thoughts upon earth, a punishment felt on reflection to be overwhelming in view of the possibilities of humanity, is the completest gratification of desires unworthily limited:

> Thou art shut
> Out of the heaven of spirit; glut
> Thy sense upon the world; 'tis thine
> For ever—take it![3]

On the other hand, the soul which has found in

---

[1] *Old Pictures at Florence*, xvi. f.
[2] *A legend of Pornic*, 20.
[3] *Easter Day*, xx.

success not rest but a starting-point, which refuses to see in the first fruits of a partial victory the fulness of its rightful triumph, has ever before it a sustaining and elevating vision:

> What stops my despair?
> This:—'tis not what man Does which exalts him, but what man Would do![1]
>
> All I could never be,
> All, men ignored in me,
> This, I was worth to God, whose wheel the pitcher shaped.
>
> Then welcome each rebuff
> That turns earth's smoothness rough,
> Each sting that bids nor sit nor stand but go!
> Be our joys three-parts pain!
> Strive, and hold cheap the strain;
> Learn, nor account the pang; dare, never grudge the throe!
>
> For thence—a paradox
> Which comforts while it mocks—
> Shall life succeed in that it seems to fail:
> What I aspired to be,
> And was not, comforts me;
> A brute I might have been, but would not sink i' the scale[2].

So far the cause of failure lies mainly in the man himself. He is conscious of a potency, a promise unfulfilled, and he trusts to Him who gave it for fulfilment. But the failure may lie in those for

[1] *Saul*, xviii. [2] *Rabbi Ben Ezra*, 25, 6, 7.

whom the patriot, or the lover, or the poet works and
suffers. Even so the assurance is the same:

> "Paid by the World—what dost thou owe
> Me?" God might question: now instead,
> 'Tis God shall repay! I am safer so[1].

> If you loved only what were worth your love,
> Love were clear gain, and wholly well for you;
> Make the low nature better by your throes!
> Give earth yourself, go up for gain above![2]

> His [God's] clenched Hand shall unclose at last,
>   I know, and let out all the beauty;
> My poet holds the Future fast,
>   Accepts the coming ages' duty,
> Their Present for this Past[3].

Meanwhile the work, even as it has been accomplished, does not perish from the earth. Of him who has striven faithfully, the words supposed to be addressed by David to Saul are true in due measure:

>   Each deed thou hast done
> Dies, revives, goes to work in the world...so, each ray of thy will,
> Every flash of thy passion and prowess, long over, shall thrill
> Thy whole people, the countless, with ardour, till they too give forth
> A like cheer to their sons: who in turn fill the South and the North
> With the radiance thy deed was the germ of[4].

[1] *The Patriot*, vi.   [2] *James Lee*, vii. 2.
[3] *Popularity*, iii.
[4] *Saul*, xiii.   Compare *Sordello*, iii. p. 416.

III.

But while Browning recognises the reality and the glory of this subjective. immortality, he has shewn elsewhere, in *Cleon*, that it is wholly inadequate to satisfy the heart of man. He assumes, therefore, in these various studies of imperfection and failure, as prophetic of progress and attainment, the continuity of personal life through death. In such a continuity of being he also finds the assurance of the full use of powers disciplined but not called into play on earth.

There is, perhaps, little in the literary history of the Renaissance to justify the picture which Browning has drawn, in *The Grammarian's Funeral*, of the perfect self-sacrifice of the scholar as realised then. But the thoughts expressed in the poem find a partial embodiment at all times. A large proportion of a student's labour must - be in preparation for tasks which he cannot accomplish. His material may remain for others; but the experience, the insight, the delicate tact, the accumulated enthusiasm which he has gained in long years, pass away with him. The example, indeed, abides for us; but this is not all. There will yet be, as we believe, a field for the exercise of every power which has been trained and not called into service. What has been consecrated cannot be wasted:

Yea, this in him was the peculiar grace
*   *   *   *   *
That before living he'd learn how to live—
    No end to learning:

> Earn the means first—God surely will contrive
>   Use for our earning.
> Others mistrust and say, "But time escapes!
>   Live now or never!"
> He said, "What's time? Leave Now for dogs and apes!
>   Man has Forever."
> Was it not great? did not he throw on God
>   (He loves the burthen)—
> God's task to make the heavenly period
>   Perfect the earthen?
> Did not he magnify the mind, shew clear
>   Just what it all meant?
> He would not discount life, as fools do here,
>   Paid by instalment[1].

But the preparation and discipline of intellect is subordinate to the preparation and discipline of feeling. The end of life is, as we have seen, the learning love—the learning God—and that in a large degree through human fellowship. *Omne vivum ex vivo*— "life is the one source of life"—is an axiom true in the spiritual as in the physical order. An intellectual result may be the occasion, but it cannot be the source of a moral quickening. Man's spirit enters into communion with the Spirit of God directly, or with the Spirit of God acting through men. A soul meets the soul which its nature needs, and receives its quickening influence; and this is its confession:

> Life will just hold out the proving
>   Both our powers, alone and blended;

---

[1] *A Grammarian's Funeral*, i. pp. 281 ff.

And then, come the next life quickly!
This world's use will have been ended[1].

And so again, in the enjoyment of a perfect sympathy the poet can say:

My own, see where the years conduct!
At first, 'twas something our two souls
Should mix as mists do; each is sucked
In each now; on, the new stream rolls,
Whatever rocks obstruct[2].

This happy issue, however, is not always gained. The soul may recognise its need and also that which will satisfy it, and yet fail to gain what is wanting. And what then? Is all the fruit of self-questioning, and self-devotion, and self-surrender to be lost? *Evelyn Hope* is the answer. The lover, by the side of the dead girl who could not have known his love, replies for us:

No, indeed! for God above
Is great to grant, as mighty to make,
And creates the love to reward the love:
I claim you still, for my own love's sake!
Delayed it may be for more lives yet,
Through worlds I shall traverse, not a few:
Much is to learn, much to forget
Ere the time be come for taking you.
So hush,—I give you this leaf to keep—
See, I shut it inside the sweet, cold hand!
There, that is our secret; go to sleep!
You will wake, and remember, and understand[3].

---

[1] *Cristina*, viii. Compare v.   [2] *By the Fireside*, xxvi.
[3] *Evelyn Hope*, iv. vii. Contrast *Too Late*, D.P. 57 ff.

IV.

Here we might well stop. We have followed in outline the thoughts which Browning offers to us on the unity of life, the discipline of life, the continuity of life, a unity which enables us to regard every condition of labour as contributing to its efficiency, a discipline which, through spiritual intercourse, fashions us to the Divine likeness, a continuity which abides through cycles of change passing all imagination. The unity, the discipline, the continuity rest upon and express that Divine Love, of which love in man is at once the offspring and the evidence. So we rise to the highest:

Do I find love so full in my nature, God's ultimate gift,
That I doubt His own love can compete with it? here, the parts shift?
Here, the creature surpass the Creator,—the end, what Began?

*   *   *   *   *   *

I believe it! 'tis Thou, God, that givest, 'tis I who receive;
In the first is the last, in Thy will is my power to believe.

*   *   *   *   *   *

Would I suffer for him that I love?—so would'st thou —so wilt thou!
So shall crown thee the topmost, ineffablest, uttermost crown—
And thy love fill infinitude wholly, nor leave up nor down
One spot for the creature to stand in[1]!

[1] *Saul*, i. ff. 93.

BROWNING'S VIEW OF LIFE. 275

> So, through the thunder comes a human voice
> Saying: "O heart I made, a heart beats here!
> Face, My hands fashioned, see it in Myself,
> Thou hast no power, nor may'st conceive of Mine,
> But love I gave thee, with Myself to love,
> And thou must love Me who have died for thee[1]!"

And what does the poet say of the end? For that which is evil there is judgment of utter destruction; for that which is good, purifying. So it is that chastisement is often seen to come through the noblest part of a character otherwise mean, because in that there is yet hope:

> You were punished in the very part
> That looked most pure of speck,—the honest love
> Betrayed you,—did love seem most worthy pains,
> Challenge such purging, as ordained survive
> When all the rest of you was done with[2]?"

And on the whole:

> There shall never be one lost good! What was shall live as before;
> The evil is null, is nought, is silence implying sound;
> What was good shall be good with, for evil, so much good more;
> On the earth the broken arcs: in the heaven a perfect round.
>
> The high that proved too high, the heroic for earth too hard,
> The passion that left the ground to lose itself in the sky,

[1] *An Epistle*, i. 343. [2] *The Pope*, 1229 ff.

Are music sent up to God by the lover and the bard;
  Enough that He heard it once; we shall hear it by-and-by.

And what is our failure here but a triumph's evidence
  For the fulness of the days[1]?

   My own hope is, a sun will pierce
     The thickest cloud earth ever stretched;
   That, after Last, returns the First,
     Though a wide compass round be fetched;
   That what began best, can't end worst,
     Nor what God blessed once, prove accurst[2].

These thoughts, which I have endeavoured simply to set forth and not to criticise, come to us in the words of our own time. They are clothed in images which are familiar to our own experience. Our hearts in the main, I believe, respond to them as interpreting the fulness of our lives, our trials, and falls, and aspirations; as expressing our trust through disappointment, and our ideal aims in spite of imperfection. And, as it seems to me, they help us to understand better, that is with a more real and vital intelligence, some parts of our Faith in which alone, as far as I can see, they find their solid foundation.

[1] *Abt. Vogler*, ix. ff.   [2] *Apparent Failure*, vii.

THE RELATION OF CHRISTIANITY TO ART.

ἐκ μεγέθους καλλονῆς κτισμάτων ἀναλόγως
ὁ γενεσιουργός αὐτῶν θεωρεῖται.

WISD. xiii. 5.

NO student of the apostolic writings can fail to find himself sometimes confronted by the question Does the teaching of the New Testament cover all the interests of human life? and more particularly Does the New Testament, does Christianity as laid down there in its broad outlines, leave scope for the free development of Art? This latter question deserves consideration. It is not enough that it should have been practically answered by general consent: the answer thus given includes many elements which tend at least to create misgivings as to its soundness; and it is, superficially at least, in conflict with the most prominent utterances of early Christian feeling. The main issue is not whether the Christian spirit encourages that temper which is the strength of the artist, but whether it recognises his work as contributory to the fulfilment of man's destiny. There can be no doubt that truth, sympathy, reverence, will characterise all effort which deserves the name of Christian; but it is not at once obvious that in the face of the overwhelming moral problems of life Christian effort can be properly directed to the pursuit of Art.

Thus there is the suggestion if not the distinct appearance of a conflict between man's constitution and the Gospel. He is born with artistic instincts and powers; and these, it may be alleged, are not directly taken into account by the records of the Faith.

The apparent contrast requires to be stated a little more in detail.

On the one side it is certain that Art corresponds with essential parts of our nature. Men universally seek particular combinations of form, colour, sound; and the pleasure which these give can be deepened and extended through the study of the principles by which they are ruled. Men can be trained to a keener and finer perception of beauty. There is then here a force of influence which cannot be overlooked in the discipline of life.

And more than this, the complex scene in which we are placed requires to be revealed to us. We are not at once able to enter into the manifold aspects of Nature which we can recognise when they are pointed out. There is something of disorder and disproportion in the impression which we first receive from the world about us. The "form" of things needs some interpretation; and the particular interpretation which we adopt has helped and will help to make us what we are and what we shall be.

For the physical effects which Art produces exercise a profound moral and spiritual influence upon character. It is unnecessary to attempt to make any comparison of the relative power of external nature and society upon the education of the soul. It is enough that both have their due office in moulding the ideal man. Remove the discipline of one or the other, and the man is weaker and poorer however successfully he cultivates the self-centred virtues on which he has concentrated himself. It may be necessary to "cut off the right hand" or to "pluck out the right eye," but he who is forced to do so enters into life "maimed."

This expressive image seems to carry with it a full recognition of the manifold activities of eye and hand, of the power of seeing beauty and setting it forth, as belonging to the completeness of man. And if under the actual conditions of life it is through sense, which Art uses as its organ, that the most obvious and universal dangers come to men, the natural conclusion seems to be that this fact shews convincingly the paramount importance of the study of Art. In this region we need peculiarly to be trained in order that we may enjoy rightly; and not be called upon to sacrifice that which was capable of ministering to a richer service.

Such reflections, indicated in the briefest summary, serve to shew that Art justly claims a permanent place in the highest training of men; but on the other hand it may be urged that, with the exception of music, there is no recognition of the office of Art in the New Testament. One or two illustrations from engraving (Hebr. i. 3) or painting (Hebr. viii. 5; x. 1) are all that it contains. The imagery of the Apocalypse—as the cubic city (Apoc. xxi. 16)—is symbolic and not pictorial.

And not only so, but it seems as if representative Art were distinctly condemned. It is difficult to give any sense to "the desire of the eyes," which St John declares to be "not of the Father but of the world" (1 John ii. 16), which shall not include works of sculpture and painting; and at first sight the revelation of the transitoriness of that out of which they spring appears to carry with it the sentence of their rejection.

Nor can any stress be laid upon the partial recognition of the service of Art in the Old Testament. The system of the old Covenant was essentially external. It spoke through symbols. But it might be argued, not unreasonably, that, as Christianity is essentially spiritual, it is likely that it would be independent of all illustrations from Art.

These are the elements of the contrast which have to be reconciled. The reconciliation, to anticipate the result of our inquiry, lies in the central message of Christianity, "the Word became flesh." By that fact the harmony between the seen and the unseen

CHRISTIANITY TO ART. 281

which had been interrupted was potentially restored. Creation in all its parts was made known as a revelation of Him through whom it was called into being. But the reconciliation here as elsewhere lies in transfiguration. The passage to life is through death. The old had to pass away that the new might find its proper place. This truth has even now not been fully mastered; but it will be seen more clearly if we first consider the position of Art in relation to Christianity in the apostolic age (I), and the character of Christian Art in the first four centuries (II), and then attempt to determine the relation of Christianity to Art (III), and the peculiar office of Art (IV).

I.

The position of the early Christian teachers towards Art was determined under two powerful and conflicting influences. In no other region of human activity were the Shemitic and Hellenic tendencies more directly at variance. Each bore witness to a partial truth; and in the apostolic age each had reached its complete development.

For the Jews imitative Art had practically no public existence. In the absence of satisfactory evidence it is impossible to say how far Architecture and Music found free and characteristic expression. But in spite of the very narrow range within which Jewish Art was confined it embodied a principle which enters into the life of Art. The commandment which forbade the making of any graven image or likeness was not observed in the Sanctuary itself. By this exception it was made evident that the enactment was directed against accidental abuses of imitative Art and not against the Art itself. At the same time the manner in which Art was employed served to embody another thought. The description of the decorations of the Tabernacle and of the Temple brings out plainly the idea that representations of outward things, and the manifold combination of materials, which found place there, were designed to suggest more than the simple figure or effect. Whatever there was of grandeur or beauty in "the ordinances of divine service" pointed beyond itself. Natural forms and elements were used to indicate the unseen. How this could be is still powerfully shewn in the works of Egyptian Art, which constrain the spectator to rise beyond that which he looks upon to something which can find no adequate expression externally. The figures of gods and men alike—Pasht or Rameses—are above all things symbols of character. They cannot be taken simply as efforts to present direct and complete portraitures of the beings whom they call up before the soul. Later experience indeed proved that there were possibilities of deep corruption in the promiscuous use of such images of the mysteries of life as were presented in the accompaniments of Egyptian worship. The conception was noble but it was unfitted for common use. So it was that the sacred legislation of Israel kept the conception and guarded it jealously. The employment of the symbolic figures in the sanctuary of the Temple, by emphasizing this exception to the general law[1], kept the Jew from the desecration of the symbol, and preserved for him in its purity the thought which it enshrined. He learnt from the records of the Old Testament that it was the Divine will that in the unapproachable darkness of the Holy of Holies the costliest works of Art should render service before the revealed Presence of the Lord. No human eye could rightfully ever again trace the lineaments of those cherubim and palm-trees and open flowers when they were once placed in the oracle, but it was enough to know that they were there. In no other way could the Truth be more eloquently or solemnly enforced that the end of Art is to witness to the inner life of Nature and to minister to GOD. The repetition of the forms in the Holy place kept the memory of them fresh in the minds of the priests[2]. Their significance could not be mistaken. By that offering of the best which he could command simply for the Divine glory Solomon declared to his people for all time the consecration of Art, and he declared not obscurely that

[1] The twelve oxen which supported the Molten Sea in Solomon's Temple (1 K. vii. 25; 2 Chron. iv. 4 f.; Jer. lii. 20) are a perplexing exception to the law. The twelve lions on the steps of the royal throne (1 K. x. 18 ff.; 2 Chron. ix. 18 f.) form a corresponding exception in the civil use of Art. The Brazen Serpent was a work of a wholly different order; as also was "the Teraphim" of David (1 Sam. xix. 13).

[2] According to 2 Chron. iii. 14, cherubim were wrought on the veil.

it is the office of Art to reveal the meaning of that which is the object of sense. Circumstances delayed for ages the fruitfulness of the idea; but it remained and remains still; and few can think of all that was implied by the adornment of that august chamber lighted only by the splendour of a manifested Presence of GOD or the glow of the kindled incense (Apoc. v. 8) without feeling that it has a lesson for those to whom Art is appointed work. Philosophers and poets have dwelt often upon the veiled statue at Sais: there is an open secret in the sacred gloom of the Holy of Holies more sublime and more inspiring.

The Jewish repression of imitative Art, which the Law still hallowed for the highest service, corresponded with the spiritual conception of GOD which was the endowment of His "people." Spiritual Religion could not at that stage of its development admit the habitual use of painting or sculpture. With the Greeks on the other hand imitative Art was the characteristic embodiment of the Nature worship which underlay their life. The form of beauty was for them not the symbol but the direct representation of the godlike. The statue was the final expression of the artist's thought, and his consummate skill enabled the spectator to rest in it. Humanity was made the measure of the divine; and under these conditions anthropomorphism became a fatal temptation. At the same time Greek Art, if premature and perilous in regard to the complete spiritual training of man, witnessed to a part of the truth affirmed in the record of Creation which is most commonly forgotten. The form of man, the visible expression of what he is essentially embodied under the conditions of time, answers to "the image of GOD" in which he was made. So far the Greek was right in seeking for traits of divinity in human beauty. The source of error, from which flowed the stream of later corruption, was that he regarded these as fixed and final. He failed, necessarily failed in the way of nature, to claim recognition for the fulness of the truth that man made in the image of GOD has to grow into His likeness: that all that is noblest in form or present embodiment is preparatory to something yet unseen and higher: that Art in its greatest achievements must be prophetic, must not rest in a victory but reveal that which is unattained[1].

It would be difficult to overrate the skill with which Greek sculpture of the best period represents strength in majestic repose, and feeling under sovereign control; but all, so to speak, lies within the figure before us. "The gods have come down to us in the likeness of men;" and we look no further. At first the spiritual, religious element is supreme, as in all living Art; but with the decay of faith that which is sensuous usurps the place of the spiritual, and Art which takes man as the standard of the divine cannot

[1] This is only one application of the general law that man cannot find rest in the finite. The key to the understanding of Ecclesiastes lies in the recognition of this truth which the Book illustrates from many sides. Comp. Eccles. iii. 11.

but fall. A single illustration will be sufficient to indicate my meaning. This is given in a crucial shape by the treatment of Aphrodite in the earlier and later schools. The physical beauty of the Medicean Venus has lost all the pure sovereign majesty of the Aphrodite of Melos, which is worthy to be an ideal of "woman before the Fall [1]."

It is unnecessary to trace the decay of Greek Art. It retained to the last the gift of physical beauty, but in the apostolic age it had become the servant of the luxury of the Empire. Starting from a human ideal it became enslaved to man. So far as it had a place in popular worship it brought down the divine to the level of a corrupt life.

This being so the antagonism of early Christians to contemporary Art was necessarily essential and absolute. Before Art could be placed in its true position there was need of a complete change of centre. For this the stern discipline of Judaism had made provision. The lesson of consecration which had been kept in silent witness for long ages could be applied now that "the Word had become flesh." By that fact a new meaning was given to the beauty which the Greek artist had felt for, and an immeasurable scope was opened for the ministry of nature to GOD which the Jewish legislator had declared in symbols. But death is the condition of resurrection. There is indeed a continuity through death; but a

---

[1] Kraus (F. X.), *Die Christliche Kunst*, s. 22.

formal severance from the past was the prelude to the new birth of Christian Art.

II.

It will be seen from what has been already said that Christianity had to recognise and reconcile the partial and contrasted aspects of imitative Art which had found expression in Judaism and Hellenism. Christian Art embodies the twofold conception of the spiritual destiny of the visible, and of a spiritual revelation through the visible. The central fact of the Christian Faith gives a solid unity to both truths.

The realisation of such an idea of Art can of necessity only come slowly and through the course of life, not by any definite and conscious effort but in the gradual conquest of humanity. The beginning was made when St Paul established Christian Churches in Ephesus, Athens, Corinth, and Rome. The end is still far off, even if it has come from age to age more clearly into view. When the Church first appeared openly in the Empire it had already the outlines of a system of Art which had been drawn in the times of darkness and suffering. In the first stage of such a progress the inspiring thought is supreme: the perfection of form comes later.

It is however extremely difficult to trace the course of Christian Art in the ante-Nicene age. The literary evidence is extremely scanty; and it naturally deals for the most part with the dangers and abuses of popular Art. Even in the present age little could be gathered as to the place which is occupied by Art in ordinary Christian life from the works of theological controversy and general instruction. But the stern warnings of a man like Tertullian are evidently directed against influences and practices which he felt to be powerful if not dominant. Christian artists did not scruple to continue their profession even when they were admitted to the ministry[1]. The painter Hermogenes is condemned for the use which he made of his art, but the art itself is not proscribed[2]. It may also be fairly concluded from the denunciations of female luxury that other adornments of life besides rich dresses and jewels found admission into Christian households; and excess and extravagance imply a temperate use. It is also of interest to notice that Tertullian mentions incidentally "paintings on chalices[3]," and in especial the image of "the Shepherd," which he speaks of as a usual subject[4].

The scanty notices of Christian Art at Alexandria are of the same character as those in Tertullian. The

---

[1] Tertull. de idol. 3 ff., adleguntur in ordinem ecclesiasticum artifices idolorum. Comp. de spectac. 23. A Christian sculptor is represented at his work on a sarcophagus assigned by De' Rossi to the third century. See Northcote and Brownlow, ii. p. 236. The subject was first engraved by Fabretti, *Inscr. Ant. N.* cii. p. 587, who describes the sarcophagus as "ex cœmeterio Helenæ."

[2] Tertull. adv. Hermog. i. pingit illicite, that is, by painting pagan subjects.

[3] de Pudic. c. 7, picturæ calicum.

[4] *id.* c. 10, pastor quem in calice depingis.

CHRISTIANITY TO ART. 289

language of Clement shews clearly that many Christians did not scruple to wear heathen gems; and when he defines the subjects which might rightly be admitted in consideration of their typical significance, he accepts a principle which is capable of a very wide application[1].

At the same time it is evident from Origen's eloquent vindication of the spiritual service of Christians—the spiritual altar, and sacrifices and images of GOD—that no religious use was as yet publicly made of imitative Art[2]. Nor can it be doubted that the feeling of the great teachers of the African Churches was decidedly adverse to the pursuit of Art[3]. The influence of Judaism was so far prevailing. Local circumstances probably in this case checked what might have been expected to be the natural result of Alexandrine thought.

The position of the Italian, and specially of the Roman Church, seems to have been somewhat different. Among the earliest Italian converts were members of noble families who brought with them the influence of cultivated taste, and at once found a place for the ministry of Art. But here again the evidence is limited in range. It is derived almost exclusively from paintings in the Catacombs, and mainly from the Catacombs of Rome; so that the simplest remains of Christian Art are necessarily con-

[1] Clem. Alex. Pæd. iii. 11, § 59, p. 289 P.
[2] Orig. adv. Cels. viii. 17 ff. Comp. de Orat. 17.
[3] Clem. Alex. Protr. i. § 62, p. 54 P.

fined in scope. They throw no light upon its domestic use, nor do they furnish any measure of its actual extent in subject or in prosecution. Moreover many of the paintings have been retouched at later times, and some which are commonly reckoned among the earliest are of uncertain antiquity.

In spite of these drawbacks however the paintings in the Catacombs appear to give a fair representation of the character and spirit of Christian Art in Italy. They extend in date over the whole history of the early Church, though the earliest works are very few, from the beginning of the second century onwards, and include works of the greatest rudeness and of high artistic merit.

The earliest Roman example which is known, the decorations of the most ancient part of the cemetery which bears the name of Flavia Domitilla, are, as it appears, a unique monument of the primitive patrician Church of the Imperial City. In this case it may be supposed that the converts had the means for readily securing the services of a good artist, and an impartial judge pronounces the work to be such as would not discredit a painter of the best age[1]. Both in general style and subject these decorations closely resemble contemporary pagan works, but there are sufficient traces of characteristic subjects to establish their Christian origin[2].

[1] Mommsen, *Cont. Rev.* May 1871, p. 170.

[2] Northcote and Brownlow, ii. 120 ff. Garrucci, *Storia dell' Arte Cristiana*, I. 19.

CHRISTIANITY TO ART. 291

The decorations of the Catacombs of St Januarius at Naples and of chambers in the cemetery of St Callixtus at Rome are even more completely classical in treatment. The artist acting under Christian instruction has followed as far as he could the custom of his time, using freely conventional ornaments, birds and flowers and masks, which were consistent with Christian feeling, and introducing subjects which marked the faith of those for whom he worked[1].

[1] Schultze, *Die Katakomben*, 90 ff.; Garrucci, Tavv. 90—98.
Northcote and Brownlow, ii. pp. 18 ff.; Garrucci, Tav. 26. Compare Garrucci, Tavv. 13, 20, 37, 38, 88 for other examples of a classical type, and the beautiful pagan decorations of the tomb in the Via Latina (Parker, *Tombs*, pl. xiv. ff.).

The following classical subjects may be specially noticed:
ORPHEUS.

S. Domitilla, Northcote and Brownlow, p. 31.
S. Callixtus, North. and Br. *Pl.* xviii. 2 (as Good Shepherd). Bottari, lxxi.
The figure occurs also on a Lamp, D.C.A. 922.
PSYCHE.

S. Domitilla, North. and Br. 33; Schultze, *Die Katakomben*, 98.
S. Gennaro, Naples. Schultze, *Tab.* v.; id. *Die Kat.* s. 93. Compare North. and Br. p. 239 (sarcophagus).
DIOSCURI.

Arles; sarcophagus. LeBlant, *Les Sarc. Chrét. d'Arles*, xxiii.
ULYSSES and the SIRENS.

Crypt of Lucina: sarcophagus: North. and Br. p. 240.

A very remarkable series of scenes from the Gospel History is found in the Catacomb of Prætextatus. They are unfortunately only imperfectly known. From the drawings published by Garrucci, they appear to represent (1) Christ

The other examples of painting in the Roman Catacombs are of inferior artistic merit, being provided by poorer converts. But the same general features are preserved throughout. Christians used as far as they could the resources of popular art, and even adopted some current subjects which were capable of a Christian interpretation. There was no chasm of separation between Christianity and Art except that which was fixed by the ordinary subservience of Art to idolatrous purposes[1].

At the beginning of the fourth century, when the

and the woman of Samaria; (2) The healing of the woman with the Issue; (3) The Baptism. The last subject is debated, but De' Rossi's idea that it represents the striking of the Lord with the reed is wholly at variance with the cycle of subjects in early Art, and with the appearance of the dove in the picture.

The drawing seems to be singularly good; and the figure of the Lord is of a youthful classical type. Schultze, *Die Kat.* 145; North. and Br. 143 ff.

Schultze points out that Christian artists borrowed ornamental figures from classical myths which embodied beliefs about the dead: a. a. O. 98 ff.

[1] *E.g.* Garrucci, Tavv. 8, 12. None of the groups of figures seem to shew real artistic merit, unless it be the Madonna in the Cemetery of Priscilla as interpreted in Northcote and Brownlow, ii. pl. vii.; yet contrast the photograph in Parker's *Catacombs*, pl. ii.

The marvellously beautiful group of the Shepherd and the Sheep in the tomb of Statilius Taurus (B.C. 30) is wholly unapproached by any Christian work. Parker, *Tombs in and near Rome*, pl. xix.

There are examples of decorations in Jewish and Mithraic

Christian Society had emerged from obscurity and began to erect dignified places for worship, it was natural that Christians should introduce into their churches the Art which had decorated their tombs. The famous Canon of the Synod of Elvira was evidently not directed against a prospective or imaginary danger, but against an actual and probably a growing practice. There can be no real doubt as to its meaning, whatever opinion may be held as to its wisdom and its authority. The Synod absolutely forbids the painting of pictures on the walls of churches, in order to guard against the representation of the objects of worship[1]. Primitive feeling shrank, most justly, I believe, from the portraiture of Divine Persons. Perhaps there were already symptoms that this reserve was likely to be broken. So it seemed better to exclude pictures from the churches altogether than to run the risk of injuring the sensibility of faith.

There was perhaps something of the sternness of African Christianity in the Canon of Elvira. It may have been called for by peculiar local perils. It is

tombs closely analogous to those of the Christian tombs: Garrucci, Tavv. 493 ff.

[1] Conc. Illib. Can. 36. *Ne picturæ in ecclesia fiant.* Placuit picturas in ecclesia esse non debere, ne quod colitur et adoratur in parietibus depingatur. Comp. Dale, *Synod of Elvira*, p. 289 n.

The Canon is most strangely quoted by Northcote and Brownlow (ii. p. 4) as "one which forbad 'pictures to be placed in a church, or that which is worshipped and adored to be painted on the walls.'"

therefore of more interest to notice a similar expression of feeling from an opposite quarter. This is found in a letter addressed by Eusebius of Cæsarea to the Empress Constantia, which was brought forward at the Second Council of Nicæa. In this Eusebius seems to speak according to the general feeling of the time. The empress had requested a likeness (εἰκών) of Christ. What do you mean by a likeness of Christ? is the answer of Eusebius. Not of course the image of Him as He is truly and unchangeably; nor yet of His human nature as it has been glorified, of which the overpowering splendour of the Transfiguration offered some pledge and likeness. It must then be an image of the frail mortal flesh which He bore before His Ascension. But such images are forbidden by the Mosaic Law. They are nowhere to be found in churches; and it is notorious that with us alone they are forbidden. "Some poor woman," he goes on to say, " brought to me two painted figures, like philosophers, and ventured to say that they represented Paul and the Saviour; I do not know on what ground. But to save her and others from offence, I took them from her and kept them by me, not thinking it right in any case that she should exhibit them further (εἰς ἑτέρους ὅλως ἐκφέρειν), that we may not seem like idolaters to carry our GOD about in an image." The images of Simon Magus and Mani may be worshipped by their followers. "But such objects are forbidden us. Since we confess that our Saviour is GOD and Lord we prepare ourselves to see Him as

GOD, using all zeal to purify our own hearts, that if so be when purified we may see Him. For *Blessed are the pure in heart because they shall see God.* And if in addition to this hope (ἐκ περιουσίας) before that vision which shall be 'face to face' you set high value on the images of the Saviour, what better artist can there be than the GOD-WORD Himself[1]?"

Such judgments were however unable to stem the tide of popular feeling which soon set in. The revolution in the Empire, which was marked and crowned by the conversion of Constantine, introduced new and perilous elements into the Christian body. The intense spirituality of the first ages was lost. Paganism passed not yet wholly conquered under the yoke of the Church. Within less than a century the representations of sacred scenes obtained for good and evil a recognised place in Christian sanctuaries. The innovation was not accomplished without resistance. The familiar anecdote of Epiphanius († 402) is a kind of summary of the controversy. This zealous and rigid bishop when visiting a village church in Palestine found there a veil "bearing a fanciful image of Christ (imaginem quasi Christi) or some Saint," for this detail he could not remember. He at once tore it asunder, and ordered the guardians of the church where it hung to use it for the shroud of a pauper. Nor was any further remonstrance made than that he should supply a new one, which he did through the Bishop of Jerusalem, begging him to warn the priest

[1] Euseb. Ep. ad Const. Migne, *Patrol. Gr.* xx. 1515 ff.

in charge of the church not to hang there veils, "which are contrary to the Christian religion[1]."

But in spite of such isolated action, and the traditional practice by which it was supported, pictures found a recognised place in sacred buildings even in the lifetime of Epiphanius. Three illustrations will be sufficient to shew how far their use was extended in the West and in the East. Paulinus († 431), who was a scholar of Ausonius and of consular rank, devoted himself and his fortune to the service of the Church. He took for his special hero Felix, a martyr of Nola, whose grave he decorated with noble buildings while he celebrated his praises in a long series of poems. In one of these he describes in some detail the pictures with which he had adorned the cloister of the church[2]. The series included the events of the Pentateuch, and of the Historical Books of the Old Testament[3]. By means of these representations he

[1] Epiph. Epist. ad Joann. Hier. § ix. (iii. 390, ed. Migne).
[2] xxvii. (De S. Felice carm. natal. ix.) 511 ff.
Nunc volo picturas fucatis agmine longo
Porticibus videas, paulumque supina fatiges
Colla, reclinato dum perlegis omnia vultu.
[3] Qui videt hæc vacuis agnoscens vera figuris
Non vacua fidam sibi pascet imagine mentem.
Omnia namque tenet serie pictura fideli
Quæ senior scripsit per quinque volumina Moses,
Quæ gessit Domini signatus nomine Iesus...
Jam distinguentem modico Ruth tempora libro,
Tempora Judicibus finita et Regibus orta,
Intentis transcurre oculis: brevis ista videtur
Historia, et magni signat mysteria belli... *id.* 514 ff.

hoped to attract and instruct the crowds of ignorant rustics who visited the shrine of St Felix[1]. Each scene had, as he describes it, a certain fitness for enforcing some particular lesson, the new creation, the offering of Isaac, the continence of Joseph, the overthrow of Pharaoh[2], the separation of Ruth and Orpah[3]. He admits that the experiment was an unusual one[4]; and it does not appear that he introduced into his decorations any scenes from the Gospel history. His language indeed implies that he shared to some extent the feeling expressed by Eusebius as to representations of the Lord[5].

[1] Propterea visum nobis opus utile, totis
Felicis domibus pictura illudere sancta;
Si forte attonitas hæc per spectacula mentes
Agrestum caperet fucata coloribus umbra,
Quæ super exprimitur titulis ut littera monstret
Quod manus explicuit...   *id.* 580 ff.

[2] De genesi, precor, hunc orandi collige sensum,
Ne maneam terrenus Adam...
Hostia viva Deo tanquam puer offerar Isac...
Sit mihi castus amor, sit et horror amoris iniqui...
Sit mihi ab Aegypto bonus exitus...   *id.* 607 ff.

[3] Nonne, precor, toto manet hæc discordia mundo,
Parte sequente Deum, vel parte ruente per orbem?
id. 537 f.

[4] Forte requiratur quanam ratione gerendi
Sederit hæc nobis sententia pingere sanctas
Raro more domos animantibus adsimulatis.
id. 542 ff.

[5] Hæc tibi, Christe Deus, tenui facilique paratu
Pro nobis facimus; nec enim te, summe Creator,

The contemporary evidence of Gregory of Nyssa († c. 400) shews that in some places at least the range of subjects had been already enlarged. In commemorating Theodorus he has given a description of a picture of his martyrdom, which in its intense realism no less than in its subject is foreign to the spirit of early Christian Art. The artist, he says, had imaged in glowing colours the heroic acts of the martyr, his struggles, his pains, the brutal forms of his persecutors, their insults, the flaming furnace, the blessed consummation of the soldier of Christ. Painting, he adds, even in silence can speak upon the wall, and do great service[1].

> Facta manu capiunt, toto quem corpore mundus
> Non capit.

In his restoration of the old Basilica Paulinus introduced "the two Testaments," but his language is very obscure:
> tribus in spatiis duo Testamenta legamus;
> Hanc quoque cernentes rationem lumine recto,
> Quod nova in antiquis tectis, antiqua novis lex
> Pingitur; est etenim pariter decus utile nobis
> In veteri novitas, atque in novitate vetustas.

Compare also xxviii. 22—27.

In the apse of the Basilica at Funda he represented the idea of the Passion as it is found on sarcophagi:
> Sanctorum labor et merces sibi rite cohærent,
> Ardua crux pretiumque crucis sublime corona.
> Ipse Deus, nobis princeps crucis atque corona,
> Inter gloriferi cæleste nemus paradisi,
> Sub cruce sanguinea niveo stat Christus in agno,
> Agnus ut innocua injusto datus hostia leto.
>
> (*Ep.* xxxii. 17.)

---

[1] Greg. Nyss. de S. Theod. Mart. iii. p. 733 (ed. Migne).

About the same time Asterius, bishop of Amasea, gives a strange description of popular extravagance. Men and women wore robes embroidered with all kinds of subjects "as if it were not enough to have the walls of their houses decorated with pictures." The more pious, he adds, choose scenes from the Gospels, and think that in so doing they dress themselves in a way to please God. "If they follow my advice, let them sell such garments and honour the living images of God. Do not paint Christ, for the one act of humility of His Incarnation, which He voluntarily undertook for us, is sufficient, but bear in thy soul and carry about spiritually (νοητῶς) the incorporeal Word[1]."

Not long afterwards there is evidence that still more remarkable freedom was used in ecclesiastical ornament. Olympiodorus consulted Nilus († 430) on the decorations which he proposed to place in a great church to be erected in honour of the martyrs. It was his design to represent on both sides of the Sanctuary (ἱερατεῖον) scenes of hunting and fishing, with representations of various animals and fish; and to erect in "the common house" "a thousand crosses, and histories (ἱστορίας) of all kinds of birds and beasts and reptiles and plants." "In answer to your letter," so Nilus writes, "I should say that it would be puerile and childish that the eye of the faithful should wander over such subjects. It befits a strong and manly character to fashion one single cross at the

[1] Hom. de div. et Laz. p. 167, Migne (*Patrol. Gr.* xl.).

east of the most sacred precinct (τοῦ θειοτάτου τεμένους)...and to fill the holy sanctuary (τὸν ναὸν τὸν ἅγιον) on both sides with histories of the Old and New Testament by the hand of a skilful artist, in order that those...who are unable to read the divine Scriptures may by looking at the paintings call to mind the courage of men who have served the true God and be stirred to emulation of their heroic exploits[1]."

In the time of Augustine the African Church had yielded to the growing fashion. Speaking of the Sacrifice of Isaac he says "that it was sung in many "tongues, painted in many places[2]." And he bears witness that the fashion had brought the results which earlier Christians had dreaded: "I know many," he writes, "who worship tombs and pictures[3]."

---

[1] Nilus, Epp. iv. 61. The letter was brought forward at the Second Council of Nicæa. In the following letter Nilus speaks of a young monk who recognised a martyr who appeared to him from having seen him often represented "in the paintings" (ἐκ τοῦ πολλάκις τὸν χαρακτῆρα τοῦ ἁγίου ἐπὶ τῶν εἰκόνων τεθεᾶσθαι). The phrase sounds like one of a later time. But Chrysostom bears witness to the custom in his Homily on Meletius (ii. 2, p. 516, ed. Migne); he says that the portrait of that Saint was drawn on "rings, seals, bowls, and chamber walls."

[2] c. Faust. xxii. 73. Compare also De cons. evv. i. x. 16, Sic omnino errare meruerunt qui Christum et apostolos ejus non in sanctis codicibus sed in pictis parietibus quæsierunt; nec mirum si a pingentibus fingentes decepti sunt.

[3] de Mor. Eccles. Cath. i. 34 (75) novi, multos esse sepulcrorum et picturarum adoratores. The famous phrase "picturæ

The remains of early Christian Sculpture are singularly few. This may be due partly to the costliness of such works, and still more to the nature of the Art itself. Sculpture far more than painting was identified with idolatry. The aversion from "the graven image" has perpetuated itself in the Greek Church[1], and even to the present time Sculpture is for the most part inspired by the spirit of the old world. A single ideal figure, the Good Shepherd of the Vatican, which seems to have been suggested by the type of the Hermes Kriophoros, is referred to the fourth century[2]; part of a single portrait statue, that

(imagines) sunt idiotarum libri" is often referred to Augustine, but, as far as I know, wrongly.

[1] I am informed that statues are used as ornaments of Russian churches, as (for example) on the outside of the Isaac Church at St Petersburgh. I may add here that a friend, who has given a considerable amount of study to the monuments of early Celtic hagiology, especially of the Scoto-Irish school, informs me that, as far as his reading has extended, he "cannot remember meeting with any mention of a sacred picture or image, unless it be in one passage in the Life of Brigid by Cogitosus, a work which Colgan attributes to the last quarter of the sixth century. It is there stated that in the church of Kildare, in which the body of Brigid was still lying buried in the time of the author, the *paries tabulatus*, which separated the eastern part from the twin naves, was *decoratus et imaginibus depictus, ac linteaminibus tectus* (Cogitosus, cap. xxxv., in the *Trias Thaumaturga*, p. 523). But what subjects these *imagines* depicted is not hinted: it is possible that only flowers, or, at most, figures of angels, are meant."

[2] According to Eusebius (Vit. Const. iii. 497) Constantine set up in the market at Constantinople "the representation of

of Hippolytus, is referred to the fifth century. To these two works may be added a small statue of the Good Shepherd found at Seville, and perhaps the famous bronze statue of St Peter; and the list of the extant Christian statues of the first five centuries is complete[1]. The other early works of sculpture are sarcophagi, one of which belongs to the third century[2].

the Good Shepherd familiar to students of Scripture (τὰ τοῦ καλοῦ ποιμένος σύμβολα, τοῖς ἀπὸ τῶν θείων λογίων ὁρμωμένοις γνώριμα), and a gilded bronze figure of Daniel with the lions."

[1] The two other figures of the Good Shepherd which remain (Appell, *l. c.* p. 5) are hardly so early. A statuette of St Peter (Appell, p. 6) which was once at Berlin appears to be of early date; but is known only by engravings.

[2] It is dated 273. See Le Blant, *Étude sur les Sarcophages Chrétiens de la ville d'Arles*, p. iv.; and compare *id.* pl. xxxiv. Le Blant assigns to the same age the sarcophagus of Livia Primitiva, which bears a rude representation of the Good Shepherd between two sheep, a fish and an anchor: *l. c.* Bottari, T. xxxv. 2.

Garrucci's fifth volume contains the sarcophagi. A very careful and valuable list and description is given by Dr Appell, *Monuments of Christian Art*, 1872.

Prof. Ramsay has shewn me a drawing of a most interesting relief which is probably the oldest remaining specimen of Christian sculpture. It is found on a monument erected by "Abercius a deacon, to himself, his wife, and his children," and represents a small figure with one arm laid across the breast standing between two profiles of a man and a woman executed on a larger scale. These profiles are evidently portraits, and that of the woman has considerable artistic merit. Prof. Ramsay placed the work c. 200. [He inclines now to a later date.]

In spite of the limited scope which sarcophagi offered to the artist the sculptures which they present are of great interest as confirming the general impressions conveyed by the remains of early Christian painting. The sarcophagi of Helena and Constantina, the mother and daughter of Constantine, are perfectly classical in character. The vine and winemaking which are represented on the latter recall the earliest wall-paintings. Such objects lend themselves readily to a Christian interpretation while they are not distinctively Christian. In other cases classical imagery is found to which a Christian meaning can only be given with difficulty[1]. But for the most part the same scenes are found as in the Catacombs, and they are treated in the same manner. The sculptor brought to his work the experience and the traditions of ancient art, as far as they still survived, and used them for the expression of new ideas[2].

Meanwhile Christian Architecture had made vigor-

[1] *E.g.* The figures of the Dioscuri on a sarcophagus at Arles. Le Blant, pl. xxiii. pp. 38 ff. On the use of classical details see Le Blant, *l. c.* Introduction, pp. x. f.; 19.

[2] Some examples shew considerable artistic merit. For example a sarcophagus in the Lateran Museum, given in Northcote and Brownlow, ii. 255; Parker, pl. xvii.; Bottari, T. xxxiii. The sarcophagus of Junius Bassus (A.D. 359) shews thoughtful work. It is hard to understand how other engravings come to represent Daniel as nude, according to all but universal custom, while Parker's engraving "taken from a photograph" (pl. xiii.) represents him as fully clothed. Dr Appell says that the figure is modern. (*Monuments of Christian Art*, p. 10.)

ous progress. When the persecution of Diocletian broke out at Nicomedia (A.D. 303), "a most lofty temple" there was one of the first objects of destruction. At that time it is evident that the religious buildings of Christians were of considerable importance; and the church which Paulinus erected at Tyre not many years afterwards (A.D. 313) probably only reproduced the type of earlier works of which no detailed description has been preserved. Eusebius has fortunately given an account of this which proves beyond question that Christians were ready to devote the costliest work to purposes of Divine worship[1]. The central door was decorated "with plates of bronze and reliefs" (παραπήγμασί τε χαλκοῦ σιδηροδέτοις καὶ ποικίλμασιν ἀναγλύφοις). Elaborate carvings of wood were freely used. The roof was made of cedar. And Eusebius taxes the powers of his rhetoric to represent the splendour of the effect produced both by the costliness of the materials and by the beauty of the workmanship. The external magnificence was indeed designed, if we may believe him, to attract passers by and lead them to enter the sacred precincts[2].

The church of Paulinus was a genuine expression of Christian feeling. Less stress can be laid on the

[1] *H. E.* x. 4.

[2] Euseb. *l. c.* ὡς ἂν μὴ παρατρέχῃ τις ὅτι μὴ τὴν ψυχὴν κατανυγεὶς πρότερον μνήμῃ τῆς τε πρὶν ἐρημίας καὶ τῆς νῦν παραδόξου θαυματουργίας, ὑφ᾽ ἧς τάχα καὶ ἑλκυσθήσεσθαι κατανυγέντα καὶ πρὸς αὐτῆς τῆς ὄψεως ἐπὶ τὴν εἴσοδον προτραπήσεσθαι ἤλπισεν.

evidence furnished by the works of Constantine at Jerusalem. These so impressed Eusebius that he suggests that they may have been prefigured by the prophets in their description of the New Jerusalem[1]. No kind of rich decoration was spared. The interior walls were encrusted with variegated marbles. The carved ceiling was gilded throughout. The semicircular apse was adorned with twelve columns, supporting as many silver vases which the Emperor "presented " as an offering to his GOD." And Eusebius says that he could not enumerate the other gifts " of gold and " silver and precious stones " with which the building was enriched[2].

The works of Constantine at Rome seem to have been of a similar type; and the drawings of the original Basilica of St Peter which have been preserved are so full of beauty that it is difficult not to feel that the present building has been dearly purchased by the loss of the greatest of his churches.

The development of Christian Architecture gave occasion to the first original effort of Christian Art, the application of Mosaic on a large scale to wallpictures. The earliest remaining examples are in the churches of St Constantia and St Maria Maggiore at Rome; and one of the most beautiful in the tomb of Galla Placidia at Ravenna[3]. This form of art, it is

[1] Vit. Const. ii. 33.

[2] *Id.* 34—40. Bingham (*Antiquities*, viii. § 5) has given an interesting early inventory of Church vessels.

[3] There is a drawing of this Mosaic in D. C. A. ii. 6, 1328,

THE RELATION OF

obvious, lends itself naturally to conventional representation; and it is not unlikely that the later Mosaics preserve unchanged the earliest types as they were successively fixed.

One example deserves to be specially noticed, that on the apse of the church of St Pudentiana at Rome. No existing work gives a better idea of the peculiar spirit and power of early Christian Art. The treatment is conventional without being lifeless. A spiritual purpose is dominant without destroying the natural dignity of the figures and the grouping. The spectator is forced by the beauty of that which he sees to look beyond to that which is suggested[1].

There are very few traces of the domestic Art of the early Christians. Clement of Alexandria gives a list of subjects which might properly be engraved on rings; and existing specimens present nearly all the types which he allows[2]. Many early Christian lamps

and a large coloured drawing at South Kensington. It is excellently described in Woltmann and Woermann, *Hist of Painting*, London, 1880, i. 167 f.

[1] There are valuable representations of early Mosaics in the South Kensington Museum. See *Christian Mosaic Pictures* by J. W. Appell, Ph. D., 1877.

Garrucci devotes his fourth volume to Mosaics.

[2] For the history and remains of early Christian glyptic Art see C. W. King, *Antique Gems and Rings*, ii. § vii. pp. 24 ff. London, 1872; and Dr Babington's article *Gems* in D. C. A.

A simple enumeration of the subjects of the small collection of early Christian gems in the British Museum will give a fair idea of the general character of these works.

1. A dove, olive branch and star (ruby).

CHRISTIANITY TO ART.

are works of considerable merit[1]. And one of the gold coins of Constantine offers a unique and most

2. A fish, olive, pastoral staff.

3. A fish and anchor, with the word ЄΠΙΤΥΝΧΑΝΟΥ (D. C. A. p. 714).

4. A cross, fish and dove (D. C. A. p. 713).

5. Two fish (ascending and descending) and a bowl.

6. An anchor between two dolphins with the letters A. P. L.

7. An anchor between two fish.

8. ΙΧΘΥC enclosed between two olive branches (sard).

9. An anchor-cross with two doves resting on the arms, two fish (ascending and descending), and two palms.

10. Good Shepherd under an olive with two doves (hæmatite).

11. Good Shepherd between two sheep: very rude.

12. Good Shepherd with IH ΧC: very rude.

13. Good Shepherd, with sheep and two lambs, under a tree with a dove: very rude.

14. Good Shepherd and Jonah cast out by the monster: a dove with olive branch: a palm and gourd with a star between: in the centre the monogram.

15. Two parts: above, the Good Shepherd and Jonah under the gourd: below, an anchor, dove, branches, fish, figures kneeling, a figure floating above.

16. A Cross, which has become a living tree, with a dove resting upon it. (This is a singularly interesting device.)

17. Two sheep between two palms: very well executed.

18. Chariot with two horses and angel.

19. Four sheep with collars.

20. The temptation.

21. Cross with the Chrisma (sapphire).

22. Palm between two branches.

23. Palm tree, two branches and two birds with inscription: very rude.

[1] See Dr Babington's article in D. C. A.

beautiful embodiment of a Christian thought. The Emperor is represented as "looking upwards in the "attitude of prayer:" so, Eusebius says, he wished to express his faith[1].

The rapid sketch which has been given of the progress of Christian Art in different directions will be sufficient to indicate the circumstances under which it gained finally a recognised place in Christian life, and especially in Christian worship. It was, as we

[1] Vit. Const. iv. 15. An engraving of the coin, which does not do it justice, is given in D. C. A. *Money*, Fig. 23. Dr Babington (D. C. A. i. p. 720) refers to an agate in which the Emperor is represented in the same way.

Some other coins of Christian emperors deserve mention as illustrating the symbolism of Christian Art. Most conspicuous among these is the small "third brass" coin of Constantine, bearing on the reverse the words *spes publica* with the labarum, the spiked end of which pierces the serpent (D. C. A. *s.v. Labarum* and *Money*, fig. 16). A variation of this design Constantine is said to have set over the portal of his palace (Euseb. Vit. Const. iii. 3). The old device of the phœnix with the legend *Felix temporum reparatio* occurs on coins of Constans and Constantius. On coins of the two Eudoxias Victory is represented inscribing the letters of the sacred monogram on a shield. On a coin of Valentinian III., which has the common legend *Victoria Augusti*, Satan takes the place of the barbarian whom the Emperor treads under his feet. At last the head of the Lord, of a singularly dignified type, appears on a gold coin of Justinian II. Compare C. W. King, *Early Christian Numismatics*, pp. 35 ff.

A very complete account of the interesting Christian glass work is given by Dr Babington in D. C. A. (*Glass*). See also Garrucci, Tom. iii.

have seen, fashioned on classical models; it inherited the use of classical methods; it incorporated some of the familiar subjects of classical use[1]; but at the same time it embodied, even if only in an elementary form, the power of a new life. It was conventional and it was symbolic. By these characteristics it claimed effectually the office of interpreting the invisible through the visible, of giving predominance to the spiritual idea over the external appearance, of advancing from within outwards, from the thought to the expression. The means adopted for securing these ends belong, no doubt, to the infancy of Christian Art. Efforts which were arrived at directly and simply in the first stage of the new artistic life can be secured now without any sacrifice of the freedom or of the fulness of the artist's labours. But this fact does not deprive the earliest works of their distinctive meaning and importance.

Early Christian Art is conventional. This is true both as to the choice and as to the treatment of subjects. It is indeed necessary to remember that our illustrations are chiefly drawn from the Catacombs, from tombs and sarcophagi. But when allowance is made for the limitation of the artist's freedom by the nature of his work, it seems certain that other influences must have kept him within the narrow circle of subjects to which he confined himself. He made a new departure in Art, though perhaps unconsciously, and strove to call attention to the divine element in life.

[1] See p. 343, n. 1.

For this purpose it was necessary to take a few familiar subjects which could easily be made to express a universal spiritual truth. Scenes and figures came in this way to express great thoughts; and when this correspondence between facts and ideas was established in a few cases, a lesson of wide application was surely taught.

Thus it is that a few subjects from the Old Testament and a few from the New Testament are repeated both in painting and sculpture with almost wearisome monotony. Among these three scenes from the history of Jonah ((*a*) Jonah cast out of the ship; (*b*) disgorged by the sea-monster; (*c*) resting under the gourd), Daniel between two lions, Noah in the ark, the Feeding of the multitudes and the Raising of Lazarus are perhaps the most frequent in early works; and next to these the Fall, Moses striking the rock, the Three Children in the furnace, Job in his distress, the Sacrifice of Abraham, the Ascension of Elijah, the Adoration of the Magi, the Miracle of Cana[1]. It is very remarkable that only one representation of David

---

[1] Lists of examples of these different subjects are given in various writers. It is sufficient to refer to Canon Venables' articles *Fresco* and *Old Testament* in D. C. A., and Mr Tyrwhitt's article in the same work on the different subjects. See also C. J. Hemans, "The Church in the Catacombs," *Cont. Rev.* Oct. 1866.

How great was the tendency of the subjects to become fixed is shewn by the identity of the decorations of two sarcophagi, one at Rome (Bottari, xxiv.) and the other at Arles (Le Blant, ix.).

is referred to by the historians of early Christian Art[1].

The treatment of these subjects offers little variation. Jonah is always represented nude, and the sea-monster seems to have been modelled on the type of that found in representations of Andromeda. Daniel, nearly always nude, stands in the attitude of prayer between two lions placed symmetrically. Lazarus is drawn like a mummy, and his tomb commonly appears like a small chapel, while the Lord holds a rod in hand. The Magi are dressed in Persian (Phrygian) costume. The treatment of the Good Shepherd offers a partial exception to the general uniformity. In addition to the commonest type in which He bears the lamb over His shoulders, the Shepherd is represented with the pipe, and leaning on His staff, and with goats[2]; and on a sarcophagus He appears in three separate forms[3]. It is not difficult to see the special colouring which is given in each case to the common thought. Elsewhere there is little change; and anyone who examines the work of Garrucci will feel the truth of the words used at the Second Council of Nicæa, "the making of pictures is not the invention of artists but the admitted legislation and tradition of the Catholic Church[4]."

[1] See p. 315, n. 5.

[2] Compare Northcote and Brownlow, ii. p. 24. Bottari, lxxviii., lxxx., xcvii., ciii., cv., cxiii., cxvi., cxviii., cxliii., cxlv., clv., clxxii., clxxix.

[3] Bottari, clxiii.

[4] Οὐ ζωγράφων ἐφεύρετις ἡ τῶν εἰκόνων ποίησις ἀλλὰ τῆς

This view as it was maintained by the artists of the Greek Church was necessarily fatal to Art. The conventionalism of early work was no more than a first step in the new life. Conventionalism was the condition of Symbolism, that is of the simplest assertion of the spiritual purpose of Art. But when the end was gained, the provisional restriction of subjects ceased to be necessary.

We are thus brought to the second characteristic of early Christian Art: it was symbolic. There is no doubt some exaggeration in the theory, which has gained the support of De' Rossi, that Christian artists worked under the direction of theologians and embodied definite schemes of doctrine in their pictures. But it is impossible to study the cycle of subjects in connexion with early Christian literature and not feel that the artists embodied thoughts which their religious services brought before them. Scenes in the Old Testament shadowed forth truths of the Gospel and illustrated the reality of the one purpose underlying all life. By repeating these it was not difficult to suggest the thought of the correspondence between different stages in the fulfilment of the divine will, of the inner meaning of ordinary events, of the way in which things are set "one over against another." The offering of Isaac indicated as much as the early believer thought could be safely indicated, in a direct representation, of the Lord's Passion. The deliver-

καθολικῆς ἐκκλησίας ἔγκριτος θεσμοθεσία καὶ παράδοσις. Conc. Nic. II. *Act.* vi. (Concil. viii. 1085, *ed.* Colet.)

ance of Noah from and by the waters was an eloquent symbol of salvation in the Church "through water." The four rivers of Paradise suggested thoughts of the streams of grace flowing to the Church through the Gospel and the Gospels. The domestic feast, and the feeding of the multitudes called up recollections of the provision which the Lord had made and still continues to make for the material and spiritual sustenance of His people. Above all the familiar figure of the Good Shepherd brought together the imagery of the Old Testament and the experience of daily life, and in some degree perhaps symbolic forms of ancient art[1]. In one subject at least the imagination of the old world was allowed its full right. The myth of Orpheus expressed with far-reaching pathos the faith of man in a restored order of creation; and the Christian artist gladly accepted the pictured parable of which his faith gave the meaning.

The reality of this definite symbolism is placed beyond all question by the direct testimony of the monuments themselves. In several cases St Peter, "the leader of the New Israel," is represented under the figure of Moses striking the rock. Not only is the figure of Moses commonly given in the conventional type of St Peter, but the identification is completed by the addition of the name, Peter[2]. In other

[1] On the relation of the Good Shepherd to the Hermes Kriophoros see Northcote and Brownlow, ii. pp. 26 ff.

[2] Compare Northcote and Brownlow, ii. frontispiece, and p. 180; Le Blant, *Sarc. Chrét.* p. xxii.; pp. 36 f.

examples Christ Himself appears as Moses[1] and again as Abraham[2]. Elsewhere, as when a young Christian man in the attitude of prayer occupies the place of Noah in the ark, the lessons taught by the experience of the old saints are brought down into actual life[3].

An illustration of a different kind is furnished by the sarcophagus of Bassus. On this, in the small reliefs which fill the spandrils of the arcade, a sheep occupies the place of the divine representation in the familiar cycle of subjects. A sheep receives the Law,

[1] Garrucci, lv. 2; xliii. 1.
[2] Garrucci, t. xliii. 1.
[3] It is enough simply to refer to the unquestioned symbolism of "the Fish" (ΙΧΘΥC). Except in scenes of "fishing" this figure hardly comes within the proper scope of Art, though it illustrates the attitude of the artist. Compare D. C. A. *s. v.* The most remarkable use of "the Fish" which I have seen is in a picture from Cyrenaica, where several distinct kinds of fish are combined with a figure of the Good Shepherd (Garrucci, tav. 105 c). Fishing and Baptism are combined: Garrucci, vii. 2. Figures of some very curious gems with the "Fish" are given in D. C. A. i. p. 713. Le Blant (*Sarc. Chrét.* Intr. § 5) has pointed out the remarkable correspondence between the subjects on sarcophagi and the historical references in the Offices for the dead. His last words are well worth quoting: Mais, je le répète, ce qui me semble dominer dans le cycle des représentations figurées sur les tombes, c'est l'idée même dont s'inspirent les liturgies funéraires et qui fit mettre aux lèvres du preux Roland ce cri suprême; O notre vrai Père, toi qui ressuscitas saint Lazare d'entre les morts et qui défendis Daniel contre les lions, sauve mon âme et protége-la contre tous périls (p. xxxix).

strikes the rock, administers Baptism, multiplies the loaves, raises Lazarus. So the unity of the working of GOD throughout the Old and New Testaments is vividly brought out[1].

When the general principle is once recognised it is scarcely possible to overlook the combination of thoughts which is indicated by definite groupings of types, such as Moses striking the rock and the raising of Lazarus[2]; Moses striking the rock and Baptism[3]; Christ teaching in the centre, and grouped round the sacrifice of Abraham, the feeding of the multitudes, Moses striking the rock, Noah, the Three Children[4]; and again, Orpheus in the centre, and around David with the sling[5], Moses striking the rock, Daniel, the raising of Lazarus, separated by four pastoral scenes[6]; yet again, the Good Shepherd in the centre, and around the raising of Lazarus, Moses striking the rock, the healing of the Blind, Job[7]. In one example Daniel, the Good Shepherd, and Jonah cast to the whale occur in a continuous picture[8].

[1] Compare Northcote and Brownlow, ii. p. 260.

[2] Bottari, t. cxxix.

[3] Le Blant, xv.

[4] Bottari, t. lix.; Garr. xxiv.

[5] Bottari says that this is the single representation of David with which he is acquainted in early Art (p. 32). May not the figure really be that of the Sower?

[6] Bottari, lxiii.; Garr. xxv.

[7] Bottari, xci., Garr. xl. Other examples are given, Garrucci, xliii.; xlviii.; li. (Bottari, cxviii.).

[8] Bottari, t. clxx.

The symbolism of Christian Art is one expression of another mark by which it is distinguished, its reserve. This characteristic is specially illustrated by the treatment of subjects from the Gospels, and especially of the Person of the Lord. As early as the second century Gnostic sects had alleged portraits of the Lord[1]. Such representations were foreign to the mind of the Church. They do not occur in works connected with the Catholic Communion till the fourth century at the earliest, and then in conventional types[2]. At the same time the figures of the Lord which appear commonly on sarcophagi shew Him as a youthful figure of a pure classical form with no attempt at realistic portraiture[3]. It is no doubt due to the

[1] Iren. i. 24, 25. Compare D. C. A. *Gems*, i. p. 721.

[2] Compare Northcote and Brownlow, ii. 216 ff.; Pearson *On the Creed*, p. 88 note; and the articles by Mr Tyrwhitt and Archd. Cheetham in D. C. A. i. pp. 874 ff.

The famous statue at Cæsarea (Euseb. vii. 18) cannot in any case be regarded as contravening the general statement.

I do not enter on the question of the date of the legendary portraits of the Lord. The two specimens on "cloth" reproduced by Mr Heaphy in his work on *The Likeness of Christ* (edited by W. Bayliss, London, 1880), from the originals at St Peter's at Rome, and St Bartholomew's at Genoa, are most remarkable works. I know nothing in early Christian Art at all resembling the former in style. Those who have seen "the Holy Face" at Lucca speak of it as being no less impressive.

[3] A very fine example is found on the sarcophagus of Junius Bassus. Appell, p. 9; Bottari, xv.; Parker, xvii. See also Bottari, xxxiii. Another remarkable example is given in Bottari, liv With these may be compared the corresponding

reverent shrinking from all representations of the Lord in His human Presence that scenes from the Gospel history were with very few exceptions carefully avoided.

A rude sketch of the Nativity is found upon a fragment of a sarcophagus dated A.D. 343[1]. There are representations of the visit of the Magi of as early a date[2]. Other scenes, except the Raising of Lazarus, are very rare and of isolated occurrence.

In this connexion the early treatment of the Passion is of the deepest interest. One of the earliest representations of the subject is of singular beauty and impressiveness. It is found on a sarcophagus preserved in the Lateran and referred to the fourth century[3]. The face of the sarcophagus is divided by columns into five compartments. The two end compartments shew on one side Christ, a youthful figure, led by a soldier, and Pilate washing his hands; on the other Christ crowned by a soldier with a crown not of

---

figures of the bearded Christ; Le Blant, pl. iv.; Bottari, xxi., xxii., xxiii., xxv., xxviii. The distinction which has been drawn between the beardless and bearded figures as expressing the human and divine aspects of Christ's Person (see Le Blant, p. 25) does not seem to hold good.

[1] Northcote and Brownlow, ii. 235.

[2] The occurrence of the Star in the group noticed above, p. 343, n. 2, seems to shew that that really represents the visit of the Magi.

[3] Appell, p. 21; Parker, xv.; Northcote and Brownlow, ii. 253. Compare Paulinus, *Ep.* xxxii. 17, quoted above, p. 346 n.

thorns but of flowers, and Simon the Cyrenian bearing His Cross[1]. In the centre is the Cross terminated by the sacred monogram encircled by a wreath. On the arms of the Cross two doves are resting, and beneath are two figures of the Roman guards, one watching and one sleeping. So the whole story of sadness and joy, of suffering and glory, of death and triumph, is eloquently told.

This representation of the Passion was widely spread, though without the accompanying scenes[2].

In one example below the Cross, in the place commonly occupied by the two guards, the Lord is represented appearing to two women[3]. In another the crowned Cross is the object of devout contemplation to the apostles, who stand six on either side with their right hands upraised, while from above out of the starry heaven a hand places a crown upon the head of each[4].

Another treatment of the idea of the Passion, which occurs on the sarcophagus of Anicius Probus, who died

---

[1] This is well pointed out by Le Blant, *Sarc. Chrét.* p. 18. His engraving p. xxxiii. is admirable. The smaller size and dress of the figure bearing the Cross leave no doubt as to the artist's meaning.

Le Blant observes that this is the single example in which any incident of the Passion subsequent to the appearance before Pilate is represented in early art (*l. c.*).

[2] Examples are given by Garrucci, tavv. 349—353; 403.

[3] Bottari, t. xxx.; Garrucci, t. cccl.

[4] Le Blant, pl. xiv. A small engraving of this work is given in D. C. A. i. p. 108.

in 395, is scarcely less beautiful. In this case also the face of the sarcophagus is divided into five compartments. The two on either side are occupied each by two disciples. In the centre one, which is wider, the Lord appears between St Peter and St Paul. He stands, a graceful youthful figure, upon a mound from which flow the four streams of the new Paradise: in His left hand He holds the roll of the Gospel, and in the right a jewelled cross[1].

The full meaning of this representation is brought out more clearly in other examples, where the Lord stands on the mound, and by Him a Lamb bearing the Cross upon its head[2]. The same thought is indicated by a Lamb standing in front of the Cross; or by a Lamb with a cruciform nimbus which stands upon a mound from which issue the four rivers[3]; and less distinctly by a Cross or the Chrisma between two lambs[4].

Yet more significant and touching is a representa-

[1] Bottari, t. xvi. A similar group with the addition of two palm trees is found on another sarcophagus; Bottari, t. xxxv.

[2] Bottari, tavv. xxi., xxii., 1. With this may be compared the rude, almost startling, figure of Christ throned with the Chrisma upon His head: Le Blant, pl. xxvii.

[3] Garrucci, t. ccclvi.; t. 355.

[4] Garrucci, tavv. 10, 303, 337, 345, 389, 393, 422, 426.

On the cover of an Evangelarium at Milan are several typical scenes from the Lord's Life; but there is no Crucifixion. In place of this there is a Lamb in the centre with a wreath: Labarte, *Hist. des Arts industriels...* 1864; pl. vi.; Garrucci, t. 454.

tion of the Passion which is found on a slab preserved in Wirksworth Church, Derbyshire. The slab was found some years ago buried under the floor of the Chancel. The work is rude, and was probably executed by some English sculptor of the ixth or xth century, but the design is of a much earlier date, and may reasonably be referred to an Italian artist of the vith or viith century.

The larger portion of the slab which remains is in good preservation, and contains scenes from the Life of the Lord; among others less distinct, the Nativity and the Ascension in a most suggestive juxtaposition, the Feet-washing and the Burial, and between these a symbolic image of the Passion. On the centre of a plain Greek Cross is laid the figure of a dead lamb. As far as I can learn the conception is unique[1]. The drooping head and the bent legs of the victim tell of death with eloquent force; and under this limited aspect it is perhaps allowable to present for contemplation the Dead Christ[2]. No one, I think, can regard

[1] The image of the *Living* Lamb is found on the centre of the Vatican Cross (D. C. A. 1, 513) and elsewhere. A very striking example occurs in a bas-relief on the Ciborium at St Mark's Venice: Grimouard de St Laurent. *Iconographie de la Croix*...in Didron's *Annales Archéologiques*, xxvi. p. 213 (Paris, 1869). It is said that the Face of the Lord is represented as the intersection of the arms of the Cross in the Transfiguration at Ravenna: D. C. A. p. 494.

[2] I feel unable to believe that a gem representing the Dead Christ (D. C. A. i. p. 718) can be as early as the ivth century.

it without feeling that we have lost greatly by substituting a literal representation for such a symbol[1].

The same spirit of reserve which led Christian artists to shrink from direct representations of the Lord's sufferings, kept them also from representing the sufferings of His martyrs. A single painting in the Cemetery of St Callixtus is supposed to portray the trial of Christian confessors[2]. And a single gem, a new-year's gift, of unusually good execution, which is referred to the age of Constantine, represents an actual martyrdom, perhaps that of St Agnes[3]. It seemed enough for the most part to represent the death and deliverance of martyrs by the type of the Three Children.

In correspondence with the reserve of early Christian Art we may also notice its joyousness. The reserve was a natural consequence of the vivid realisation of spiritual truth: the aim of the artist was, so to speak, to let earth speak of heaven and not to confine heaven in forms of earth. The joyousness was another manifestation of the same faith. In spite of appearances the Christian believed that the victory

[1] This is not the place to enter on the history of the direct representations of the Crucifixion, first ideal and then realistic. The subject is of deep theological importance, but it belongs wholly to a later period than that with which we are concerned here. The essay of M. Grimouard de St Laurent referred to in note [1], p. 320, is a valuable contribution to the history, but by no means exhaustive.

[2] Northcote and Brownlow, i. pl. 8, ii. 173.

[3] D. C. A. i. p. 719.

over sin and death was already won; and he gave expression to his conviction. The characteristic words 'in pace' which marked the 'rest' of the believer were reflected in all the associations of death. The painful literalism which deforms many of the monuments of the xvth and xvith centuries found no place in the vth and vith, and still less in earlier times. The terrible pictures which Tertullian drew of the sufferings of persecutors, and the scarcely less terrible descriptions by Augustine of the sufferings of the wicked were not as yet embodied by Art. No attempt was made to give distinctness to the unseen world. It is doubtful whether there are any representations of angels earlier than the latter half of the fourth century, and it seems certain that there are no representations of powers of evil, other than the natural serpent, till a later date.

By that time the work of early Christian Art was ended.

III.

From what has been said it will appear that the relation of Christianity to Art is that which it holds generally to life. It answers to a fresh birth, a transfiguration of all human powers, by the revelation of their divine connexions and destiny. The pregnant words of St Paul, 'old things (τὰ ἀρχαῖα) passed away: behold, they have become new,' have an application here. There is no loss, no abandonment of the past triumphs of thought and insight and labour, but they

CHRISTIANITY TO ART.   323

are quickened by a new power; and disclosed in a new position with regard to the whole discipline of man. Christian Art is the interpretation of beauty in life under the light of the Incarnation. The ministry of the beautiful in every shape, in sound, in form, in colour, is claimed for GOD through man.

The realisation of this idea must necessarily be slow, but it is impossible that the facts of the Incarnation and Resurrection can leave Art in the same position as before. The interpretation of Nature and the embodiment of thought and feeling through outward things must assume a new character when it is known not only that Creation is the expression of the will of GOD, and in its essence 'very good,' but also that in humanity it has been taken into personal fellowship with the Word, through whom it was called into being. Such a revelation enables the student to see in the phenomena of the visible order Sacraments, so to speak, of the spiritual and unseen, and free him from bondage to 'the world' while he devotes himself with devout enthusiasm to the representation of the mysterious beauty which it contains. The Old Testament teaches us to regard Creation as an embodiment of a Divine thought, marred by the self-assertion and fall of its temporal sovereign: the New Testament teaches us to see it brought again potentially into harmony with GOD through the Blood of Him who is its Eternal Author and Head (Col. i. 14—23).

The Gospel therefore seeks the service of Art in the sensible proclamation of its message. The spirit must clothe itself in some way, and the dress may help to emphasise salient features in that which it partly veils. No doubt it is true that the spirit can in any case illuminate that in which it is confined; but it is no less true that it has a necessary tendency to fashion its own shrine, even as the soul "doth the body make[1]."

The early controversy as to the outward appearance of the Lord illustrates this twofold truth[2]. Some argued from the description of "the servant of the Lord" that the Son of man had "no form or comeliness," "no beauty that we should desire Him." And others replied that it could not but be that perfect holiness should become visible in perfect beauty. To the spiritual eye, we feel, there would be no final antagonism in the two statements. And Art by spiritual sympathy is able to guide the spectator to a right vision of that which is not naturally discerned.

---

[1] A remarkable and somewhat obscure passage of Athenagoras points to one aspect of this truth in the discussion of the objects of worship in præ-Christian times. After quoting the famous lines from the Melanippe of Euripides (ὁρᾷς τὸν ὑψοῦ τόνδ᾽ ἄπειρον αἰθέρα...) he says τῶν μὲν γὰρ οὔτε τὰς οὐσίας, αἷς ἐπικατηγορεῖσθαι τὸ ὄνομα συμβέβηκεν, ὑποκειμένας ἑώρα... τὸν δὲ ἀπὸ τῶν ἔργων (sc. ἑώρα), ὄψει τῶν ἀδήλων νοῶν τὰ φαινόμενα, ἀέρος, αἰθέρος, γῆς (*Legat. pro Christ.* c. 5). To the true spiritual eye natural phenomena reveal something of the Divine character more really than any creation of the imagination of man.

[2] On the appearance of the Lord compare the Oxford translation of Tertullian, note F, pp. 252 ff.

Or, to present the same thought from the opposite side, as all Art brings the ideal, in some sense, before us in a material form, and preserves for earth a definite place in the present order, so Christian Art is characterised by the endeavour to present "in many parts and in many fashions" that view of Creation wherein it is shewn in "earnest expectation" "waiting for the revelation of the sons of GOD" (Rom. viii. 19). In other words Christian Art treats its subject as that which has partly lost and is partly striving towards a divine type, not self-complete and not an end, and seeks to make clear the signs of the true character and the true goal of all with which it deals. It is directed not to humanity and nature in themselves, but to humanity and nature as revelations of the Divine.

Such an effort is obviously of universal application. Christian Art, like Christianity itself, embraces all life. The inspiration of the new birth extends to every human interest and faculty. Christian Art, as Christian, does not differ from classical Art in range of subject but in its prevailing treatment. It will indeed happen again and again that "the soul naturally Christian" unconsciously fulfils its high office of spiritual interpretation in classical works, but Christian Art exists by and for this. And there is nothing to which the office does not apply, nothing in which it does not find scope for exercise. The joys and sorrows and energies of men, the manifold forms and varying moods of nature, all have their "religious" aspect, if religion be, as it assuredly is, the striving towards the unity of man, the world, and GOD. Music, which is, as it were, the voice of the society, and architecture which is as its vestment, have in all their applications a religious power. This Christianity affirms as its postulate, and by affirming determines its relation to Art.

The fulfilment of this universal claim, as has been already said, will be necessarily slow. The conquest of life for Christ is gradual and not without reverses. New forces are not subdued without a struggle, and old forces, which have been subdued, not unfrequently rise up again in dangerous rebellion. More than once the fanatical iconoclasm of a false Judaism, and the sensual nature worship of a false Hellenism, have troubled the development of Christian Art. No struggle indeed has been fruitless; but even now we cannot dare to say that the office of Art is frankly acknowledged, or the exercise of Art spiritually disciplined.

The development of Christian Art has been gradual, and it has been unequal in different branches. The social Arts, if I may so describe them, Music and Architecture, were soon welcomed by the Church and pursued in characteristic forms. It is not too much to say that modern Music is a creation of the Church; and the continuous and rich growth of Christian architecture up to the Renaissance in types of varied beauty is in itself a sufficient proof of the power of the Faith to call out and train the highest genius in Art. The advance of painting and sculpture was checked perhaps in a great degree by the influence of Eastern asceticism. Both were treated as subsidiary to architecture, which was preeminently the Art of the Middle Ages; but some of the single statues of the XIIIth century contain a promise, not yet fulfilled, of a Christian Art worthy to crown that of Greece. Meanwhile a new style of painting was being prepared by the illumination of manuscripts, in which not only scenes and persons but small natural objects, flowers and insects, were treated with the utmost tenderness and care. Here again the Renaissance checked the direct development of the twofold promise over which the student lingers in admiration and hope as he regards at Bruges side by side the works of Van Eyck and Memling.

The forces of the Renaissance have not yet been completely assimilated. The wealth of ancient material then poured at once before Christian Artists hindered their normal progress; but they have moved since along their proper lines and the Past contains the assurance that "all things" are theirs.

So much at least the history of Christianity fairly shews, that nothing which is human lies beyond its range. It lays the greatest stress upon practical duties, upon "the good part" of moral discipline, but none the less it finds place for the satisfaction of what we regard as less noble instincts. The single incident recorded in the Gospels in which the Lord received a costly offering seems to illustrate the principles which hallow even the simplest gratifications of sense. When Mary lavished the precious spikenard over the Head and Feet of her Master, "the house," St John tells us, "was filled with the odour of the ointment." It was natural that the thought of the Apostles should find expression by the lips of Judas. "Why was not this ointment sold for three hundred pence and given to the poor?" "To what purpose was this waste?" And the judgment was given: "Verily I say unto you, wheresoever this gospel shall be preached in the whole world, there shall also this that this woman hath done, be told for a memorial of her." The fragrance was most transitory, but it was diffusive: the waste was most complete, but it gave clear witness of love, of that highest love of which the chief reward is that it should be known that its object inspired the devotion of perfect sacrifice. So it is with every work of Christian Art. It aims not at a solitary but at a common enjoyment: it seeks to make it clear that all to which it is directed has a spiritual value able to command the completest service[1].

[1] This is the lesson of the soul in *The Palace of Art*.

"Make me a cottage in the vale," she said,
    "Where I may mourn and pray.
Yet pull not down my palace towers, that are
    So lightly, beautifully built:
Perchance I may return with others there
    When I have purged my guilt."

IV.

Christianity, it has been seen, claims the ministry of Art in the whole field of life. What then is the peculiar office of Art? It is in a word to present the truth of things under the aspect of beauty, to bring before us the "world as GOD has made it" where "all is beauty." The fulfilment of this office involves the exercise not only of insight but of self-control. Man and nature are evidently disordered. The representation of all the phenomena of life would not be the representation of their Divine truth. Love therefore, a looking for the highest good of the whole, will guide and limit the search after beauty to which Art is directed.

In the imitative arts, painting and sculpture, the effort to make visible the truth of GOD in man and in nature is immediate and direct. In the creative arts, music and architecture, the effort is to find an expression, an embodiment, harmonious with the truth of things for elementary emotions and wants. Men in society seek a common voice, a common home: the hymn and the temple belong to the first stage of the state. But in these arts there is necessarily more freedom and variety than in those which are directly imitative. The application of the general laws of Art to them is complicated by many physical influences. It is best then to endeavour to determine the office of Art by a consideration of the imitative arts, and specially of painting, which is both richer than sculpture in its effects and wider in its range.

In three most suggestive studies of painters of the Renaissance Browning has marked with decisive power the mission of Art, and the grounds of its failure. He has not crowned the series by a portraiture of the ideal artist, but it is not difficult to gather his lineaments from the sketches of the other three. In "Fra Lippo Lippi" the poet vindicates the universality of Art answering to the fulness of life, and yet plainly indicates the peril which lies in this frank recognition of "the value and significance of flesh." In "Andrea del Sarto" he shews the power of faultless execution neutralised by the deliberate acceptance of a poor and selfish motive. In "Pictor ignotus," the loftiest ideal and the fullest power of imagination and execution are supposed to be combined, but the artist shrinks from facing a world sordid proud and unsympathising, and buries his work in obscurity.

It would not be possible to describe the artist's feeling more truly than in Lippi's words:

> This world's no blot for us
> Nor blank: it means intensely, and means good:
> To find its meaning is my meat and drink.
>
> So it is that for him to see the world is to see
>
> The beauty and the wonder and the power,
> The shapes of things, their colours, lights and shades,
> Changes, surprises—and GOD made them all...
> ... paint any one, and count it crime
> To let a truth slip.

If it be said that nature is before us, and that the artist can neither surpass nor reproduce it, the answer is complete:

> we're made so that we love
> First when we see them painted, things we have passed
> Perhaps a hundred times nor cared to see;...
> ... Art was given for that:
> GOD uses us to help each other so,
> Lending our minds out.

It is therefore faithless disloyalty to the Creator to seek to "paint the souls of men" by disparaging their bodies. Even if such a thing as soulless beauty were possible, the devout spectator would "find the soul he wants within himself, when he returns GOD thanks."

These pregnant words describe the manifold field of Art, its peculiar interpretative power, and its moral effect, but in connexion with a perfect, an unfallen, world. They take no account of the sorrows and failures which come from "what man has made of man;" and the circumstances under which they are spoken give powerful emphasis to the reality of that disorder in life which imposes on Art the necessity of discipline. There must indeed be no violent suppression of any part of true nature in the endeavour to gain the highest lesson of earth, but the divine meaning must be sought through the traces of the divine ideal, so that the artist "makes new hopes shine through the flesh they fray."

The failure of Lippi springs from a reaction against conventionality. In the assertion of the divine glory of Nature he overlooks the reality of corruption. The failure and the success of Andrea del Sarto are of a different kind. There is in him no sense of an illimitable progress of Art as it "interprets GOD to men." "I can do," he says, "do easily,

> what I know,
> What I see, what at bottom of my heart,
> I wish for, if I ever wish so deep."

The last words give the clue to his position. He has deliberately, irrevocably, limited his idea by an unworthy passion. In earth and in heaven, as he looks forward, he accepts defeat as the consequence: so he chooses. He has fettered himself and strives to think that "GOD laid the fetter."

But none the less he is conscious that his matchless power was given him for something nobler. He recognises truer greatness in pictures less perfect than his own. The complete fulfilment of his design is his condemnation:

> a man's reach should exceed his grasp,
> Or what's a heaven for? all is silver grey,
> Placid and perfect with my art—the curse!

He had said of the Madonna, which was but the image of his wife,

> It is the thing, Love! so such things should be—

but yet looking back to the early and unsullied days

he thinks, addressing Lucrezia, how he

> could paint
> One picture, just one more—the Virgin's face,
> Not your's this time!

The artist has need of discipline: he has need of devotion to an unattainable ideal: he has need also of un-selfregarding courage. The pathos of earthly passion in the confession of Andrea is less touching than the self-effacement of "the unknown painter," who, conscious of power and purpose, keenly alive to the joy of triumphs which he might secure, yet shrinks from the cold hard criticism of the crowd, "as from the soldiery a nun," and chooses for his works silent unnoticed decay. He has failed to acknowledge the reality of his mission. The right question for him was not how men would judge him, whether "their praise would hold its worth," but whether he had a trust to discharge, different from that monotonous task which he took to himself, painting

> ...the same series, Virgin, Babe and Saint,
> With the same cold, calm, beautiful regard.

It might have been that "merchants would have trafficked in his heart;" but they could not have disguised the heart's teaching. It might have been that his pictures would have lived with those who

> count them for garniture and household-stuff,

but no dull eye could have extinguished the light of his interpretation of life. The work of the artist is a battle, not without loss and suffering, and he must bear its sorrows, just as he must exercise the patient self-control of one who has to recover an image partly marred and defaced, and to keep in vigorous activity his loftiest aspiration.

All nature, all life, so far as it can be presented under the form of beauty, is the field of Art. But the beauty which is the aim of Christian Art is referred to a Divine ideal. It is not "of the world," as finding its source or its final measure there, but "of the Father," as corresponding to an unseen truth. The visible to the Christian eye is in every part a revelation of the invisible. The artist, like the poet, sees the infinite in things, and, under the conditions of his works, suggests it.

So far the artist's pursuit of beauty is limited. The boundaries within which he is confined will not always be the same, but they will always have the same relation to moral discipline. They will correspond with the circumstances of the time. And the discipline of sense has a positive and not only a negative value. It brings into healthy action a power of goodness which a rigid asceticism keeps unused and tends to destroy. In this way Christianity is able to give back, as has been already indicated, what was lost by the corruption of the old Aryan passion for Nature. All that was at first referred to limited divinities is shewn to be essentially an expression of one Divine Will. The spiritual signs may be greatly obscured: they may not be in every case distinctly discoverable; but the assurance of the significance and purpose of the whole cannot but illuminate the study of every part.

And while the field of Christian Art is in one sense limited by the recognition of a spiritual destiny of all its fruits, it is, in another sense, unlimited. The understanding of Nature is deepened and enlarged with the progress of life. Every discovery as to the history of creation, sooner or later, places new forces in the artist's hands. It may be some detail as to the formation of rocks, some law as to the arrangement of leaves and branches, some phenomenon of light or vapour, which has been more firmly seized; and shortly the painter's interpretation of the landscape will offer a fuller truth. The instructed eye will discern the importance of some minute effect and the artistic instinct will know how to convey it to the ordinary spectator[1].

For the artist has both to interpret and to embody. He has to gain the ideal of his subject, and then he has to present it in an intelligible shape. He has to give the right effect and to call out the right feeling. He has, as it were, to enter within the veil, and coming forth again to declare his heavenly visions

[1] When the Turner Collection was first exhibited at Marlborough-House I remember examining a sketch-book which contained some studies of laurel bushes. At the side was a note to the following effect: "N.B. The under-side of a laurel-leaf does not shine." It would be interesting to know how Turner conveyed the effect which he noticed.

to men. He is not a mirror but a prophet. The work of the photographer may help him, but it in no sense expresses his aim, which is not reproduction but translation. He has abdicated the office of an artist who simply repeats for the mass of men what they see themselves. The artist bids them behold the ideal as it is his privilege to realise it. He strives to make clear to others what his keener sensibility and penetrating insight have made visible to him. There is, as in every true poem, an element of infinity in his works. They suggest something beyond that which they directly present: something to be looked for, and felt after, thoughts which they quicken but do not satisfy. So it is that

> Art may tell a truth
> Obliquely, do the thing shall breed the thought,
> Nor wrong the thought.

This consideration places in a true light the danger of the popular realism in Art. There is a charm, no doubt, in being enabled to see some scene far removed from us in time or place as it would have presented itself to an ordinary observer; but exactly in proportion to the grandeur of the subject such a superficial portraiture is likely to be misleading. The spectator is tempted to rest in that which he understands at once; and the loftier though vague impression which he had before is lost and not assisted by the external details which profess to give the literal truth. Or, to put the truth in another light: the divine act was fitted to convey the divine meaning at the time of its occurrence, in relation to those who witnessed it, but a realistic representation could not give the same impression to a different age.

This is signally the case with scenes in the Gospel History. The early Church by a right instinct refrained from seeking any direct representation of the Lord. It was felt that the realistic treatment of His Person could not but endanger the living sense of the Majesty which the Church had learnt to recognise. By no effort could the spectator in a later age place himself in the position of the disciples before the Passion and the Ascension. The exact reproduction, if it were possible, of what met their eyes would not produce on him the effect which they experienced. The scene would require artistic interpretation in order that the idea might be preserved.

A great artist can alone determine what the law of interpretation must be, and even then he will not himself always obey it. Two illustrations taken from the commonest of sacred subjects, the Madonna and the Crucifixion, may serve to bring out the thought which I wish to emphasise. In the *Madonna della Seggiola* Raffaelle has given an exquisite natural group of a Mother and Child, overflowing with human tenderness, affection and proud joy, and we look no further: in the *Madonna di San Sisto* he has rendered the idea of divine motherhood and divine Sonship in intelligible forms. No one can rest in the individual figures. The tremulous fulness of emotion in the face of the Mother, the intense far-reaching gaze of the

Child, constrain the beholder to look beyond. For him too the curtain is drawn aside: he feels that there is a fellowship of earth with heaven and of heaven with earth, and understands the meaning of the attendant Saints who express the different aspects of this double communion. It may well be doubted whether the Crucifixion is in any immediate shape a proper subject for Art. The image of the Dead Christ is foreign to Scripture. Even in the record of the Passion Death is swallowed up in Victory. And the material representation of the superficial appearance of that which St John shews to have been life through death defines and perpetuates thoughts foreign to the Gospel. The Crucifixion by Velasquez with its overwhelming pathos and darkness of desolation, will shew what I mean[1]. In every trait it presents the thought of hopeless defeat[2]. No early Christian would have dared to look upon it. Very different is one of the earliest examples of the treatment of the Crucifixion on the Sigmaringen Crucifix[3]. In that life, vigour, beauty, grace, the open eye, and the freely outstretched arm, suggest the idea of loving and victorious sacrifice crowned with its reward. This

[1] A small engraving is given in Mrs Jameson's *History of the Lord*, ii. 205.

[2] The Lord's words in the Gospel narrative speak of the uttermost conflict as over before the physical Death: ἵνα τί με ἐγκατέλιπες;

[3] Mrs Jameson's *History of the Lord*, ii. 330. It is, I fear, doubtful whether the youthful figure is correctly given.

is an embodiment of the idea: the picture of Velasquez is a realisation of the appearance of the Passion.

If the view of Art which has been given is correct, its primary destination is public and not private, and it culminates in worship. Neither a great picture nor a great poem can be for a single possessor. So it has been at all times when Art has risen to its highest triumphs. But as an element of worship Art must be seen to be distinctly ministerial. In every form, music, painting, sculpture, it must point beyond the immediate effect. As long as it suggests the aspiration "to Thy great glory, O Lord," it is not only an offering, but a guide and a support. When it appears to be an end idolatry has begun.

The artist, we have seen, must use every fresh help and discovery: he must make evident new thoughts or illuminate thoughts which are imperfectly understood. It is clear therefore that he cannot follow one constant method in the fulfilment of his office. His work will be accomplished according to the conditions of his time. He will choose that mode of presenting the truth that he sees which is on the whole likely to be most effective. As a teacher, with a limited and yet most noble range of subjects, he will consider how he can best serve his age. Nothing short of this conviction can overcome the influence of fashion, or sustain that resolute purpose which bears temporary failure.

I have touched only upon the highest forms of creative Art. The principles by which these are animated apply also with necessary modifications to the humbler types of decorative art. The problems which these raise are in many respects more difficult and of wider application than those connected with the artistic interpretation of nature and life. It is no affectation to speak of the moral influence of colours and shapes in the instruments and accessories of everyday life. Here also there is room for a manifold apprehension and embodiment of truth. If once thoughtfulness of workmanship could be placed in general estimation before richness of material, a legitimate and fruitful field would be opened for domestic Art. When Greek Art was greatest it was consecrated to public use; and one chief danger of modern society is lest the growth of private wealth should lead to the diversion of the highest artistic power from the common service, and at the same time leave the appropriate labours of domestic art unencouraged.

This however is not the place to pursue the questions which are thus opened for inquiry. It is enough to have shewn that Christian Art is a necessary expression of the Christian Faith; that the early antagonism of Christianity to ancient Art was an antagonism to the idolatry, the limited earthliness, of which it was the most complete expression; that from the first beginnings of the Faith there were strivings after an Art which should interpret nature and life as a revelation of GOD, leading the student through the most patient and reverent regard of phenomena to the contemplation of the eternal; that the consecration of Art, involved in the facts of the Christian Creed, limits the artist only in the sense that a clear exhibition of the ideal saves the beholder from following wayward and selfish fancies.

The works of the greatest masters of the Middle Ages, of the greatest masters of the Renaissance, and the statement holds good still, shew how constantly foreign elements, fragments of the old life, not wholly transfigured, intrude themselves into that which as a whole belongs to a new order. Here perhaps traces of sensuousness, there traces of unlicensed satire, reveal disturbing forces in the artist's soul which are yet powerful enough to make themselves felt. But it is true, I believe, without exception that the noblest works, those on which we look with the deepest gratitude, drawing from them new powers of spiritual vision, new convictions of a spiritual world about us, are those which are most Christian.

CHRISTIANITY AS THE ABSOLUTE RELIGION.

CHRISTIANITY claims to be a Gospel; to offer to men that which answers to their needs; to disclose in a form available for life eternal truths which we are so constituted as to recognise, though we could not of ourselves discover them. Its verification therefore will lie in its essential character; in its fitness to fulfil this work, which is as broad as the world. And it may be worth while, in the presence of much apparent misunderstanding, to endeavour to indicate the points which must be noticed in any fair estimate of its relations to modern thought.

I assume that men are born religious. By this I mean that they are so constituted as to seek to place themselves in harmony with the powers without them, and to establish a harmony between the forces which are revealed in their own persons. The effort to obtain this twofold harmony will be directed by many partial interpretations of the phenomena of existence. The results of experience gained during the life of humanity and during the life of the indi-

CHRISTIANITY AS THE ABSOLUTE RELIGION. 343

vidual present the elements with which religion has to deal in various lights. Children and childlike races have of necessity different conceptions of self and the world and GOD—the final elements of religion—from those which belong to a maturer age or to a later period of national growth. The religion which is able to bring peace at one stage of human development may be wholly ineffective at another.

When, therefore, we look for a religion which shall perfectly satisfy the needs of men, we look for one which is essentially fitted for the support of man as man; which is able to follow him through the changing circumstances of personal and social growth, able to bring from itself new resources for new requirements, able to reveal thoughts out of many hearts, and to meet them with answers of wider knowledge. Such a religion must have a vital energy commensurate with all conceivable human progress.

And yet again: the perfect religion must not only have the power of dealing with man and men throughout the whole course of their manifold development; it must have the power of dealing with the complete fulness of life at any moment. It must have the present power of dealing with the problems of our being and of our destiny in relation to thought and to action and to feeling. The Truth which religion embodies must take account of the conditions of existence, and define the way of conduct, and quicken the energy of enterprise. Such Truth is not for speculation only: so far it is the subject of Philosophy. It is not for discipline only: so far it is the subject of Ethics. It is not for embodiment only: so far it is the subject of Art. Religion in its completeness is the harmony of these three, of Philosophy, Ethics, and Art, blended into one by a spiritual force, by a consecration at once personal and absolute. The direction of Philosophy, to express the thought somewhat differently, is theoretic, and its end is the true, as the word is applied to knowledge; the direction of Ethics is practical, and its end is the good; the direction of Art is representative, and its end is the beautiful. Religion includes these several ends, but adds to them that in which they find their consummation, the holy. The holy brings an infinite sanction to that which is otherwise finite and relative. It expresses not only a complete inward peace, but also an essential fellowship with GOD.

Every religion, even the most primitive, will exhibit these three aims, these three elements, at least in a rudimentary form: the perfect religion will exhibit them in complete adjustment and efficacy. A perfect religion—a religion which offers a complete satisfaction to the religious wants of man—must (to repeat briefly what has been said) be able to meet the religious wants of the individual, the society, the race, in the complete course of their development and in the manifold intensity of each separate human faculty.

This being so, I contend that the faith in Christ, born, crucified, risen, ascended, forms the basis of this perfect religion; that it is able, in virtue of its essential character, to bring peace in view of the problems of life under every variety of circumstance and character—to illuminate, to develop, and to inspire every human faculty. My contention rests upon the recognition of the two marks by which Christianity is distinguished from every other religion. It is absolute and it is historical.

On the one side, Christianity is not confined by any limits of place, or time, or faculty, or object. It reaches to the whole sum of being and to the whole of each separate existence. On the other side, it offers its revelation in facts which are an actual part of human experience, so that the peculiar teaching which it brings as to the nature and relations of GOD and man and the world is simply the interpretation of events in the life of men and in the life of One who was truly Man. It is not a theory, a splendid guess, but a proclamation of facts.

These, I repeat, are its original, its unalterable claims. Christianity is absolute. It claims, as it was set forth by the Apostles, though the grandeur of the claim was soon obscured, to reach all men, all time, all creation; it claims to effect the perfection no less than the redemption of finite being; it claims to bring a perfect unity of humanity without destroying the personality of any one man; it claims to deal with all that is external as well as with all that is internal, with matter as well as with spirit, with the physical universe as well as with the moral universe; it claims to realise a re-creation co-extensive with creation; it claims to present Him who was the Maker of the world as the Heir of all things; it claims to complete the cycle of existence, and shew how all things come from GOD and go to GOD.

Christianity is absolute: it is also historical. It is historical, not simply in the sense in which (for example) Mohammedanism is historical, because the facts connected with the origin and growth of this religion, with the personality and life of the Founder, with the experience and growth of His doctrine, can be traced in documents which are adequate to assure belief; but in a far different sense also. It is historical in its antecedents, in its realisation, in itself; it is historical as crowning a long period of religious training, which was accomplished under the influence of divine facts; it is historical as brought out in all its fulness from age to age in an outward society by the action of the Spirit of GOD; but, above all, and most characteristically, it is historical, because the revelation which it brings is of life and in life. The history of Christ is the Gospel in its light and in its power. His teaching is Himself, and nothing apart from Himself; what He is and what He does. The earliest creed—the creed of our baptism—is the affirmation of facts which include all doctrine.

Dogmatic systems may change, and have changed so far as they reflect transitory phases of speculative thought; but the primitive Gospel is unchangeable as

ABSOLUTE RELIGION.

it is inexhaustible. There can be no addition to it. It contains in itself all that will be slowly wrought out in thought and deed until the consummation.

In this sense, Christianity is the only historical religion. The message which it proclaims is wholly unique. Christ said, *I am*—not I declare, or I lay open, or I point to, but *I am*—the Way, the Truth, and the Life.

At first sight, the two characteristics of Christianity which I have laid down, that it is absolute and that it is historical, appear to be inconsistent. It may seem that a revelation which is not only given under particular conditions of time and place, but also expressed under those conditions, must be limited; that the influence and the meaning of a life, however powerful and sympathetic, must grow fainter in the course of centuries, and cannot extend, even if it has the capacity for extending, through all being.

It is a partial and suggestive answer to such objections that, since we have to consider a final revelation given to man, to man as he is in the fulness of his being, such a revelation must come through a true human life; and further, that what is offered to us in a representative life has contact with all life, as the one life is unfolded in its manifold richness; that nothing in the whole realm of Nature can be alien from man, who gathers in himself an epitome of Nature; that nothing, therefore, is incapable of sharing in the consecration and transfiguration by which he is ennobled.

But the complete answer lies in the personality of Him who lived Man among men. *The Word*, we read, *became flesh*. Here lies the secret of the power of that one true life. The Son of man was also Son of GOD. The Incarnation and the Resurrection reconcile the two characteristics of our faith—they establish the right of Christianity to be called historical, they establish its right to be called absolute.

We are not now concerned with the "evidence" for these transcendent facts, but I may make one remark which is of considerable importance. There cannot possibly be any antecedent objection to them. They are as unique as the universe itself. There is no standard of experience to which we can bring them, and pronounce in virtue of the comparison that they are "preternatural."

And it may be added that the antithesis of the finite and the infinite which they combine underlies all thought, all life. The antithesis exists; consciousness witnesses to it; Christianity meets it, announcing the vital union of the two terms as the fundamental Gospel, not as a speculation but as a twofold fact. By the Incarnation it gives permanent reality to human knowledge; by the Resurrection it gives permanent reality to human life.

Thus, the Incarnation and the Resurrection furnish the basis for a religion which is intensely human, and which, at every moment, introduces the infinite and the unseen into a vital connexion with the things of earth—a religion which illuminates the dark clouds that lie over our work, which offers an ideal wherein we can recognise the fulfilment of the destiny of humanity, which supplies an inspiration of power flowing from a divine fellowship—a religion, in other words, which is a complete satisfaction of the religious needs of man.

Let me endeavour to make these statements a little clearer in detail. Men, as we have seen—men, as born for religion—are born for knowing, for feeling, for acting; they need light, they need an ideal, they need power. And (this is my contention) the historic Gospel brings the light, the ideal, the power which they need—the light, the ideal, the power which we ourselves need in this crisis of our trial.

1. Men need light. No one can look either within or without and fail to see clear marks, not only of imperfection, but of failure. No one can study the pictures which great writers draw of the destiny of humanity, and not feel that the features which he recognises have been grievously marred. There is a terrible contrast between man's power and man's achievements; there is a terrible contrast between that which (as we are made) we feel must be the purpose of Creation and the facts by which we are encountered. Viewed in themselves, the phenomena which suggest a design of love in the order of the world issue in deeper sorrow. Naturally—and the words have a manifold application—death closes all. There is not, I think, a more impressive image in literature than that in which Dr Newman describes

the first effect of the world upon the man who looks there for tokens of the presence of GOD. "It is," he says, "as if I looked in a mirror and saw no reflection of my own face." This is the first, the natural effect.

But the record of the life of Christ, the thought of the presence of Christ, changes all. Christ, as He lived and lives, justifies our highest hope. He opens depths of vision below the surface of things. He transforms suffering; He shews us the highest aspirations of our being satisfied through a way of sorrow. He redresses the superficial inequalities of life by revealing its eternal glory. He enables us to understand how, being what we are, every grief and every strain of sensibility can be made in Him contributory to the working out of our common destiny.

Such reflections have a social, and they have also an individual, application. It was, as we read in St Paul, the good pleasure of GOD "*to sum up all things in Christ*," and "*through Him to reconcile all things to Himself*."

This purpose is, in potency, already accomplished in Him. In one sense all is done already; in another sense, all has still to be realised. The fact at least of a fellowship of earth and heaven is given us in life; and we can all strive towards the sense of the new unity. Under this broadest aspect, the fact of Redemption carries us back to the fact of Creation, and we are enabled to see how the will of GOD is wrought out in spite of man's self-assertion.

We may not indeed be able to penetrate very far

into these great mysteries. We shrink rightly from confining, by any theory in the terms of our present thoughts, truths which pass into another order. But the vision which we can gain is sufficient to change the whole aspect of life. Let us once feel that the anguish of creation is indeed the travail-pain of a new birth, as Scripture teaches, and we shall be strengthened to bear and to wait. And, as I said, these larger sorrows—sorrows which form a heavy burden to many of us—find a counterpart in the single soul. And here again light is thrown upon the discipline of personal suffering through the work of Christ. That reveals to us the love from which it flows, and the perfection to which it is able to minister. Again, we may not be able to see far into the application of these lessons; but it becomes intelligible that if the virtue of Christ's life and death was made available for man through suffering—if it was through suffering that He fulfilled the destiny of man fallen—the appropriation of that which He has gained may be carried into effect through the same law. The mystery of the forgiveness of sins is fulfilled, and we can bear cheerfully the temporal consequences of sin.

In both respects, in regard to personal sufferings and to social sufferings, it is enough to remember that He who was the "Man of sorrows," He who "*was a propitiation for our sins, and not for ours only, but also for the whole world,*" first revealed the Fatherhood of GOD.

These considerations, which I can only indicate

in the faintest outline, prove our first point. We need light, as conscious of failure in ourselves, sensible of failure around us; and Christianity takes the fullest account of this great gloom and illuminates it.

2. But in the next place, as men—as men in our essential constitution, and not only as fallen men—we need an ideal which may move us to effort. Now here, up to a certain point, there is no difference of opinion.

It is generally agreed that the type of character presented to us in the Gospels is the highest which we can fashion. The Person of the Lord meets us at every point in our strivings, and discloses something to call out in us loftier endeavour. In Him we can discover in the most complete harmony all the excellences which are divided not unequally between man and woman. In Him we can recognise the gift which has been entrusted to each one of us severally, used in its true relation to the other endowments of humanity. He enters into the fulness of life, and makes known the value of each detail of life.

And what He is for us, He is for all men, and for all time. There is nothing in the ideal which He offers which belongs to any particular age, or class, or nation. He stands above all and unites all. That which was local or transitory in the circumstances under which He lived, in the controversies of rival sects, in the struggles of patriotism, in the isolation of religious pride, leave no colour in His character.

All that is abiding, all that is human, is there without admixture, in that eternal energy which man's heart can recognise in its time of trial.

So it is that the Person of the Lord satisfies the requirement of growth which belongs to the religious nature of man. Our sense of His' perfections grows with our own moral advance. We see more of His beauty as our power of vision is disciplined and purified. The slow unfolding of life enables us to discern new meaning in His presence. In His humanity is included whatever belongs to the consummation of the individual and of the race, not only in one stage but in all stages of progress, not only in regard to some endowments but in regard to the whole inheritance of our nature enlarged by the most vigorous use while the world lasts. We, in our weakness and littleness, confine our thoughts from generation to generation, now to this fragment of His fulness and now to that; but it is, I believe, true without exception in every realm of man's activity, true in action, true in literature, true in art, that the works which receive the most lasting homage of the soul are those which are most Christian, and that it is in each the Christian element, the element which answers to the fact of the Incarnation, to the fellowship of GOD with man as an accomplished reality of the present order, which attracts and holds our reverence. In the essence of things it cannot be otherwise. Our infirmity alone enfeebles the effect of the truth which we have to embody.

3. "Our infirmity." Here again the historic Gospel comes to our aid. We need light; and, as we have seen, it makes a sun to rise upon our darkness. We need an ideal; and it lifts up before us a Person in whom, under every variety of circumstance, we recognise the divine likeness for which we were created. We also need power. It is true that we instinctively acknowledge the ideal in Christ as that which interprets perfectly our own aspirations. No accumulation of failures can destroy the sense of our destiny. But alone, in ourselves, as we look back sadly, we confess that we have no new resource of strength for the future, as we have no ability to undo the past. The loftiest souls apart from Christ recognise that they were made for an end which "naturally" is unattainable. They do homage (for example) to a purity which they personally dishonour. This need brings into prominence the supreme characteristic of the faith. Christ meets the acknowledgment of individual helplessness with the offer of fellowship. He reveals union with Himself, union with GOD, and union with man in Him, as the spring of power, and the inspiration of effort. The knowledge which flows from the vision of the world as He has disclosed it is not simply for speculation: the glory of the image of man which He shews is not for contemplative admiration. Both are intensely practical. Both tend directly to kindle and support love in and through Him; and love, which is the transfiguration of pain, is also strength for action and motive for action.

ABSOLUTE RELIGION.

In this way believing in Christ—believing in Christ, and not merely believing Christ—brings into exercise the deepest human feelings. It has been excellently laid down by one who was not of us, that "the solution of the problem of essence, of the questions, Whence? What? and Whither? must be in a life and not in a book." For the solution which is to sway life must have been already shewn in its sovereign efficacy. And more than this, it must have been shewn to have potentially a universal and not only a singular application. And this is exactly what the Gospel brings home to us. He who said, "I came forth from the Father, and am come into the world; again I leave the world, and go to the Father," illuminated the words by actions which made known the divine original and the divine destiny of man. The Son of man did not separate Himself from those whom He was not ashamed to call brethren. He bade, and bids, them find in His humanity—His "flesh and blood"—the support of their own humanity. In His life, for our sakes, the heavenly interpreted the earthly. He called out, and He still calls out in us, as we dwell upon the records of the Gospel, the response of that which is indeed kindred to Himself, of that which becomes one with Himself.

The sympathy which is thus awakened by Christ makes known to the soul its latent capacities. Again and again our own experience startles us with unexpected welcomes to the highest thoughts and claims. Even in ordinary life contact with nobler natures arouses the feeling of unused power, and quickens the consciousness of responsibility. And when union with the Son of man, the Son of GOD, is the basis of our religion, all these natural influences produce the highest conceivable effect. We each draw from fellowship with the perfect life that which our little life requires for its sustenance and growth.

Such considerations enable us to understand a little better than we commonly do those two words of St Paul, "*in Christ*," which form an implicit creed. We come to see that they correspond with the fact of a larger life to which our lives are contributory, a life which reaches potentially to all redeemed beings, a life which takes into itself all that is harmonious with its character, and conveys of its infinite wealth to each fragment included in its organization.

The revelation which places us in direct connexion with unfailing power supplies us also with a sovereign motive. When we accept such a revelation, the same instinct which constrains us to labour for ourselves constrains us to labour for others. To labour for others is, we then see in literal truth, to labour for ourselves. The separate consciousness of the individual parts of the body of Christ does not modify their inter-dependence, but gives a new meaning to the social destination of work. There is, we know, no pain which the devotion of love is unable to transfigure; and it is this devotion which the Christian conception of humanity and nature is essentially fitted to stir and to deepen. Not by accident, not by a remote or precarious deduction, but directly, in its simplest announcement, the Gospel proclaims that we are members one of another, and that all creation waits for the manifestation of the sons of God.

And it is obvious that this belief in the solidarity of life, if once we could give it vivid distinctness, is able—perhaps is alone able—to deal with the evils which spring from selfishness. It enables us to estimate rightly the burden of poverty and the heavier burden of wealth, when we take account of the conditions under which the one life is fulfilled in many parts. It quickens that keen sense of responsibility to God which best regulates the use of large means; and it quickens that conviction of Divine fellowship which brings dignity even to indigence. And meanwhile it delivers us from the bondage of material standards, when it makes known all that is of the earth as that through which the spiritual is brought within our reach.

If now I have succeeded in any degree in marking clearly the lines of thought which I have wished to trace, we shall see that the capacity of Christianity to illuminate, to guide, to inspire, belongs to its very nature; that we cannot hold our Faith without finding in it light to dispel the heaviest clouds of life, an ideal to keep before us the divine purpose of creation, power to support us in our strivings to fulfil God's will; that, when it fails us in theory or in deed, we have so far limited or misunderstood or misused it.

In other words we shall see that Christianity is the perfect religion.

It gives stability and energy to thought, and feeling, and action. Nothing can be without its scope, but to all things transitory it adds the element of the infinite.

It supplies the foundation of perfect freedom in absolute self-devotion. It ennobles dependence as the correlative of social fellowship. It presents the total aspect of being not as a conflict but as a unity. Politicians aim at "the greatest happiness of the greatest number," but we have a surer and wider principle for our guidance, that the happiness of the whole is the happiness of all.

But it will be said that the theoretic claims of Christianity are paralleled by the claims of other religions; that they are disproved by the crimes of Christians. I notice the objections only to point out that they do, in fact, if fairly examined, confirm my position with overwhelming force. If it could be shewn that the vital force of any other great religion was alien from Christianity; if it could be shewn that the crimes of Christians arose from that which is of the essence of their Faith, then the objections would be weighty; but if, on the other hand, it is obvious that the religions of the world each touched the hearts of men by a power of order or devotion, of sympathy with nature or of surrender to a supreme King, then each præ-Christian religion becomes a witness to the Faith which combines these manifold powers in a final unity; if it is obvious that the excesses of Christian men and Christian States are in defiance of the message of the Incarnation, then they only prove that the approach to the ideal is slow, and that it rises above attainment to condemn and to encourage. So it is that the gathered experience of men bears testimony to the truth of Christianity, both when it records anticipations and when it records corruptions of its teaching. In the one case it shews the Gospel as satisfying the cravings of men, and in the other as judging their self-will and selfishness.

And at the same time the wide, frank questionings of history which lead to these results, the attempts, however imperfect, to bring our Faith into actual contact with the most varied facts of life, reveal its breadth and grandeur and vitality. We are all tempted to limit our conception of its efficacy by our personal requirements. We forget that it is directed not only to the redemption of man as fallen, but to the consummation of man as created. It requires a serious effort to look beyond ourselves, our nature, our age, and recognise how it meets wants which we have not felt, how it disciplines powers with which we are not endowed, how it supplements our offerings by the fruits of other service. The effort is difficult, but it brings for its reward a calm assurance which is as firm as the far-reaching foundation of human experience on which it rests.

So it may well be that some of the lines of thought which I have endeavoured to indicate—only to indicate—may be strange; but I know that they are worth following. I know that they are able to bring home to us with irresistible force the conviction that Christianity has a message for us; that the Holy Spirit is speaking to us with a voice which we can interpret; that the currents of action and thought by which we are swayed can be so guided as to generate a divine light; that the conceptions of the dependence of man upon man, and of man upon nature, of a fundamental unity, underlying the progress of phenomena, which are taking place about us, illuminate mysteries of apostolic teaching; that the theology which expresses the temporal apprehension of the facts of revelation advances still, as it has advanced from the first, with the accumulated movement of all ancillary sciences.

Such convictions restore to us the position and the spirit of conquerors—the only position, the only spirit which befit our Faith. We are, we must be, as believers in Christ, in the presence of a living, that is, of a speaking GOD. Nothing, indeed, can be added to the facts of the Gospel, but all history and all nature is the commentary upon them. And the loftiest conceptions of human destiny and human duty cannot but be quickened and raised by the message which reaches through the finite to the infinite, through time to eternity: "In the beginning was the Word, and the Word was with GOD, and the Word was GOD. . . . And the Word became flesh, and tabernacled among us." Our imaginations are

ABSOLUTE RELIGION. 361

dull and undisciplined. We can hardly for a brief moment strive to realise what this Historic Gospel means. Yet even so in the still silence it makes itself felt. Then we confess that nothing beautiful, or true, or good, which lies within the range of human powers, can be outside its hallowing influence; that it calls for an expression in doctrine, and in conduct, and in worship, which exercises the utmost gifts of reason, and will, and feeling; that it restores to man the Divine fellowship which has been interrupted by sin; that it discloses the importance of the present through which the interpretation of the eternal comes to us; that it confirms the value of the individual by revealing his relation to a whole of limitless majesty; that it offers a sovereign motive for seeking the help of unfailing might; that it asks, guides, sustains the ministry of all life, and the ministry of every life; and, therefore, that it is a complete satisfaction of the religious needs of men.

BENJAMIN WHICHCOTE[1].

THERE can, I think, be no better omen for the future of our lecture-room than that we should first hear in it words of a former Provost through whom some of the noblest thoughts of Cambridge found shape and expression in an age of unparalleled distress and anxiety, BENJAMIN WHICHCOTE.

Whichcote was one of those men whose work is their life. Such benefactors are naturally forgotten, though their work lives on, if they do not find a sympathetic biographer, and the only memorials of Whichcote's life which we have are the funeral sermon of Abp. Tillotson, transcribed with a few additions and paraphrases by Allen, and the short but careful notice prefixed by Dr Salter to Whichcote's correspondence with Tuckney. But these scholars witness to Whichcote's power, and a well-known passage of Burnet has preserved a clear if brief judgment of the labours of our Provost.

[1] A Lecture given at the opening of the new Lecture Room, King's College, Oct. 13, 1885.

When describing the effects of the Restoration upon the English clergy Burnet writes: "with this great accession of wealth [from the fines raised on the Church estates] there broke in upon the Church a great deal of luxury and high living on the pretence of hospitality; while others made purchases and left great estates, most of which we have seen melt away. And with this overset of wealth and pomp, that came on men in the decline of their parts and age, they who were now growing into old age became lazy and negligent in all the true concerns of the Church: they left preaching and writing to others, while they gave themselves up to ease and sloth. In all which sad representation some few exceptions are to be made; but so few that if a new set of men had not appeared of another stamp the Church had quite lost her esteem over the nation. These were generally of Cambridge, formed under some divines, the chief of whom were Drs Whitchcot, Cudworth, Wilkins, More, and Worthington. Whitchcot was a man of rare temper, very mild and obliging. He had great credit with some that had been eminent in the late times; but made all the use he could of it to protect good men of all persuasions. He was much for liberty of conscience; and being disgusted with the dry systematical way of those times, he studied to raise those who conversed with him to a nobler set of thoughts, and to consider religion as a seed of a deiform nature, to use one of his own phrases. In order to this he set young students much on reading the ancient

Philosophers, chiefly Plato, Tully, and Plotin, and on considering the Christian religion as a doctrine sent from GOD, both to elevate and sweeten human nature, in which he was a great example, as well as a wise and kind instructor[1]."

Every detail of Whichcote's life which has been recorded serves to confirm this estimate of his character and influence and line of thought. The period through which he lived made his work in every way specially important. It was fitted to try to the uttermost the power of calm and comprehensive moderation. The vigour of his manhood was passed in a time of revolution, in which every opinion and institution which had been held sacred in the past was questioned or overthrown. He saw the rise of a new philosophy, of a new civil constitution, of a new ecclesiastical organization; and in part he saw the old restored. As an undergraduate at Emmanuel he might have met Milton at Christ's and Jeremy Taylor at Caius. As a Fellow he was the tutor of Wallis, Culverwel, John Smith, Worthington and Cradock: the friend of Cudworth and More. The date of his ordination by Williams, Bishop of Lincoln, coincided with that of the imposition of the ship-money (1636). He was appointed Provost in the year when Descartes published his Principles of Philosophy (1644). He was created D.D. with those friends who had taken a leading part in the Westminster Assembly. His controversy with Tuckney took place in the year of the

[1] *History of his own Time*, i. 186 f., Orig. edit.

battle of Worcester and the publication of Hobbes' Leviathan (1656): his death in the year of the execution of Lord W. Russell and the Oxford declaration in favour of passive obedience (1683).

Through these stirring crises of thought and action Whichcote held on his way, unchanged except by silent and continuous growth.

Trained, as it seems, in a Puritan family and entered at Cambridge on the Puritan foundation of Emmanuel College, he extended his sympathies from the first beyond the narrow limits of the opinions of those about him. "From your first coming to Cambridge," his Emmanuel tutor Tuckney writes, "I loved you, as finding you then studious and pious, and very loving and observant of me." However, he goes on to say, "I remember I then thought you somewhat cloudy and obscure in your expressions; but I then left you. Since I have heard, that when you came to be lecturer in the College you in a great measure for the year laid aside other studies and betook yourself to Philosophy and Metaphysics[1]."

And Whichcote himself does not dissemble the differences by which he was separated from his early teachers, while he acknowledges his debt to them with singular tenderness. "I have borne you reverence," he writes to Tuckney, "beyond what you do or can imagine, having in me a living and quick sense of my first relation to you; and of all men alive, I have least affected to differ from you; or to call in

[1] *Correspondence*, p. 36.

question what you have done or said or thought; but your judgment I have regarded with reverence and respect. I do not, I cannot, forget my four first years' education in the University under you; and I think I have principles by me, I then received from you[1]."

Nevertheless, while he writes with reverent love for his old master, he maintains that he has gained a nearer view of the truth. "I cannot," he says, "return to that frame of mind.... you .. seem to advise me to. I have had, in the former part of my life, experience thereof; and having freely and fully delivered myself up to GOD to be taught and led into truth, my mind is so framed and fashioned by Him .... that I can no more go back than St Paul, after Christ discovered to him, could return into his former strain[2]."

The circumstances indeed in which he was placed made a larger, a more human, faith necessary. A serious thinker, removed from the turmoil of affairs, could not but look earnestly in such an age for some stable foundation for life. Controversy had issued in an anarchy of sects. Authority had been invoked on opposite sides with peremptory sternness. Enthusiasts had ventured to claim for their extravagance the title of inspiration. Theology, systematised with logical precision in the Westminster Confession, had failed to cover or to meet the facts of daily experience. It was not then strange that one whose work was in the calm seclusion of the Eastern University

[1] *Correspondence*, pp. 6 f.   [2] *Ib.*, p. 115.

should attempt once more to look fairly at "all reasons;" not strange that he should seek to co-ordinate the conflicting phenomena which he regarded from afar: not strange that he should find in character and conduct the test of truth which he required.

"*I act therefore I am*[1]" was the memorable sentence in which he echoed and answered the *cogito ergo sum* of Descartes. But then, as he paraphrases the memorable sentence, I act not as my own maker, not as my own sustainer, but as the creature and servant of Him who is the original of all and will be final to all: who is "to be adored as the chiefest beauty and loved as the first and chiefest good:" who hath given us a large capacity which He will fulfil and a special relation to Himself which He will answer[2].

Thus Whichcote's whole teaching may be described as an expansion of Tertullian's appeal to the "testimonium animæ naturaliter Christianæ." As a College Lecturer (we have seen) he turned aside from Protestant Scholasticism to 'Philosophy and Metaphysics[3].' As Vice-Chancellor he deliberately justified his choice. And we must not fail to take account of the originality of his position. By this appeal to reason he traversed the one conclusion in which the most powerful representatives of English thought in his day outside Cambridge were united. Bacon and Hobbes, Puritans and Prelatists, agreed in

[1] *Sermons*, iii. 241.   [2] *Ib.*, ii. 61; 94.
[3] *Correspondence*, p. 36.

treating philosophy and religion as things wholly different in kind. The extreme schools on each side concurred in "wounding virtue," by destroying the belief that it was in any way suited to our nature and constitution[1] as a source of good or happiness. Against both Whichcote stood forth in the phrase of Lord Shaftesbury as "the preacher of good nature," yet so that he never contemplated man apart from GOD, abhorring and detesting in his own vigorous words "all creature-magnifying self-sufficiency[2]." According to his judgment, in a phrase which his opponents accused him of quoting "over-frequently," reason was the candle of the Lord, lighted by GOD and lighting us to GOD, *res illuminata illuminans*[3]. "I count it true sacrilege," he writes, "to take from GOD to give to the creature, yet I look at it as a dishonouring of GOD to nullify and make base His works, and to think He made a sorry, worthless piece, fit for no use, when He made man[4]." "This," he says again, "I dare defend against the whole world, that there is no one thing in all that religion which is of GOD's making that any sober man in the true use of his reason would be released from, though he might have it under the seal of heaven." He held that the vision of the Lord in glory to St Paul was not more convincing than the exhibition of the Gospel to the Soul[5]; and on the other hand, that no miracle can warrant our belief unless it be in con-

[1] Shaftesbury, *Preface*, pp. xi. f.   [2] *Correspondence*, p. 100.
[3] *Aphorism*, 916.   [4] *Correspondence*, p. 112.
[5] *Sermons*, iii. 88.

junction with a doctrine worthy of GOD[1]. "And to me it seems"—so he declares with stern indignation—"to be one of the greatest prodigies in the world that men that are rational and intelligent should admit that for religion which for its shallowness, emptiness, and insignificancy, falls under the just reproof and conviction and condemnation of reason; religion which makes us less men: religion unintelligible or not able to give satisfaction to the noble principles of GOD's creation[2]." That is "not an action of religion which is not an act of the understanding: for that is not a religious act which is not human[3]."

Such convictions, which Whichcote is never weary of repeating, help us to understand how he was a thinker rather than a reader in an age pre-eminent for learning. In one of his letters to Tuckney, who had referred his opinions to the influence of the contemporary Arminian and High Church writers, he says: "Truly, Sir, you are wholly mistaken in the whole course of my studies. You say you find me largely in their [the Remonstrants] *Apologia*. To my knowledge I never saw or heard of the book before [which Tuckney says was greedily 'bought and read by his friends']; much less have I read a tittle of it. I should lay open my weakness if I should tell you how little I have read of the books and authors you mention: of ten years past [since 1641] nothing at all.... Truly I shame myself to tell you how little I have

[1] *Aphorisms*, 1177.   [2] *Sermons*, iii. 249.
[3] *Ibid.* i. 151 f.; 157.

been acquainted with books, but for your satisfaction I do. While fellow of Emmanuel College employment with pupils took my time from me. I have not read many books but I have studied a few. Meditation and invention hath been rather my life than reading..." At the same time he mixed much with men, and in conversation, he adds significantly, "I rather affect to speak with them who differ from me than those who, I think, agree with me[1]."

So it was that alone of the group of scholars with whom he is associated, Tuckney, Hill, Arrowsmith on the one side, Cudworth, Smith, More on the other, Whichcote published nothing. The only writings of his which have been preserved in a complete form are four letters to his old tutor, Dr Tuckney, which deal with the main points at which he was at issue with orthodox Puritanism. Many of his Sermons were published after his death, partly from notes of his hearers and partly from his own notes; and besides these twelve centuries of "aphorisms" were taken from his papers, of which the greater part are found literally or substantially in his other remains. But though these materials are fragmentary and in part confused it is not difficult to gain a clear view of his opinions. His frequent repetitions, his bright epigrams, his earnest simplicity, bring his main thoughts vividly before the reader; for when he spoke from the pulpit he appears to have laid aside the technical forms of expression which sometimes on

[1] *Correspondence*, pp. 53 ff.

other occasions provoked the criticism of his contemporaries. Nor can I see any need for Lord Shaftesbury's apology for "the unpolished style and phrase of an author who drew more from a College than a Court; and who was more used to School-learning and the language of a University than to the conversation of the fashionable world," as likely to "ill-recommend his sense to the generality of readers [1]." I should have ventured to say that there are few prose writers of any time from whom one could gather more "jewels five-words-long" than from Whichcote. Here are a few as they are numbered in Salter's collection:

He that repents is angry with himself: I need not be angry with him (1142).

Heaven is first a temper and then a place (464).

No one reverenceth a wicked man: no not a wicked man himself (252).

In worldly and material things what is used is spent: in intellectuals and spiritual things what is not used is not had (1111).

A covetous man equally enjoys having nothing and having all things (600).

We must be men before we can be Christians (997).

It is the chiefest of good things for a man to be himself (416).

Where there is most of GOD there is least of self (911).

GOD takes a large compass to bring about His great works (903).

[1] *Preface*, p. xv.

No man can command his judgment: therefore every man must obey it (871).

He that takes himself out of GOD'S hands into his own, by and by will not know what to do with himself (819).

He that is full of himself goes out of company as wise as he came in (675).

Whosoever scornfully uses any other man disparages himself the human nature (126).

Men have an itch rather to make religion than to use it (36).

Every man hath himself as he useth himself (341).

For about ten years Whichcote worked at Cambridge as Fellow and Tutor of Emmanuel. In 1643 he took the living of North Cadbury in Somersetshire, which was afterwards held by Cudworth. But in the next year he was called back to Cambridge to take the Provostship of our College from which Dr Collins had been ejected.

"The choice," it is said, "was perfectly agreeable to Dr Collins himself, but not quite so to Whichcote." However, when after careful deliberation he accepted the invidious honour, his conduct fully justified his decision. As Provost, Tillotson says, and Allen adopts his words, "he was a most vigilant and prudent governor, a great encourager of learning and good order, and by his careful and wise management of the estate of the College, brought it into a very flourishing condition and left it so."

At the same time he made generous provision for Dr Collins, for "by the free consent of the College there were two shares out of the common dividend allotted to the Provost, one whereof was constantly paid to Dr Collins, as if he had been still Provost."

"And as he was not wanting either in respect or real kindness to the rightful owner, so neither did he stoop to do anything unworthy to obtain [the] place; for he never took the Covenant; and not only so, but by the particular friendship and interest which he had in some of the chief visitors, he prevailed to have the greatest part of the Fellows of [the] College exempted from that imposition, and preserved them in their places by that means." "And this," Allen adds, "does Walker reasonably assign as the main cause why so few of this numerous society were sent a begging in those destroying times, which almost laid waste the University, for their unalterable steadiness to the established Church and State."

It is therefore with good reason that Tillotson remarks, "I hope none will be hard upon him, that he was contented upon such terms to be in a capacity to do good in bad times." Or, as Allen paraphrases the clause, "as those times would not endure the orthodoxy of Dr Collins and it was absolutely necessary some person should supply such a vacancy, and if good men cannot be prevailed on worse men would, I cannot apprehend such imputation can be justly fastened on our reverend Doctor for suffering himself to be an instrument under wicked magistrates perpetually labouring to work good out of their sinister machinations."

"Besides his care of the College," Tillotson continues, "[Whichcote] had a very great and good influence upon the University. Every Lord's day in the afternoon, for almost twenty years together, he preached in Trinity Church, where he had a great number not only of the young scholars but of those of greater standing and best repute for learning in the University, his constant and attentive auditors; and in those wild and unsettled times contributed more to the forming of the students of that University to a sober sense of religion than any man in that age."

Whichcote's activity and position as Provost of King's brought his peculiar opinions into prominence. Little by little his old Puritan friends hung back from him, grew silent and reserved in his presence, murmured and criticised him among themselves; and at length on the occasion of his Commencement Sermon as Vice-Chancellor in 1651, Dr Tuckney frankly expressed, in a letter on the next day, his dissatisfaction with his teaching 'on the use of reason in religion, on the differences of opinion among Christians, on the reconciliation of sinners to GOD.' A correspondence followed which is a model of lofty and generous controversy. It closed without changing the position or lessening the affection of the disputants. "Could I syllabically and to a tittle have said as you said, *non reclamantibus judicio et conscientia*," Whichcote writes as his last words, "I

was under a temptation to do it through the respect and honour I bear to your person; and a desire in me to keep all fair. Sir, wherein I fall short of your expectations I fail for truth's sake, whereto alone I acknowledge myself addicted. So justifying nothing contrary to my due respect to your person whom I honour and shall most readily serve, I take leave[1]."
Five years afterwards Whichcote joined in electing Dr Tuckney to the Regius Professorship of Divinity.

The controversy with Tuckney enables us to picture the keen questionings which occupied the leaders of thought at Cambridge in the last year of the Commonwealth. Well would it have been if all could have shared Whichcote's spirit. If I provoke a man, he used to say, he is the worse for my company, and if I suffer myself to be provoked by him I shall be the worse for his.

In this respect Tillotson writes: "Though Whichcote had a most profound and well-poised judgment yet was he of all men I ever knew the most patient to hear others differ from him, and the most easy to be convinced when good reason was offered; and, which is seldom seen, more apt to be favourable to another man's reason than his own."

A simple but characteristic anecdote has been preserved which illustrates this trait of his character. Once he was, it is said, engaged in a conversation with Peter Sterry upon some abstruse points of divinity, and when Sterry explained himself with

[1] *Correspondence*, p. 134.

great ease and cleverness "the Doctor rising from his seat and embracing him expressed himself in this manner: Peter, thou hast overcome me: thou art all pure intellect."

In this way ready to learn even to the last, gladly confessing that no man gains so much in any way as by teaching, Whichcote was able to sympathise with the "young scholars," who flocked to hear him, and with the young divines of whom he was a great encourager and kind director. He had the characteristics of the true master, tender in his patience, strong in his wisdom, generous in the use of his endowments, so that his greater pupil Smith could say that "he lived upon him[1]."

The Restoration put an end to this happy activity at Cambridge. "He was removed from the Provostship by special order of the King[2];" but I can well believe that it cost him far less to be deprived of the office than it had cost him to assume it. Still, "though removed he was not," Sadler says, "disgraced or frowned upon; so far from it he was on the contrary only called up from the comparative obscurity of a University life to a higher and more conspicuous station." He was in fact appointed two years afterwards (1662) to St Anne's, Blackfriars. But his connexion with Cambridge and the College was not broken; and when his church was destroyed in the

[1] *Aphorisms*, Pref. xviii.

[2] See the interesting correspondence and documents in Heywood's 'King's College.'

great fire he came down to Milton, of which he held the sinecure rectory, having been presented to it on the death of Dr Collins. Here "he preached constantly, and relieved the poor, and had their children taught to read at his own charge; and made up differences among the neighbours."

His last charge was St Lawrence, Jewry, where he had the general love and respect of his parish; and where he found a "very considerable and judicious auditory, though not very numerous, by reason of the weakness of his voice in his declining age."

Whichcote's true work was done at Cambridge, and he closed it there.

"He died," Tillotson writes, "in the house of his ancient and most learned friend, Dr Cudworth, Master of Christ's College, like a primitive Christian." Allen, adds..."After receiving the sacrament he said to Dr Cudworth, I heartily thank you for this most Christian office. I thank you for putting me in mind of receiving this sacrament...He disclaimed all merit in himself...He expressed likewise great dislike of the principle of separation; and said he was the more desirous to receive the sacrament that he might declare his full communion with the Church of Christ all the world over. He disclaimed popery, and, as things of near affinity with it, or rather parts of it, all superstition and usurpation upon the conscience of men."

If you have followed the outline which I have drawn, I shall be disappointed if you are not proud of our Provost of two centuries and a half ago; if you do not sympathise with him; if you do not feel that he has a message to us. The fragmentariness and informality of the records of Whichcote's teaching obscure in some degree its scientific merits; but it is not difficult to see that he takes into account the manifold elements which enter into the problems of morality with a breadth of view which, as far as I know, is found only in his pupil Smith, till it appears again, though with more sombre effects, in Bp Butler. As compared with the abstract school of Clarke he insists on the coordination of all human faculties and endowments. He finds the expression of humanity in action and not in thought. He comes before GOD in the fulness of his whole nature. In the picture which he draws of man's moral constitution he has many points of coincidence with Shaftesbury, who "searched after and published" a volume of his Sermons in 1698; but Whichcote does not like Shaftesbury hide the darker side of life. He recognises harmony as the essential, divine law of the universe, but he never fails to recognise that it has been disturbed. His hope, as far as he defines it, lies in the efficacy of the discipline of GOD, which, he seems to imply, must sooner or later secure its end.

What then would he say if he were with us to-night? What thoughts would he strive to associate with a room which as we trust will be a fruitful scene of learning and teaching? I do not doubt as to the answer. He would tell us, as often as we meet here, to remember that man is made for truth, to recognise it and to embody it. He would tell us that truth is one in all its variety of parts, answering to the fulness of our nature. He would tell us that truth is not simply an intellectual result but a moral force, the very soul of action.

The foundation of Whichcote's teaching is the postulate or axiom that man was made by GOD to know Him, and to become like Him. Of this truth man, he affirms, is himself the witness. "GOD is the centre of immortal souls.". . . "If GOD had not made man to know there is a GOD, there is nothing that GOD could have demanded of him, nothing wherein He might have challenged him, nothing that He could have expected man should have received of Him[1]." As it is "the truth of the first inscription," as Whichcote calls it; "the light of GOD's creation;" "the true issue of reason;" the facts that GOD is; that every fellow-man, as man, claims our respect; that every man must reverence himself; or, in other words, the three duties of godliness, righteousness, and sobriety, are, he shows, such that you must unmake man if you deny them[2]. Truth and goodness, right and justice, are a law with GOD, unchangeable as He is. The reasons of things are eternal; they are not subject to our power; we practise not upon them. "They are as much our rule as sense is

[1] *Sermons*, iii. 144.

[2] *Ibid.* iii. 22 ff.; 120 f. *Aphorisms*, 630, 126, 211, 989. *Sermons*, iii. 422.

to sensitives, or the impetus of nature to inanimates." It is our wisdom to observe them, and our uprightness to comply with them. If we think otherwise than they require, we live in a lie[1].

So far we remain as we were created. For the Fall has not altered the destination of man nor obliterated his knowledge of it. "The idolatry of the world," as Whichcote profoundly remarks, "hath been about the medium of worship, not about the object of worship[2]." The testimony of conscience—our "home-GOD," as he calls it[3]—still remains. Great hopes and great aspirations contend in the human heart with the sense of weakness and failure. Sin, however familiar, is "unnatural," "contrary to the reason of the mind which is our governor, and contrary to the reason of things which is our law." Wrong-doing is evil, not only because GOD has forbidden it, but by its intrinsic malignity[4].

These truths involve, as it is evident, consequences of infinite moment. The results of actions are like the actions themselves. Sin carries with it inevitably the seeds of misery; virtue the seeds of joy. For happiness and misery hereafter are not simple effects of Divine power and pleasure; they

---

[1] *Sermons*, i. 68, 71. *Aphorisms*, 258. Comp. 116, 257, 333, 455, 456. *Sermons*, iii. 92; i. 149, 386, 253; ii. 397. *Aphorisms*, 157, 797. *Sermons*, iii. 91, 372, 387 f.

[2] *Sermons*, iii. 202. [3] *Ibid*. i. 40. Comp. *Aphorisms*, 1092.

[4] *Sermons*, i. 212; iv. 192. *Aphorisms*, 212, 523. *Sermons*, ii. 397. *Aphorisms*, 918.

have a foundation in nature[1]. It is impossible to make a man happy by putting him into a happy place unless he be first in a happy state[2]. "Heaven," as he tersely says, "is first a temper and then a place[3]." "Heaven present is our resemblance to GOD;" and "men deceive themselves grossly when they flatter themselves with the hopes of a future heaven, and yet, by wickedness of heart and life, do contradict heaven present[4]." So far therefore as man has lost the Divine image, happiness for him is inherently impossible.

Here, then, by the contemplation of the original facts of nature, we are brought face to face with the great enigma of life. How can man, fallen, sin-stained, estranged from GOD, gain his true end? The "truth of first inscription" witnesses inexorably against him. Whichcote points to the answer which lies in the "truth of after revelation." · This is "the soul's cure[5]." By this we are assured of forgiveness upon repentance and faith in Christ, and of needful help in the struggle of life; things credible indeed, yet such that nothing short of the Mission of the Son of GOD could have established them solidly.

By this Mission, GOD has re-established His loving purpose. The light of reason is supplemented by the light of Scripture[6]. To use the former is to do no disservice to grace, for GOD is acknowledged in both;

[1] *Sermons*, ii. 198.   [2] *Aphorisms*, 216.   [3] *Ibid*. 464.
[4] *Sermons*, ii. 196. Comp. iv. 255.   [5] *Ibid*. iii. 20.
[6] *Aphorisms*, 109, 778, 920.

in the former, as laying the groundwork of His creation; in the latter, as restoring it[1]. And this second gift is as universal and as real as the first. "When God commands the sinner to repent, this supposes either that he is able, or that God will make him so[2]."

Revealed truth, as Whichcote holds, differs from natural truth "in a way of descent to us" but is equally "connatural" to man[3]. "Though they [revealed truths] be not of reason's invention, yet they are of the prepared mind readily entertained and received[4]." ..."For men are disposed and qualified by reason for the entertaining those matters of faith that are proposed by God[5]." So false is it that the matter of our faith is unaccountable, or that there is anything unreasonable in religion, that there is no such matter of credit in the world as the matters of faith; nothing more intelligible[6]. "Nowhere is a man's reason so much satisfied[7]." If he be "once in a true state of religion, he cannot distinguish between religion and the reason of his mind; so that his religion is the reason of his mind, and the reason of his mind is his religion.... His reason is sanctified by his religion and his religion helps and makes use of his reason." Reason and religion in the subject are but one thing[8].

---

[1] *Sermons*, i. 371.   [2] *Aphorisms*, 516, 811.

[3] *Sermons*, iii. 20.   *Aphorisms*, 444.   *Sermons*, iii. 213, 388. *Letters*, p. 47.   [4] *Sermons*, iii. 23.

[5] *Aphorisms*, 644. Comp. 99.

[6] *Sermons*, iii. 23 f.; i. 71, 74.   [7] *Aphorisms*, 943.

[8] *Sermons*, iv. 147.

"Truth is so near to the soul, so much the very image and form of it, that it may be said of truth that as the soul is by derivation from GOD, so truth by communication. No sooner doth the truth of GOD come into the soul's sight, but the soul knows her to be her first and old acquaintance. Though they have been by some accident unhappily parted a great while, yet, having now through the Divine Providence happily met they greet one another, and renew their acquaintance as those that were first and ancient friends.... Nothing is more natural to man's soul than to receive truth[1]...."

Our reason, therefore, "is not laid aside nor discharged, much less is it confounded by any of the materials of religion; but awakened, excited, employed, directed, and improved by it; for the .... understanding is that faculty whereby man is made capable of GOD and apprehensive of Him, receptive from Him and able to make returns upon Him[2]...." Religion is the living sum of these manifold activities. It is not "made up of ignorant well-meanings or ... slight imaginations, credulous suspicion or fond conceit;" that is superstition; "but of deliberate resolutions and diligent searches into the reason of things, and into the rational sense of Holy Scripture[3]." We must then study it till the reason of our minds receives satisfaction; for till then we cannot count it our own,

---

[1] *Sermons*, iii. 17 f. Comp. i. 353.
[2] *Ibid.* iv. 139 f.   [3] *Ibid.* iv. 151.

nor has it security and settlement[1]. We must have a reason for that which we believe above our reason[2]. It is the peculiarity of human nature that man, through the reason of his mind, can come to understand the reason of things; and there is no coming to religion but this way[3]. The riches of earth can be left and inherited; the wealth of the soul must be won[4].

Thus there is laid upon every one, according to the measure of his opportunity, the duty of personal inquiry. To neglect this is to incur the guilt of superstition, or insincerity, or self-conceit[5]. The use of private judgment requires, no doubt, far more preparation and diligence than men commonly suppose, a larger comprehension of facts, a more patient weighing of deductions; but it is a fundamental duty[6]. "If you see not well," Whichcote writes, "hear the better: if you see not far, hear the more. The consequence of truth is great; therefore the judgment of it must not be negligent[7]." "He that believes what GOD saith without evidence that GOD says it, doth not believe GOD, while he believes the thing which comes from GOD[8]." By a natural re-action, "he that is light of belief will be as light of unbelief[9];" and

---

[1] *Sermons*, iv. 149. *Aphorisms*, 1089. *Sermons*, iv. 292.
[2] *Aphorisms*, 771.   [3] *Sermons*, iv. 142.
[4] *Sermons*, iv. 141.   [5] *Ibid.* ii. 387; iv. 337 ff.
[6] *Ibid.* ii. 38. *Aphorisms*, 622. *Sermons*, iii. 416.
[7] *Aphorisms*, 1090.   [8] *Ibid.* 977.
[9] *Ibid.* 292.

"of all impotences in the world credulity in religion is the greatest[1]." "It doth not, then, become a Christian to be credulous[2]."

In virtue of this continuous obligation we work from first to last, and GOD also works. Belief and repentance are vital acts[3]. The selfsame thing that is in us called virtue, as it refers to GOD, is grace[4]. "It is far from true that man hath nothing to do upon supposition that GOD hath done all[5]." Nay, rather by the appropriation of His gifts our noblest powers find their noblest exercise; and it ill becomes us to make our intellectual faculties "Gibeonites"—in Whichcote's picturesque phrase—mere drudges for the meanest services of the world[6]. The rule of their employment even now should be their future destiny: the law of heaven should be the law of the world[7]. Can any man think, he asks, that GOD gave him his immortal spirit as salt, only to keep his body from decay[8]? Nay, he that is in a good state hath still work to do[9]. "GOD, who hath made us what we are, would have us employ and improve what we have. Faculties without any acquired habits witness for God and condemn us[10];" and "in spiritual things the paradox is true, that what is not used is not had[11]."

In this sense Whichcote held that the grand

[1] *Sermons*, iv. 143.   [2] *Ibid*. iii. 114.
[3] *Ibid*. i. 70; iii. 87.   [4] *Ibid*. ii. 205.
[5] *Aphorisms*, 179.   [6] *Sermons*, iii. 186, 220, 323.
[7] *Sermons*, iv. 435.   [8] *Ibid*. iii. 147.
[9] *Aphorisms*, 564.   [10] *Ibid*. 1088.   [11] *Ibid*. 1111.

articles of the Gospel are as natural as the precepts of the moral law. "I receive," he says, "the truth of Christian religion in a way of illumination, affection and choice. I myself am taken with it, as understanding and knowing it. I retain it as a welcome guest. It is not forced into me, but I let it in; yet so as taught of GOD; and I see cause for my continuance to embrace it. Do I dishonour my faith or do any wrong to it, to tell the world that my mind and understanding are satisfied in it? I have no reason against it; yea the highest and purest reason is for it. What doth GOD speak to, but my reason? And should not that which is spoken to hear? Should it not judge, discern, conceive what is GOD's meaning[1]?" "The reason is the only tool with which we can do man's work[2]. If GOD did not make my faculties true, I am absolutely discharged from all duty to Him[3]. For a man hath not a sovereignty over his judgment; he must judge and believe where he sees cause and reason[4]. The reason of a man's mind must be satisfied; no man can think against it[5]." But "they are greatly mistaken," he argues, "who in religion oppose points of reason and matters of faith; as if nature went one way and the Author of nature went another[6]." The facts and the commands of the Gospel equally answer to our con-

[1] *Correspondence*, p. 48.   [2] *Sermons*, ii. 407.
[3] *Ibid.* i. 170.   [4] *Ibid.* iii. 216.
[5] *Ibid.* iv. 201; ii. 29. *Aphorisms*, 942.
[6] *Aphorisms*, 873.

stitution. "When the revelation of faith comes, the inward sense, awakened to the entertainment thereof, saith Εὕρηκα: it is as I imagined: the thing expected proves: Christ the desire of all nations: that is the desire of their state: at least the necessity of their state[1]."

"Sir," he writes to Tuckney with unusual warmth, "this I would not write to you—this assertion of the office of reason in dealing with religious truth—did I not think the honour of GOD and truth engaged, the interest of souls concerned; and were not I myself so assured as that thereto, if called to it, I must give attestation with my life. Therefore, Sir, though I dearly love you in my relation to you, and highly honour you for your own worth, yet cannot I out of respect to you give up so noble, so choice a truth, so antidotical against temptation, so satisfactory, so convictive, so quietive; in so full confirmation to my mind of the truth of Christian religion. Sir, this knowledge, GOD being merciful to me, I will keep till I die, not out of worldly design but out of love to my soul[2]."

Truth, Whichcote tells us, is natural to us: it is one: and it is also practical. "I have always found," he writes, "such preaching of others hath most commanded my heart which hath most illuminated my head[3]." True knowledge involves of necessity a right affection towards the things known; for knowledge

[1] *Correspondence*, p. 102. [2] *Ibid.* p. 106.
[3] *Aphorisms*, 393.

unfulfilled is the most troublesome guest that can be entertained[1]. Or, to take another figure: Truth is a seminal principle in the mind which must bring forth fruit unless it be killed[2]. Therefore, he says, to give one application, as thou art a Christian, take up this resolution, that it shall be better for every one with whom thou hast to do, because Christ died for thee and for him[3]. And to sum up all in one pregnant sentence: "When the doctrine of the Gospel becomes the reason of our mind, it will be the principle of our life[4]." A man "cannot be at peace within himself while he lives in disobedience to known truth[5]." "Reason and argument are transforming principles in intellectual natures; and it is not possible, where men are informed and satisfied with good reason and argument, but it should work upon them[6]." So it is by action answering to knowledge that character is slowly shaped according to an inevitable law. That which is worldly in respect of the matter can be made spiritual through the intention of the agent[7]. For religion is able to possess and affect the whole man, and bring that unity to his conflicting powers whereby he gains the chiefest of good things that he is himself, his true self[8]. In this respect "we have ourselves as we use ourselves[9]." "We are not born with habits, but only with faculties." "We

---

[1] *Sermons*, iii. 61.   [2] *Ibid.* iii. 211.   [3] *Ibid.* iv. 45.
[4] *Aphorisms*, 94. Comp. 132.   [5] *Sermons*, iii. 61.
[6] *Sermons*, iv. 175.   [7] *Aphorisms*, 520.   [8] *Ibid.* 956.
[9] *Ibid.* 341. *Sermons*, iii. 224.

are so in act as we are in habit, and so in habit as
we are in act[1]." Thoughts of GOD and things divine
mightily enlarge the parts of men: on the contrary,
men's parts wither away if they be not excited and
called forth to nobler acts by higher objects. The
mind as a glass receives all images; and the soul
becomes that with which it is in conjunction.

This law of correspondence is universal, and of
immediate efficacy; but in our present state the true
issues of action are often obscured or hidden. Hereafter,
however, all will be made plain. Judgment is a
revelation of character: punishment is the unchecked
stream of consequence. Every man may estimate his
future state by his present. He will then be more of
the same, or the same more intensely. Therefore
"there must be salvation of grace as antecedent to
that of glory.... otherwise there is no salvation."
"The unrighteous are condemned by themselves
before they are condemned of GOD." A guilty conscience
hath hell within itself[2].

Such a line of argument throws light upon the
warnings of the Gospels. It shows that impenitence
in its very essence is not compassionable. Repentance
is the moral correlative to forgiveness. An
impenitent sinner cannot be pardoned, because GOD
cannot contradict Himself[3]. He cannot be reconciled

[1] *Sermons*, iii. 339; iv. 317; i. 43.

[2] *Aphorisms*, 188. *Sermons*, i. 321, 244. *Aphorisms*, 232.
Sermons, ii. 198.

[3] *Aphorisms*, 840.

to unrighteousness; and the impenitent will not be reconciled to righteousness[1]. "Though GOD should tell me my sins were pardoned," Whichcote boldly says, "I would not believe it, unless I repent and deprecate His displeasure[2]." For this reason he maintained with energetic distinctness that the work of Christ must be wrought not only *for* us but *in* us[3]. "All the world," he writes, "will not secure that man that is not in reconciliation with the reason of his own mind[4]." "It is not possible we should be made happy by GOD Himself if not reconciled to Him.... If we through the Spirit of GOD be not.... naturalized to Him,.... we shall glory but in an ineffectual Saviour[5]."

The application of the same moral law confirms also man's expectations of future happiness. The feeble strivings after GOD which have been made on earth gain their consummation in heaven. When we are born into time, that makes a great difference[6]; but born out of time into eternity makes a far greater. In our present state it is through the thought of GOD that we come to know the powers of our souls. He, their one proper object, calls them into activity. The soul of man is to GOD as the flower to the sun: it opens at His approach and shuts when He withdraws[7]. And "I am apt to think," Whichcote adds, "that in the heavenly state hereafter, when GOD shall otherwise declare Himself to us than now He doth, those

[1] *Aphorisms*, 1025. [2] *Sermons*, iii. 40. [3] *Letters*, p. 13.
[4] *Sermons*, i. 95. [5] *Ibid.* ii. 263.
[6] *Ibid.* ii. 120. [7] *Ibid.* iii. 104.

latent powers which now we have may open and unfold themselves, and thereby we may be made able to act in a far higher way....[1]." The nearer approach to GOD will give us more use of ourselves. "Oh GOD," he exclaims elsewhere, with an unconscious recollection of Augustine, "Thou hast made us for Thyself, our souls are unsatisfied and are unquiet in us, there is emptiness till Thou dost communicate Thyself, till we return unto Thee....[2]." "Self-denial, self-surrender, devotion are Thy injunctions upon us, not for Thy sake, but that we who are empty, shallow, insufficient, may go out of ourselves, and find in Thee fulness, satisfaction, abundance."

It was a necessary consequence of Whichcote's conception of the Gospel, that he regarded the moral element in it as supreme. In spite of his power to deal with the widest thoughts, he constantly checks himself that he may come to the analysis of homely duties. He regards the positive institutions of religion as absolutely subservient to moral ends. Men may not multiply them as binding[3]. "There is no Shekinah," he says, with a noble figure, "but by Divine assignation[4]." In the same spirit he pleads, again and again, against subtleties of definition, or the imposition upon others of words not found in the Bible[5]. "Where the doctrine," he says, "is necessary

---

[1] *Sermons*, iv. 196.   [2] *Ibid.* iv. 314.

[3] *Ibid.* iv. 187. *Aphorisms*, 835.

[4] *Aphorisms*, 648. *Sermons*, iii. 200.

[5] *Sermons*, ii. 390. *Aphorisms*, 573.

and important, the Scripture is clear and full:" we need not attempt to determine things more particularly than GOD hath determined them[1]. "Such determinations," he adds, sadly, "have indeed enlarged faith, but [they have] lessened charity and multiplied divisions." For our greatest zeal is in things doubtful and questionable[2]. We are more concerned for that which is our own in religion than for that which is GOD's[3]. But true teachers are not masters, but helpers; they are not to make religion, but to shew it[4]. And while men are what they are, different in constitution and circumstances, there must be differences of opinion; but these, Whichcote argues, vanish in the light of common allegiance to Christ, and contribute to a fuller apprehension of the truth[5]. In things rational as in things natural, motion is required to avert the corruption of unbroken stillness[6].

There is therefore, he concludes, "nothing desperate in the condition of good men .... The sun having broken through the thickest cloud will after that scatter the less."

Anyone who has followed this outline of Whichcote's teaching, which I have given as far as possible in his own words, will, I think, have been struck by

---

[1] *Aphorisms*, 1188; 152; 175. *Sermons*, ii. 241.
[2] *Aphorisms*, 981; 1036; 1054.
[3] *Aphorisms*, 499. *Sermons*, ii. 261.
[4] *Sermons*, i. 178.
[5] *Ibid.* iv. 204 f.; 378 f.; 380 ff. *Aphorisms*, 712.
[6] *Sermons*, i. 84.

its modern type. It represents much that is most generous and noblest in the "moral divinity" of to-day. It anticipates language which we hear on many sides. It rightly affirms in the name of Christianity much that is said to be in antagonism with it. It brings faith into harmony with moral law, both in its object and in its issues. It enables us to understand how all that we can learn of the true, the beautiful, the good, the holy, through observation and thought and revelation, is contributory to the right fulfilment of the duties of life.

Yet in spite of these characteristics of his line of thought, which are doubly attractive in a teacher singularly pure and lofty, Whichcote failed to influence English speculation permanently. It would be interesting to discover the origin of Shaftesbury's admiration for him; for his power seems to have been practically confined to those with whom he came into personal contact. He inspired his hearers, men of great and varied power, Smith and More, Worthington and Cudworth, Patrick and Tillotson; but he founded no school, and left no successors in a third generation.

The transitoriness of Whichcote's influence may be due in some degree to political causes; but it is not difficult, I think, to indicate defects in his teaching which contributed to his partial failure. He had an imperfect conception of the corporate character of the Church, and of the Divine life of the Christian Society. The abstractions of Plotinus had begun to produce in his case the injurious effects which were more conspicuous in his followers. He had little or no sense of the historic growth of the Church. His teaching on the Sacraments is vague and infrequent.

But these defects are not inherent in his principles. On the contrary, the full recognition of the Divine office of history, the full recognition of the Divine gifts of the Sacraments, present Christianity as most rational, most completely answering to the reason of things, to the whole nature of humanity and to the whole nature of man. Whichcote's principles do not require to be modified at the present day, but to be applied more widely. We can easily imagine with what enthusiasm he would have welcomed now "the infinite desire of knowledge which has broken forth in the world," to use the phrase of Patrick[1]; how he would again have warned us "that it is not possible to free religion from scorn and contempt if her priests be not as well skilled in nature as her people, and her champions furnished with as good artillery as her adversaries[2];" how he would have reiterated the burden of his lesson that "there is nothing true in divinity which is false in philosophy, or the contrary[3];" how he would have called us back from our tithings of cumin to the weightier matters of the law, judgment, mercy, and faith; how he would have constrained us with loving persuasiveness to take account of the proportion of things by the measure of life. With larger knowledge and on an ampler field we are then called upon to exercise his faith, to claim for religion,

[1] *Phenix*, ii. p. 316.   [2] *Ibid.* p. 317.   [3] *Ibid. l. c.*

in the name of the Son of Man, all things graceful, beautiful, and lovely[1]; to shew that there is nothing in it but what is sincere and solid, consonant to reason and issuing in freedom[2]. The one sure evidence of Christianity is, that to which he appealed, the power of the Christian life. If the Gospel were a soul to believers, they would be miraculous in the eyes of the world, and bring all men in to give their testimony for religion[3].

Thus Whichcote's sympathy extends beyond the limits of that one Church "which," as he says, "grows not old." "Some there are," he writes, "that are mere naturalists..... I do not blame these men as the world blames them. I do not blame them that they were very slow of faith, that they will not believe farther than they see reason.... A man cannot dishonour GOD and abuse himself more than to be light of faith. Such persons one would compassionate as soon as any men in the world. I would say to them, 'You do well as far as you go: you do well to entertain all that GOD hath laid the foundation for: you do well to follow the light of reason: but do you think that GOD can do no more? do you think that GOD did all at once?' Nay rather your own experience, if you give heed to it, will in due time reveal to you the wants which the Gospel meets[4]."

This splendid hope of growing knowledge, this certainty of the vision of GOD by the pure in heart,

[1] *Sermons*, i. 59. [2] *Ibid*. iii. 253.
[3] *Ibid*. iii. 45, 251. [4] *Ibid*. ii. 313 f.

leads me to the last passage which I wish to quote. If Whichcote failed to understand and to give due honour to the past, he had that rarer and more elevating faith in the present which is the support of generous effort. "I give much," he writes in answer to the charge of innovation, "to the Spirit of GOD breathing in good men, with whom I converse, in the present world, in the University and other where; and think that, if I may learn much by the writings of good men in former ages, which you advise me to, and, I hope, I do not neglect, that by the actings of the Divine Spirit in the minds of good men now alive I may learn more; and I must not shut my eyes against any manifestations of GOD in the times in which I live. The times wherein I live are more to me than any else. The works of GOD in them which I am to discern direct in me both principle, affection and action. And I dare not blaspheme free and noble spirits in religion who search after truth with indifference and ingenuity, lest in so doing I should degenerate into a spirit of persecution.... And I do believe that the destroying this spirit out of the Church is a piece of the Reformation which GOD in these times of changes aims at...[1]."

We shall all, I believe, gladly take the words to ourselves. In this confidence lies our strength. In such writings of the Spirit manifested in many strange ways and in unexpected quarters lies our guidance. The light of reason is not yet burnt out.

[1] *Correspondence*, p. 115.

The power of faith is not yet exhausted. The last word of GOD is not yet spoken.

In this Lecture-room, as we trust, men will hereafter see truths which have not been made known to us, truths brought from many fresh springs, πολυμερῶς καὶ πολυτρόπως, truths through which life shall be made brighter, purer, nobler. Καλὸν τὸ ἆθλον καὶ ἡ ἐλπὶς μεγάλη.

Wisdom is more mobile than any motion;
Yea, she pervadeth and penetrateth all things by reason of her pureness.
For she is a breath of the power of GOD,
And a clear effluence of the glory of the Almighty;
Therefore can nothing defiled find entrance into her.
For she is an effulgence from everlasting light,
And an unspotted mirror of the working of GOD,
And an image of His goodness.
And she, being one, can do all things;
And remaining in herself, reneweth all things:
And from generation to generation passing into holy souls
She maketh *them* friends of GOD and prophets.
For nothing doth GOD love save him that dwelleth with Wisdom.

WISDOM, vii. 24—28 (R. V.).

πολυμερῶc καὶ πολυτρόπωc πάλαι ὁ Θεὸc λαλήcαc τοῖc πατράcιν ἐν τοῖc προφήταιc ἐπ' ἐcχάτου τῶν ἡμερῶν τούτων ἐλάληcεν ἡμῖν ἐν υἱῷ.

Hebr. i. 1, 2.